CITIES OF DREAMS

By the same author
Total Man
Personality and Evolution
The Neanderthal Question
The Paranormal
Guardians of the Ancient Wisdom
The Double Helix of the Mind
The Secret Life of Humans
Creatures From Inner Space

with M.L. Kellmer Pringle
Four Years On

with Chris Evans
Science Fiction as Religion

with Rosemary Dinnage
The Child with Asthma

CITIES OF DREAMS

Stan Gooch

RIDER
LONDON SYDNEY AUCKLAND JOHANNESBURG

Rider & Co Ltd

An imprint of Century Hutchinson Ltd
Brookmount House, 62–65 Chandos Place, Covent Garden,
London WC2N 4NW

Century Hutchinson Australia (Pty) Ltd
88–91 Albion Street, Surry Hills, NSW 2010, Australia

Century Hutchinson New Zealand Ltd
PO Box 40-086, 32–34 View Road, Glenfield, Auckland 10,
New Zealand

Century Hutchinson South Africa (Pty) Ltd,
PO Box 337, Bergvlei, 2012 South Africa

First published 1989

Set in Times by Avocet Robinson, Buckingham

Printed and bound in Great Britain by
Butler and Tanner Ltd, Frome, Somerset

British Cataloguing in Publication data

Gooch, Stan, *1932–*
Cities of dreams
1. Palaeolithic civilization
I. Title
930.1′2

ISBN 0-7126-1925-9

This book is dedicated to alternative thinkers, past and present, some of whom are:

Geoffrey Ashe, Robert Briffault, J.G. Frazer, Robert Graves, Margaret Murray, Peter Redgrove, Robert Temple, James Vogh, Lyall Watson.

Contents

Introduction

Some twenty years ago a leading and respected psychologist, the late M.L. Kellmer Pringle – we were currently writing a book together – confided in me that in her view in only a few years' time we would know everything there was to know about human psychology and human society. This comment, which left me completely stunned for several days, was among the reasons why I felt I had to leave the psychological establishment.

It was, however, by no means the first such comment I had heard, either before or since, not just from psychologists, but from leading biologists, anthropologists, doctors, historians – the pillars of the academic establishment – the view that, really, we were well on the way to knowing everything about mankind. In all fields relating to human evolution, to the human psyche, it was pretty much a question only of tying up the loose ends, of a few details here, a few details there. And that would be that.

My own position was a very different one. Not only did I find myself each day learning more and more about less and less, as Murray Butler put it – but in considering the currently accepted theories in the fields of study relating to mankind, I saw only more and more inadequacy in, more and more objections to, the confident explanations on offer. Obviously I was suffering from some terminal deficiency that was going to (and indeed did) shunt me out of my then career and into the arms of the other heretics.

So to the topic of the present book. The question it puts is simply this. Is the story of the origins and development of modern mankind, that is, of ourselves, really that which we find in our present-day school books and encyclopedias? Or is it the case that these accepted accounts are in fact quite hopelessly biased and inadequate?

There is the two-part question. By the end of the book I hope the reader will feel able to give an emphatic no to the first part, and an emphatic yes to the second.

1 Suppose

Long before the arrival of the first European in the New World, the resident North American Indians there had evolved an in many ways advanced culture and civilisation. They had, after all, been in residence for some 20,000 years. Already by 10,000 BC the anthropologists record large-scale, continuous communities.

Prior to 2000 BC, these varied peoples of North America knew weaving, tent and weapon making, medicine, music and many other skills of civilisation – though, as it happens, not the art of pottery. They also had by then a complex political life, alongside rich cultural and religious traditions, and great bodies of ancient folklore reaching back to the time when their distant ancestors came first across the 'stepping stones' to the virgin continent. Some of the tribes spent much of each day, every day, in complex religious ritual, not unlike orthodox Jews and Moslems of our present time. Others, of course, were equally dedicated to hunting or warfare. Yet, we must emphasise, these same complex Indians had no written language: nor did they build any permanent dwellings.

Consider now the following hypothetical situation.

Suppose this long-lasting and widespread North American civilisation had never been contacted by any other human group. And suppose, further, that some sudden catastrophe overtook this family of nations – an unstoppable disease perhaps, or decades of severe drought, followed then by disease, we have enough such scenarios in our world today – so that all perished. And suppose then that 25,000 years pass, or even 50,000. What trace would any later explorer then find of those myriad peoples and their complex cultural life? Why, none. Effectively, none. Just a few stone or bone weapons and implements. No tents, no dancing, no stories. Only a few, silent skulls – one here in a dry, desert gully, another trampled in fragments along some former river, and look, three skulls together even in this icy northern cave. Nothing more.

Or consider, now, a slightly different scenario.

In this case the Indians are overrun by an invading and very different ethnic type. Still more, even, than the Europeans who, in historical reality, actually did overrun the Indian peoples, this hypothetical invader hates and despises all that the Indian stands for – hates even their physical appearance, their very existence. At the hands of this invader the Indians are therefore relentlessly hunted down, butchered, and erased *en masse*, along with all their culture and beliefs. (This very scenario of course actually took place when the Europeans arrived in Tasmania – we do not even need to make an effort of imagination here.) During the relatively short period of the overrunning, however, there occurs widespread rape of the Indian women, some few of whom then live to escape back to their own people. In addition, some natives are kept alive deliberately by the conquerors for general amusement, both as slaves and concubines. (Precisely these events, once again, actually occurred in Tasmania.) From these various circumstances there arises, over time, a small half-breed population, a group having very confused and uneasy social status. (One simply doesn't know quite what to do with them, or about them.) Yet some of these half-breeds do nevertheless find some sort of social acceptance, and are absorbed into the invading stock. Others, perhaps, band together, and take off on their own account.

Now, however, in our hypothetical scenario (but how hypothetical is it really, so far?) disaster overtakes the invaders themselves. Abruptly there onsets one of the frequent ice ages that have so much characterised our planet in recent geological time. In the course of only a few decades the glaciers slide massively and relentlessly down from the north. The climate is suddenly no longer temperate, but arctic and sub-arctic. Even as far down as the centre of the continent, the covering ice is literally miles high – as it was in fact in central Britain and northern Europe just a few thousand years ago. The escape route south for our invaders is ultimately barred. The far southlands, perhaps, are already occupied by other vigorous peoples.

So now in the following millennia only a rump of the once proud conquerors ekes out a subsistence existence in a bleak, inhospitable landscape. Under these conditions 5,000 years pass. Or perhaps 10,000. And then the ice cap once again suddenly, and inexplicably, withdraws back to its permanent home within the true arctic circle.

The descendants of the original invaders now flourish and multiply. In only a few millennia they have swarmed out again over the whole continent. They make rapid cultural, technical and, finally, scientific progress. They have very much 'arrived'.

Yet let us consider what kind of cultural, and biological, position prevails among them.

In these peoples' verbal traditions – and they are of course by now a family of nations rather than any single nation – we find, obviously, much reference to 'recent' history. They are rather full of themselves these last few thousand years, these very successful and dynamic years. Yet in among all the obviously fairly recent material – recent, that is, as history counts these things – we find fragments which clearly refer to some time still more distant, to a time or times of very great antiquity indeed. In some cases the people themselves claim that these fragments are very, very old. Sometimes, as well, their age can de deduced from their content – references to dateable geological events, for example, or to animals which have long ceased to exist. Nevertheless, as far as the main content of these fragments is concerned, this is so garbled, nonsensical, so altogether unlikely, that it is clearly out of the question that it can be taken in any sense literally or seriously. These 'accounts' are obviously just fantasies, fairy stories dreamed up long, long ago in primitive times of enormous ignorance.

Sometimes however, and sometimes again connected with these old fairy-tales, we find also strange, meaningless and quite often secret rituals, or arcane 'religious' statements, which are altogether at odds with the thrust of public religion and culture – even allowing for the fact that there is nowadays quite a deal of variation in the public religions and cultural practices coast-to-coast. Further again, there are one or two words in the present language family which are quite clearly from some other quite different language family. (The philologists are quite happy about this particular aspect. 'Oh, yes,' they say. 'These are indeed very old words that our language picked up somewhere long ago, no doubt from peoples that went before us – obviously, we don't know what the words mean and, in the circumstances, never will.' The words, however, often crop up in the context of the old legends, or in connection with the secret rituals.) Lastly, but importantly, among the fairly wide range of physical types in the present-day population, there occurs, very occasionally, the birth of an individual with an obviously very different physical ancestry.

None the less, it occurs to virtually no one to imagine that all these strange and in any case unimportant odds and ends might somehow belong together, somehow relate to each other. Still less does it occur to anyone to connect this rag-bag of oddities with the very old skulls and tools which the wind and rain, or actual excavation, occasionally unearth.

During the course of our second 'suppose' we have, as I now suggest, been moving steadily away from our North American Indians and their hypothetical destroyers and towards a wholly real, actual situation. We have not in any *fantasy* sense been hypothesising at all. We have been describing the actual supplanting and destruction of Neanderthal man in Europe and the Near East, some 30,000 years ago, by an invading and completely different physical and cultural type, Cro-Magnon man.*

* Already there arises here a considerable problem for orthodoxy. Orthodoxy wholly accepts that Cro-Magnon did indeed replace Neanderthal at the time and place suggested, although not necessarily by violent means. Yet if Cro-Magnon became the sole species of man a mere 30-25,000 years ago – then surely we ourselves are Cro-Magnon? But no, we are not. A few identifiably Cro-Magnonoid types have been located in western Ireland, the Canary Isles and so on – at the fringe, so to speak, of the European operation. But the rest of us are *not* Cro-Magnon – even if, certainly, we are rather more like Cro-Magnon than we are like Neanderthal. So how did Cro-Magnon disappear? Where did he go to, in what, in biological terms, is the mere blink of an eye? This considerable problem is sometimes mentioned in the textbooks, but is then set aside. The problem is one that is fully dealt with, that is, ceases to exist, in the position taken up in the present book.

Yet, one might still ask, even if these – what are they? – Cro-Magnons did violently supplant Neanderthal man in the general manner suggested – well, so what? One type of early man is supplanted by another – surely this is a matter of direct concern only to the specialist in such matters; and to the rest of us, if at all, in some popularised form for reading by the fire in the evenings?

The contentions of the present book, however, could not be more opposite. Involved are two major aspects.

The first is that the totally fortuitous biological mixing of Neanderthal and Cro-Magnon genes (for, as already proposed above, it seems that the mix occurred solely in the context of rape and slavery) produced virtually overnight the vigorous and gifted hybrid that is ourselves, modern man. This specifically biological claim will be discussed in more detail later in the book, but is not, however, its chief concern.

The second aspect, the second claim, is that, at the time of his, for him, unfortunate encounter with Cro-Magnon, Neanderthal had evolved a culture of the mind (a) not only of a very high order indeed (for as I often say, whereas we build cities of stone, Neanderthal built cities of dreams) but also (b) of a strangeness that is very hard for us to imagine or, even having imagined, to come to terms with (since we have, after all, experience of only one kind of human mind – our own).

At the purely psychological/cultural level, I suggest that Neanderthal dealt Cro-Magnon a culture-shock of such magnitude that its consequences are still with us today. Though it left little *physical* trace, there is in fact, as will be shown, not one aspect of our present lives, our attitudes and our institutions which does not today bear that ancient culture's stamp.

The assumptions that follow in the next few briefly descriptive paragraphs will be defended throughout the book. Let us take these on trust for the moment.

We may picture Cro-Magnon as a young, confident individual: a very tall, skilled hunter and fighter, and extremely talented with it – the range of exquisite flint tools Cro-Magnon produced, much superior to the merely adequate tools of Neanderthal, is already strong evidence for that claim – probably already having developed the kind of warrior ethos described, say, in the Arthurian legends. In all further probability he was a sun-worshipper, in any case a creature of the daylight, the open plains (hence his tallness, of course), and the summer: probably again believing himself to be the only type of man in existence. But now, entering Europe, he encounters a to him physically and wholly repulsive type of man, short, barrel-bodied, ugly – a type culminating in Classic Neanderthal, a truly monstrous adaptation of the general Neanderthal type to extreme ice-age conditions – who lives mainly by night, who worships the moon (who in homage to it drinks human blood, but that's the least of it, even menstrual blood isn't the worst of it), in short, a type of man whose very innate, biological instincts, let alone his culture, are the utter opposite of those of Cro-Magnon. (Why, even when submitting in combat, instead of bowing the head, or kneeling, they present the naked buttocks, as indeed they do to the very altar when at prayer.)

And then, as if coping with the Neanderthal problem were not enough, the climate itself abruptly turned on Cro-Magnon. By 20,000 BC Europe was again in the grip of a full-scale ice-age.

Well, these are some of the further 'supposes' we will be involved with throughout the book. Yet how and where shall we find our supportive evidence? What form will it take? What underpinning can we give it? For, after all, as we said, the skulls themselves are both empty and silent. (Yet we can, for instance, take a plaster cast of the brain those skulls once housed.)

In paleo-archaeology, all that this type of archaeologist finds, as a rule, are a few of the merest slivers of bone. These days too, however, he or she can also analyse soil samples, and from their present chemical composition show that these and these materials (and sometimes quite *different* materials) must once have been here. But always the smallest traces are examined, from which, nevertheless, skill allows the inference of a great deal else: how many people lived here, for how long they lived here, what they ate, what they wore. The process of inference, hopefully of legitimate inference, is one that we shall employ also.

We have too the geologist, who looks at what to us is a hopelessly jumbled scree. After a while of careful study he is able to announce: these vertical rocks here were once horizontal; these rocks on top here are actually far older than the ones below them; those rocks over there are actually upside down; and these ones here don't belong at all – they've been brought several thousand miles by glaciers and rivers. A very smiliar task as that which faces the geologist faces us when we look at the jumbled scree of legendary material. But hopefully again we shall be able to sort it into categories and ages that others will consider reasonable.

Lastly, there is the astrophysicist. He considers the faintest tendrils and echoes of radioactivity among the stars at one edge of the galaxy, and says, oh yes, these are the traces of a supernova long, long ago, which occurred at the other edge of the galaxy. And behind even such whispers he hears too the faint, unbelievably distant echoes of the original Big Bang.

A biological supernova occurred when Cro-Magnon and Neanderthal man met. We can, if we will listen, still clearly hear the echoes of that explosion and observe its after-effects - and *because* we can we (like the astrophysicist) know that the explosion did indeed once occur.

But behind these echoes and tendrils we can also then detect the still fainter traces of Neanderthal civilisation itself, and hear the still fainter echoes of falling cities of dreams.

2 Red Ochre

> *Investigations of paleolithic, mesolithic and neolithic tombs throughout the world, in every climate and continent, reveal striking similarities in the funerary habits of man. Of all their affinities none are more commonly encountered than the custom of including red pigments with the body. This took the form of lumps of red stone scattered about the grave or the liberal coating of the deceased with the ground powder of some red mineral substance. In some cases the dead were completely submerged in a mass of red ochre. So numerous are the references to these ochre interments that pages could be filled merely by quoting their provenance....* Many prehistorians have refrained from attaching any interpretation to this employment of red ochre.

The above are the words of Adrian Boshier and Peter Beaumont[15] – but the emphasis is mine – writing in the journal *Optima* in 1972. Already this brief quotation, apart from the actual mysteries it begins to reveal, at once brings out points which we shall be emphasising again and again in the present book. First, we have the observation that certain, clearly identifiable practices are found world-wide among all forms of early man ('in every climate and continent') – practices which are not just vaguely similar but 'strikingly similar'. Second, we have the observation that academics and researchers are clearly reluctant to discuss this circumstance and its implications. (We noted already a similar reluctance on the part of those concerned to discuss the disappearance of Cro-Magnon man.)

What, however, is the precise context in which Boshier and Beaumont are writing? The context is that of numerous large-scale prehistoric mines and quarries recently discovered in various parts of southern Africa. The most ancient of these mines so far found is 100,000 years old. Several others are dated variously 45,000, 40,000 and 35,000 BP (Before Present – see Chapter 3).

Yet mines? Large-scale mines? One hundred thousand years old? Surely we are speaking here of hollows or depressions in the earth's surface, which are possibly even accidental? No, we are very much not. One of the largest sites evidenced the removal of a million kilos of ore. At another site half a million stone-digging tools were found, all showing considerable wear. All of the sites in fact produced thousands of tools and involved the removal of large quantities of ore; and while some were open quarries, others had true mining tunnels. In all cases, however, these excavations had been painstakingly refilled when the site was abandoned. (Boshier later discovered why, for the modern Swazi today still work such mines, usually in secret. The in-fill, the Swazi say, is required to placate the Earth spirits, especially the great plumed serpent – to whom in any case daily offerings of meal, tobacco and water must be made.)

Is it any wonder that science and orthodoxy shun these findings, so clearly threatening, as they do, the complete destruction of currently held orthodox views of man and his evolution? For the orthodox view is that the release of manpower for community tasks other than those of basic food-gathering and survival occurred for the first time only a few thousand years ago, in south-east Europe, in the context of the first developments of agriculture and animal husbandry. Mining, specifically, is considered to have begun around 5000 BC.

Yet here in Africa, between 40-100,000 years ago, we find no less than a massive investment of manpower resources in a continuous operation (through thousands of generations of mankind) to obtain a substance of zero food value, of no discernible economic value (since the ore was not smelted into iron) and, in fact of no *practical* use whatsoever. We must not overlook, incidentally, the mining skills involved here; and the fact that while in some cases the red ochre lay exposed on the surface, in other cases it lay underground. How were the ancient miners aware of its existence? On this particular mystery we may be able to throw light.

Back, however, to the use of red ochre in funeral rites.

H.B.S. Cooke and his associates report on the oldest known human burial so far, from the Lebombo Mountains of South Africa.[37] This is perhaps as much as 80,000 years old, but certainly not less than 46,000 years. The burial is that of a small boy, interred with a sea-shell pendant – and in red ochre. These same archaeologists, incidentally, report the finding of notched bones from levels at least 35,000 years old (at Border Cave in Natal) which offer clear evidence that these early men knew how to count.

Far away from Africa, at La Chapelle-aux-Saints in southern France, a man was buried 45,000 years ago, also packed in red ochre. In Wales, from a site dated 35-25,000 years BP, we have 'the Red Lady of Paviland'. 'The bones [of this interment] were embedded in ruddle, a red micaceous iron ore, which has coloured the surrounding earth for half a yard around. The body must have been enveloped and completely buried up in this material, and the bones and the associated objects... are still encrusted with it.'[15]

P.L. Kirk reports on a large number of prehistoric Australian aboriginal burials at lakeland sites: 'At Lake Mungo... the complete skeleton of an adult male... Careful stratigraphic studies suggest that this skeleton, Mungo III, was laid in its shallow grave 28-30,000 years ago: pink staining of the soil around the skeleton indicates also that red ochre had been sprinkled over the body.'[104] The Aborigines of the Torres Straits islands, who formerly practised the actual mummification of corpses, likewise employed red ochre in their burials.

From Czechoslovakia comes the 'Fox Lady' of Dolni Vestonice, a burial dated 23,000 BP:

She had been given an elaborate burial inside one of the huts, laid in a prepared hollow on the left side in a contracted

> *position... Body and head were covered with red ochre and protected by two shoulder-blades of mammoth, one of which had a network of irregular lines incised on its surface. With the woman were placed her stone tools, and close to her left hand the paws and tail of an arctic fox, with the teeth in her other hand.*[161]

Breuil and Lantier describe a Bavarian burial, 20,000 years old. 'The skeleton of a thirty-year-old man was laid in a burial site... entirely surrounded by a pile of mammoth tusks and the whole body nearly submerged in a mass of red ochre.'[17]

The Red Indians who came to meet their first European visitors were painted red with ochre not (probably) so much for combat purposes, as in honour of these gods who had come among them: so, of course, we refer to these brown peoples as 'Red'. These same Indians placed their dead on platforms high up in the trees, after the corpses had been liberally covered with red ochre. This was obviously a very ancient practice, though equally clearly one which left no fossil traces for later discovery.

On a different tack now, from the Dordogne in France comes a flat bone on which are carved what appear to be the phases of the moon over a time period (Marshack[123]). The pattern of the markings on the bone possibly also shows the path of the moon in the sky relative to the position of the observer (see Figure 1). This artefact is dated 27,000 BP. Marshack also considered a host of other somewhat younger incised and notched bones from Europe (and one from Egypt). These, he proposes, again log aspects of the moon's intervals, and possibly also menstruation and pregnancy records. (Similar notched bone and wooden artefacts, incidentally, this time definitely connected with numerical aspects of lunar intervals, were in use in modern times among North American Indians, Australian Aborigines and on the Nicobar Islands off Thailand.) In some cases the bones had been rubbed with red ochre, so that the notches retain the substance. Here, then, is clear evidence of the religious or holy nature of these artefacts – and a first link too between the moon and red ochre. It should be noted here that the deliberate notching or scratching of bone in Europe, together with the consecrational and perhaps also 'fixing' use of red ochre, does in fact date back some 30-40,000 years.[104]

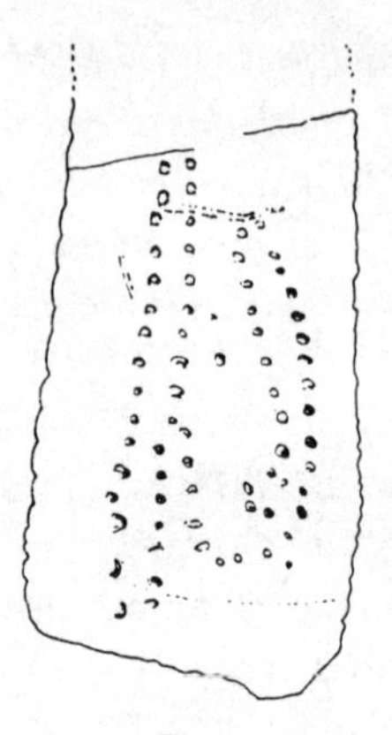

Figure 1
Paleolithic engraved bone plaque, 27,000 B.P., possibly recording phases of the moon over a time period.

A remarkable and important feature of the total story of red ochre is that its influence has never slackened throughout the whole period under discussion – from its beginnings with Neanderthal man 100,000 years ago (or earlier) right up to the present day; and in both primitive and advanced societies, as we see shortly. Raymond Dart comments:

Red ochre has a fantastic cultural evolutionary history beginning with Mousterian burial ritual and extending through its manifold late paleolithic artistic, religious, trading and bartering applications. By means of its dominating agency in the diffusion of the myths, rites and mysteries of ancient metallurgy and alchemy, it has played parts of such continuity and expanding diversity as to have rendered it unique amongst all minerals in moulding mankind's existence then and today.[14]

John Greenway writes: 'Why did this material in almost every religion since Neanderthal man invented that institution, become the most spiritually rich and magical of all substances. . . . There is no end to the myriad uses of ochre.' Greenway also has the following dramatic report concerning the influence of red ochre among Australian Aborigines today:

The most terrifying physical inquisitors in aboriginal

Australia are the little known Red Ochre Men.... It is astonishing how little is known by outsiders of the Red Ochre Men. Many whites who have learned about everything else of aboriginal life have not even heard of them, so well enforced is the omerta *among even those of the aborigines who wish the whole organisation ended.... The cult is nearly universal in aboriginal Australia.... In the deserts the Red Ochre cult moves right across the land in the course of a year, carrying its own ceremonies and myths, touching all tribes in its path, and working as a kind of ecclesiastical circuit court embodying all processes of the religious judiciary. The function of the court is to punish law-breakers – not so much the perpetrators of everyday misdemeanours like spear fights and wife-beating, but those felons who blaspheme the laws incorporated in the myths. If, for example, the young man on trial in Meekatharra had really shown the* tjurunga *[the law sticks] to women, his only chance to escape the Red Ochre Men would have been to flee from his tribal jurisdiction and live in a city or large well-policed town among other fugitives from their honour and their heritage.*

The punishments involved do include the death penalty – but that is not the worst. Far worse is when the Red Ochre Men destroy the offender's soul, so that it is of little consequence if he goes on living physically. Sometimes death is readily accepted by the offender as the price for leaving his or her soul intact.[80]

Aside from such highly secret matters, red ochre is, in any case, the most important decorative substance in use among Aborigines today in all tribal ceremony, whether that be directly religious or of the more entertaining variety. In the initial private ceremony of a boy's initiation into manhood and the religious mysteries, for example – ceremony that in all lasts almost continuously from age 14-25 – the youngster is painted all over with red ochre. He must stay away from camp and sleep by himself till the ochre wears off, and meanwhile only come to drink at the waterhole at night. New mothers also are decorated with ochre and must live in the special women's camp, as must also menstruating women and new widows. Some weeks after the birth the new father is similarly painted with ochre.

On these various occasions actual blood is also used in parallel with ochre, as it likewise is in Africa, and we know, in fact, from a variety of sources that red ochre represents blood (but whose?). One of the sources of actual blood is from circumcision of males, and from the ghastly sub-incision of the penis, which is slit open underneath from base to tip. The symbolic significance of this sub-incision is important for our general argument, and along with allied matters will concern us again later.

The influence of red ochre in historical times is not just confined to tribespeople. For example, the funeral chambers of the Chinese Shang Emperors and other aristocrats, around 1500 BC, were painted red – as were the burial tombs of Japanese, Etruscan, Greek and Roman rulers. (Here, we note, is a practice spanning two entire continents, Orient and Occident.) Homeric classical Greece, therefore, also bears the imprint of Neanderthal. Not just that, but the Pope himself is buried in a red shroud to this day. Not bad achievements for allegedly shambling and even allegedly speechless (!) Neanderthal man. Greenway, himself a Catholic, considers that the Easter ashes of Catholicism, the dab of ash on the forehead, also represent red ochre, and I agree with him. But there is far more to it all than that.

A word in passing here about alchemy. Among the various notions pursued by alchemists was that of a red powder which could turn base and leaden metals into gold. It seems clear that what we have here is a distorted and misunderstood memory of the powers of red ochre. Much else in alchemy, Gnosticism, Catharism, Freemasonry and so forth also bears examination in this and related contexts. We must realise, however, that we are seldom if ever dealing with direct memories: but rather with memories of memories of memories. Their true source and origin has been totally forgotten, and their form, like that of tortured rocks, is much distorted. Lastly here, we can note that in ancient Greece, as among African tribes today (who call it 'the essence of life'), red ochre was/is considered to have genuine medicinal properties. It is said to stop bleeding and haemorrhaging, clear blood-shot and pus-ridden eyes, cure snake bite, and correct urinary and other internal troubles. Whether such is the case or not, the belief in the powers of red ochre is clear.

So what, then, does red ochre really represent?

Everyone, both heretic and orthodox, and including the present-day users of ochre themselves, agree that it represents blood. A very common interpretation, and one that we can readily accept here, is that just as a new baby comes into the world covered with blood, so the corpse must also be covered with blood to facilitate, or perhaps cause, the re-birth of the deceased in the spirit world beyond. Birth blood is therefore one very probable meaning. A further significance (borne out also by much other evidence) is given by the Unthippa aboriginal women. They say that their own female ancestors once caused large quantities of blood to flow from their vulvas, which then formed the deposits of red ochre found throughout the world. So we can say that red ochre also represents menstrual blood: in both cases therefore female blood connected with the birth process. (We shall later be able to be even more precise and say that ochre is the menstrual blood of the Moon Mother; or more properly, the placental blood which covered the Earth when She gave birth to it.)

Yet still and all, even supposing the foregoing does indeed represent the thoughts and views of original Neanderthal in this connection, what actual *events* might have drawn him to red ochre in the first place? Do we not want, in fact demand, some very powerful reasons indeed – and indeed again, *hard*, *objective* reasons, not just fantasies or ideas – as to how and why red ochre could become a bedrock of a religion that not only totally galvanised the energies of early man for something like 100,000 years, but that then went on to fundamentally shape our own modern world – a score on which we have not yet fired even our opening salvos? Why, in short, did these ideas take hold with such *ferocity*? We turn now to some of the hard evidence.

Haematite, a Greek word meaning bloodstone, the official name for red ochre or red oxide of iron, is chemically Fe_2O_3. This chemical substance is frequently produced by the weathering of magnetite, Fe_3O_4. That is to say, when magnetite is exposed to the atmosphere at the earth's surface, it turns into haematite. Digging down through the haematite one comes upon magnetite, and it is clear that the one substance turns into the other. In his excavating of red ochre Neanderthal could not have failed to notice this phenomenon.

As it happens, however, magnetite is highly magnetic. It is what is called in historical times the lodestone (i.e. the 'leading stone'). If a small sliver of magnetite is floated on the surface tension of water, the sliver swings round until it points to magnetic north. Might it not well be that Neanderthal, accidentally or otherwise, discovered this magical property of magnetite?

There is good circumstantial evidence to suggest that indeed he did – this will later involve us in a detailed consideration of Neanderthal's view of the North. Let us imagine just in passing something Neanderthal might have imagined – that the North was the home of a Great Spirit. The Spirit often stirred, sending mankind little icy reminders of its powers; and then sometimes also, in real anger, its huge frozen hands to grip and squeeze the whole world. In those times the Sun grew weak and pale, and was sick unto death – while the Moon, however, rode on unchanged. For it was She who summoned the cold, her own elemental force, She who drew the ice back and forth across the land as easily as She drew back and forth the great waters. Suppose now that, in addition to that possible mental scenario, Neanderthal also happened upon the lodestone which (floating on water) always pointed North no matter how far you travelled into the pitiless, inhospitable arctic, where no human being could in fact live. We would begin to have some very powerful lines of reasoning here – one might almost say, lines of force.

But instead of simply speculating, let us rather look here at some recent archaeological discoveries in Central America.[184–5] Thanks to these, we now know that the Olmec Indians of Central America were using compasses – a sliver or small bar of magnetite on a piece of cork or wood, floating in a bowl of water – around 3000 years ago; and therefore at least 1000 years before their reported use by the Chinese, who are usually considered to have invented the compass. This is not at all to say, of course, that the Olmecs (or the Chinese, for that matter) only *discovered* the magnetite compass 3000 years ago – they could have had it far longer – only that we know they had the use of it at that point. One of the reasons we know this is because Olmec ceremonial centres were laid out to point a few degrees west of true north i.e. precisely to magnetic north. The specifically religious context here is, of course, of great interest to us.*

* 'A few degrees west of true north' – that true north which is marked by the 'still centre of the heavens' around which all the stars in heaven continuously revolve. Is this circumstance regarding magnetic north why the bodies in Neanderthal burials were laid on their sides, facing west? That is at least an interesting speculation.

The purely factual aspects of this particular line of enquiry do not necessarily stop there. Recent investigations of many directionally-navigating and homing creatures, ranging from sea-bacteria to the homing pigeon, have shown that these various animals possess tiny clusters of magnetite in the head, by which agency they both sense, and use for directional purposes, the Earth's magnetic field. Experimentally, a homing pigeon with a tiny bar magnet strapped to its head ceases to be able to navigate successfully. In nature, the home pigeon flying across a deposit of magnetite, haematite or other iron oxide veers about in sudden confusion, until it escapes the ore's local magnetic field.[197]

Is it perhaps possible that Neanderthal man also possessed magnetite clusters within the brain, while Cro-Magnon – like all – or like *most* of ourselves – did not? A nomadic species, such as Neanderthal apparently was, would certainly have found that endowment useful. Might such an endowment, if present, then also have enabled him to sense slight local magnetic fields – and hence locate not just underground deposits of magnetite/haematite, but also for instance running underground water, which likewise creates a tell-tale magnetic field at the surface? What we are discussing here, of course, is the ability to dowse, one which a few rare individuals do possess today. However, those inclined to be sceptical of such matters may nevertheless be impressed by a large Olmec carving in basalt of a turtle head – one of the animals known to possess the magnetite clusters. The basalt is itself rich in naturally magnetic iron, and the carving is made in such a way that the lines of magnetic force in it run to a point at the snout.

The suggestion that this ancestor of ours – and, incidentally, as of very recently, orthodoxy *does* accept the probability of interbreeding between Neanderthal and Cro-Magnon[207] – possessed an ability to sense at least some types of local magnetic-field disturbance would also offer one possible explanation of the nature of the underground 'plumed serpent' feared in Swazi folklore. But whether it is the explanation or not, the plumed serpent will prove to be another world-wide article of belief, found from Africa to China, to South America, to Australia, to Europe.

Here is a convenient moment to make a major emphasis. This is that the ideas and events discussed in this chapter are (a) a world-wide phenomenon and (b) have, therefore, persisted as ideas though vast periods of time. This second point requires further elucidation, and brings us on to more precise considerations of chronology and geography, the subject of the next chapter. The two points together, however, also beg another question. For there is an assumption here that similar ideas found in different parts of the world *can* only have arrived there through some process of dissemination. But are there any alternatives to dissemination as an explanation?

One possible explanation for similar ideas arising independently in geographically widely-separated parts of the globe is the notion of parallel evolution. It can well be argued that all human communities will and do tend to pass through similar stages in the process of evolving a complex society – and, in any case, do possess a common biology, and so common biological imperatives. Sometimes, therefore, similar ideas can arise merely coincidentally.

Certainly, one could make some such attempt at explanation in respect of, say, a world-wide preoccupation with menstruation. All peoples could and in fact would quite independently observe, for example, that pregnant women do not menstruate; that young girls do not become mothers until such time as menstruation begins; a connection between the moon's phases and both menstruation and the duration of pregnancy (subjects we shall discuss in detail later), and so on: and then from all these, to them, obviously important matters, involving of course the very existence and continuation of the tribe, spin out some roughly parallel programmes of religious explanation and observance.

Nevertheless, this initially promising and possible line of argument becomes increasingly difficult to defend as we turn to ever finer and more specific cultural detail, and as the mass of such detail relentlessly grows. Quite soon in fact the sheer weight of 'coincidence' breaks the back of any argument of parallel evolution. We are then left with the only other explanation possible: that one single, central and totally authoritative source produced the widely dispersed practices and knowledge involved.

3 Chronology and Geography

To judge the full impact of the material presented from here on we must be quite clear on the time and space scales involved.

First, notation. In respect of long periods of time, archaeologists and paleontologists employ the abbreviation BP, meaning Before Present. In the context of hundreds of thousands, and still more of millions of years, the 2000 years or so of the Christian era are a somewhat trivial irrelevance. Nevertheless, we do still need the notation BC (Before Christ) when referring to the development of the modern world (say, the last 10,000 years), if only to give us the sense of our own time, and a meaningful framework for the events of our own history as opposed to pre-history.

Turning to the actual people fixed in this amber of time, until 30,000 BP Neanderthal (*homo sapiens neanderthalensis*) is the only modern man on Earth, the first and to that point only so far discovered member of our own species. No other modern forms of man prior to this date have yet been found – aside from one or two skulls, such as that of Swanscombe man in Britain, which hint, but only hint, at a more gracile type. Before Neanderthal, and ancestral to him at around 500,000 BP, is *homo erectus*, who lived communally, knew fire and cooked his food. He is not, however, classed as *homo sapiens*. The definable Neanderthal type is in existence by perhaps 200,000 BP. Certainly by 100,000 BP he is found in considerable numbers throughout the whole of Europe, western Asia and Africa, where he is in sole charge – but not in North or South America, Australia or the Pacific, which remain empty of mankind. He is the only form of man found on Earth at this time. 'Found', we have to note, is a cautionary term. We cannot say what other finds may yet one day be made – and there does remain of course, and very much so, the problem of the physical and geographical origins of Cro-Magnon.

For Cro-Magnon (*homo sapiens sapiens*) appears abruptly, effectively from nowhere, 30,000 years ago in southern Europe. No trace of his original home site has yet been found. Partly for this reason, some authorities have tried to argue for a rapid evolution of Cro-Magnon out of a Neanderthal stock. The rapidity that would be required is, however, far too great for credibility. Ralph Solecki (see Chapter 8) states simply: 'This hypothesis has been abandoned.'*

By 25,000 BP Cro-Magnon is said to be solely dominant in Europe. This last statement, supported this time by the whole of the orthodox establishment and with no dissenting voices, is nevertheless totally incorrect. Not only are subsequent fossils found with mixed Neanderthal and Cro-Magnon characteristics (e.g. 'a man of rather primitive physical type: robust with unusually heavy brow ridges'[161]), a general circumstance very supportive for the position of this book – *but far more importantly, actual living groups of pure Neanderthals survive right up until recent historical times, in fact even up to our own present day*. The ancient Greeks, for example, report attacks on their towns by 'wild men' and, most fortunately for us, preserve portraits of the attackers on vases (see *Figure 11c*, Chapter 15). A captive wild man was brought before the Roman general Sulla in 86 BC. A thirteenth-century church in France has a fine sculpture of one (see again Chapter 15). A German anthropologist described another captured individual in 1784. Major General Topilsky of the Russian army shot and examined yet another in 1925. A group

* There is in fact not one single bone in Neanderthal that does not differ from its counterpart in Cro-Magnon (See Appendix, *Figure 12*), as does every item of software – brain, ears, eyes, gut – that we are able to reconstruct on these bones. Such total differences in such advanced creatures cannot be achieved by the processes of evolution even in the space of hundreds of thousands of years, let alone merely tens of thousands. No fewer than millions of years are required.

were seen in the Gobi desert in 1927, and described in detail; and Boris Porshnev, Director of Modern History, Moscow Academy, reports many further eye-witness accounts between 1930 and 1950.

This continued survival of Neanderthal after 25,000 BP is important to us for several reasons. First, this circumstance allows considerably more time and opportunity for interbreeding between Cro-Magnon and Neanderthal to have occurred. Second, it equally enables eye-witnesses much more time and opportunity to have viewed and described Neanderthal ceremony and magical practice, right up to and including historical time. Third, the continued existence and occasional sighting of Neanderthal very much encouraged the true-life stories of Cro-Magnon's encounter with Neanderthal to be told and re-told, stories which might otherwise, in the course of very long periods of time, have faded from the story-teller's repertoire.

Nevertheless, we must emphasise that these surviving Neanderthals live on only at the fringes of the main thrust of further human development, in fact actually in the most inaccessible areas available. All the peoples whose evolution we trace and discuss from 25,000 BP onwards are men and women essentially like ourselves – that is to say, are predominantly Cro-Magnonoid in origin and general characteristics, with, however, in different cases, varying but nonetheless always only slight admixtures of Neanderthal genes.

Turning now to our 'modern' peoples, those individuals who were subsequently to become the North and South American Indians reached the New World from what is now northern Russia by way of a land bridge, which existed from 26,000 BP (until 8000 BP). The consensus opinion is that the main migration occurred around 20,000 BP or earlier. All the migrants involved came originally not from the Russian area (they merely passed through it) but from Asia; and resemble the Mongoloids of Indonesia, Tibet and West Central Asia more than they do the peoples of Mongolia, China and Japan. This is an important circumstance.

The ancestors of the Australian Aborigines, on the other hand, probably reached their new homeland in Australia somewhat earlier, around 25,000 BP (though the oldest archaeological finds actually date from 35,000 BP). Their starting point had almost certainly been southern India. No authority in any case disputes that the Aborigines are the same physical stock as the present-day Dravidians and Veddahs of southern India. Opinion also seems to be growing that the Aboriginal language itself is related to Dravidian. (Certainly place names in Sri Lanka such as Trincomalee and Polonarua do sound remarkably Australian, and the Dravidians actually used boomerangs.) For the purposes of the present book, India is a very acceptable starting point for the Aborigines.

However, the main point to emphasise at this stage is that both the American Indian and the Australian Aborigine had each been completely encapsulated and isolated in their respective current homelands (the New World and Australia) for upwards of 20,000 years, until a few hundred years ago. They had, meantime, been without any contact with any other culture or type of man. It is clear therefore that any cultural or religious practices shown by these peoples, locked within their space-time capsules, must either have been brought with them when they first arrived; or have been independently evolved by them in the meantime.

There is another, rather briefer time-scale, in a somewhat smaller arena, which we nevertheless also very much need. This involves the languages of Europe, Russia and south-east Asia. Of these, at first sight very different languages, the large majority are in fact all members of one language family, and all descended from one common parent. This family includes Russian, Hittite, Persian, Hindi, Greek, German, French, Spanish, Swedish, English and many others. The common parent from which all these tongues descend is usually referred to as Indo-European. It is impossible to state with certainty when exactly (or where exactly) this parent language originally existed, and there was never any written form of it. Most expert guesstimates however propose Indo-European existing as one entity about 6000 years ago (that is, 4000 BC); and place its homeland somewhere north of the Black Sea. This statement however is in no way to suggest that Indo-European itself *began* as a language at that point in time. On the contrary, this was already a sophisticated and enormously complex language, with a very long history.*

* Modern Russian today, compared with modern English, is sufficiently complex to cause Russian children to be about a year behind English children in

Very probably related to Indo-European and in existence alongside it 6000 years ago (also perhaps geographically, though that is not certain) is Uralic. The Uralic family is today represented by Finnish, Hungarian, Estonian and a few other languages. A common ancestral tongue to Uralic and Indo-European would probably have existed some time between 7000-10,000 BP.

There exists also a further possible connection between Uralic/Indo-European and the Semitic-Hamitic language family, although the linguistic evidence here is admittedly only slight. However, envisaging one common ancestor for all three of these language families would take us back well beyond 10,000 BP. It is impossible to say, again, how far back. My own view (as a linguist) is however that the language of Cro-Magnon is the probable ultimate ancestor of all the languages so far mentioned in this connection, at a point some 25,000–30,000 BP.

The matters of the foregoing paragraphs are important to us for the following reason: that any parallel legends or folk-tales or fairy-tales that we find commonly distributed among European languages today must, therefore, have an age of at least 6000

achieving a similar degree of mastery of their own language. But modern Russian is nothing to the complexity of parent Indo-European. Indo-European probably had three numbers (singular, dual and plural, instead of just singular and plural), possibly three genders (as opposed to just two, masculine and feminine), and at least seven grammatical cases (as opposed to the four usually found today – nominative, accusative, genitive and dative). This situation would mean that every noun, pronoun and adjective in Indo-European would show a possible sixty-three different forms. An idea of the complexity involved here can be gained by considering the mere *eleven* possibilities of the adjective 'glad' which existed in Old English: *glaed, glaedre, glaedne, glaedra, gladu, glades, gladun, glade, gladena, glad, gladan.*

This remarkable feature of language – and one that is almost never discussed – namely that the further back in time we trace it, the more complex, and not the simpler it becomes – is not at all what we expect. Of course, once long, long ago language must initially have been fairly simple. But we would here, I suggest, be talking of antiquity of around 500,000 years, if not considerably longer. (As a matter of fact, the brain mechanisms necessary for speech have been in existence, both in our ancestors and our hominid cousins, for something like three million years.[91]) The main point for our purposes here is that the richness and complexity of the language which existed over the last many tens of thousands of years is without doubt the counterpart and reflection of a great richness and complexity of verbal and mental culture. We are absolutely wrong if we imagine early man in this extended period as being either any kind of simple-minded peasant, or dull-witted Rambo-style aggressor.

years, as far as their original form is concerned; and any legends and other verbal materials and traditions we find commonly held across European and (say) Semitic languages must then of course, in origin, be a great deal older still.

We have, then, learned something very significant in this chapter, namely that there is more than one way of reaching back into our distant past. We are, after all, not totally dependent on the skill, and the luck, of the archaeologist.

In conclusion, it should be emphasised that the languages of the North and South American Indians bear no relationship whatsoever to any of the Indo-European, Uralic or Semitic-Hamitic groups; and that the Aboriginal and Dravidian languages likewise have no relationship to them at all. Linguistically speaking, these macro-units are all watertight compartments.

How, then, shall orthodoxy account for the complex cultural and social heritage which these and indeed all other peoples of the world prove to have in common?

4 Three Ms: (1) The Hunted Maidens

The material of the next three chapters has been deliberately selected out of the mass of data on offer (hence the suggestion in the titles that the chapters are linked) because it does so self-evidently bear out the position taken up in this book, requiring little if any interpretation. It is, in short, instant and dramatic evidence of a world-wide and very ancient human legacy. It is, if you will, the Neanderthal inheritance – the document, as in a romance, discovered hidden in a forgotten book, or an old box, that suddenly visits total confusion and defeat on the false claimants to the estate. Much other evidence of the position presented in later chapters is equally compelling, equally dramatic – but some aspects of this require a structure of inference. It is material that could at first glance bear evaluation in a number of lights or several senses; though ultimately, in my opinion, only in one. So, then, on to the drama itself. We are gathered in the study.

The ancient Greeks have left us a wealth of legendary material concerned with the mythical origins of star constellations and individual stars. There are, for example, two stories (each with significant similarities) concerning the constellation called the Pleiades, a group of seven stars, of which six are readily visible, with a fainter seventh. One of the stories is as follows.

Orion the hunter came upon six sisters and their mother in a wood. Overcome with passion, he pursued the fleeing group through the forest for five years. At that point Zeus took pity on the seven women, and changed both pursued and pursuer into stars. So in the sky now we see the seven Pleiades eternally pursued by Orion the hunter.

Here, then, is the story of the origin of the Pleiades as told by the Australian Aborigines. Wurrunna the hunter was out in search of game in a strange district. Here he came upon a camp, in which however he found only seven young girls. The girls said they had come from a far country, out of curiosity, and were alone. Wurrunna decided this was a good chance to get himself a wife. By a ruse he detached two of the girls from the others and seized them about the waist, telling them they must go with him as his wives. He then told the girls to cut him some bark for the fire. As the two girls each struck a separate tree, the trees suddenly grew rapidly till their tops reached the sky. The other five sisters, who were already in the sky, now called out. At this the kidnapped pair quickly climbed the trees, and were drawn up into the heavens by their sisters, to live with them there for ever.[46]

This, now, is the story of the Pleiades as told by the Wyoming Indians of North America. There in a particular spot is a massive rock formation of volcanic origin, a natural tower of rock 865 feet high, with a flat top. The Indian legend tells how seven young girls were being pursued by a bear. They tried to save themselves by climbing up on a flat rock. But the bear could easily climb this too. So in order to save the girls the gods caused the rock to rise up far beyond the reach of the bear, pushing the girls into the sky, where they can still be seen as the seven stars of the Pleiades. (Just to cap matters here, Peter Lancaster Brown reports that the Florida Indians down in the south east – the Wyoming Indians are in the north west – have a story of the Pleiades, which they call 'the company of maidens', that is 'virtually a carbon copy' of the Greek Orion legend.)[111]

Here, then, is a most formidable mystery for orthodoxy, even if matters went no further (although they do). How can it be that three totally different ethnic groups – the ancient Greeks, the Australian Aborigines and the American Indians – living in distant, self-contained geographical areas, and separated from each other also in time by some 20,000 years (not that they were together in any conventional sense before that) nevertheless share what is basically the same legend? What are the chances of these groups having evolved the same story independently? Answer, none. Incidentally, in respect of the Greek and Australian stories, I am myself convinced that Orion and Wurrunna are the selfsame name. This, in my further view, is an actual Neanderthal word.

There is, of course, nothing in the Pleiades themselves to suggest that they are females, let alone hunted females. They are just a tiny group of seven undistinguished, fourth-magnitude stars – so not even first, second or third magnitude.

The three given accounts of the origin of the Pleiades are remarkable in the following ways. We shall find this to be the hallmark of most of the material examined throughout this book.

(1) The marked similarities between the accounts are too great to involve any possibility of coincidence or independent generation. They must, in all reasonableness, have a common point of origin.

(2) The also marked differences between the accounts are evidence of a long interval of separation from that common point of origin.

Under (1) we have the fact that the seven are always seven females, who are always hunted. They always escape their pursuer through divine or magical intervention, whereby they are raised up and placed out of reach permanently in the sky. Here they form a star cluster which, in each case, is the Pleiades. It should be emphasised again here that if this material were the only piece of solid evidence which the present book possessed, it would by itself still be enough for orthodoxy to choke to death on.

Under (2) we have the fact that in two cases the pursuers are men, in one case a bear – however, both the hunters are mythical heroes, while the bear in North America is a cult object. And in two cases the pursuit is overtly sexual, while in the third it is not. In only one of the legends, that of Orion – but more of him in a moment – is the hunter also turned into a star group. (But again, the Australian legend does have the name of the star group for its hunter.) Yet, as already suggested, we may in the circumstances also take these marked differences as supportive of our general argument: for they demonstrate that the legend has had much time to become totally embedded in the particular folk-weave of the culture in question.

As it happens, however, both the Pleiades and Orion are remarkable on many further counts.

The Pleiades are the only constellation noted and named by every culture on earth, past and present, from the most advanced to the most primitive. Thus Lancaster Brown notes: 'They were one of the most observed and discussed groups of stars in the ancient world.... Every civilisation had recorded their presence in the sky.'[111] J.G. Frazer, devoting a special section of *The Golden Bough* to an extensive documentation of the role of this star group, writes:

> *The constellation of the Pleiades plays an important part in the calendar of primitive peoples, both in the northern and southern hemisphere. Indeed, for reasons which at first sight are not obvious, savages appear to have paid more attention to this constellation than to any other group of stars in the sky.*[59]

Gleadow and others, moreover, note that the Pleiades, Orion and the Bear are the only constellations that are reliably identified by mention in the Bible – and so are effectively the only ones mentioned at all. Gleadow tells us:

> *The most famous reference occurs in the Lord's speech out of the whirlwind in the thirty-eighth chapter of Job: 'Canst thou bind the cluster of the Pleiades, or loose the bands of Orion... or canst thou guide the Bear with her train?' And there is a similar passage in the ninth chapter, verse nine, where Job says of God: 'which maketh the Bear, Orion and the Pleiades and the chambers of the south'. Also the prophet Amos exhorts us (Chapter V:8): 'Seek Him that maketh the Pleiades and Orion, and turneth the shadow of death into the morning, and maketh the day dark with night.*[60]

What an extraordinarily exalted position these biblical extracts do give to this objectively obscure little star group.

The Omagua Indians of Brazil likewise ascribed to the Pleiades a special status in human destiny. There the name of the constellation means 'Mother of those who are thirsty'. The Omagua further say that when the constellation disappears below the horizon, the snakes lose their poison; while its reappearance is held to mark the beginning of spring. (Later in the book we shall be clear that the terms 'Mother', 'snake' and the – implied – rain are all sure indicators of the influence of the moon.)

The Blackfeet Indians of North America not only know and observe the Pleiades, but celebrate their most important feast in respect of it. This is a national feast which the whole tribe turns out to celebrate. 'The women swear by the Pleiades as the men do by the sun or the morning star.' (The reference to women here is, again, important.) For the Pueblo Indians of Arizona the culmination of the Pleiades is a most important event. Reporting on this, J. Walter Fewkes (a naturalist writing in 1895) comments: 'I cannot explain its significance, and why of all stellar objects this minute cluster of stars of low magnitude is more important than other stellar groups is not clear to me.'[59] In Mexico, as in Brazil, the Indians there date the New Year from the rising of the Pleiades. With some South American tribes the word for 'year' and for 'Pleiades' is one and the same.

Before leaving the Americas, mention must be made of the great importance which both the Aztecs and the Incas attached to this constellation. The most solemn and impressive religious ceremony of the Aztecs was timed to coincide with the moment when the Pleiades were in the middle of the sky precisely at midnight. The ceremony occurred at the end of their so-called 'great period' of fifty-two years (we note, in passing, but without further comment here, that $52 = 4 \times 13$). The expectation of the Aztecs was that at this point the stars could cease to revolve, and the world come to an end.

When the critical moment approached, the priests watched from the top of a mountain the movement of the stars, and especially of the Pleiades, with the utmost anxiety. When that constellation was seen to cross the meridian, great was the joy; for they knew that the world was respited for another 52 years. Immediately the bravest and handsomest of the captives was thrown down on his back; a board of dry wood was placed on his breast, and one of the priests made fire by twisting a stick between his hands on the board. As soon as the flame burst forth, the breast of the victim was cut open, his heart torn out, and together with the rest of his body was thrown into the fire. Runners carried the new fire at full speed to all parts of the kingdom to rekindle the cold hearths; for every fire throughout the country had been extinguished as a preparation for this solemn rite.[59]

The Incas, however, invoked no such concept of a great period. They worshipped the Pleiades 'because of their curious position and the symmetry of their shape'. This is a very odd statement – for there is nothing immediately curious about the position of the Pleiades, nor anything particularly symmetrical. It looks very much here as if the Incas were either inventing reasons for their worship – or remembering reasons which no longer applied. For it is perhaps the case that the Pleiades were once symmetrical a long time ago – since we must appreciate that all the constellations are continuously altering their shape. This particular point recurs with greater force later in the chapter.

Far away from America, the Society Islanders of the South Pacific divide the year into two seasons – Pleiades above the horizon and Pleiades below. In the Hervey Islands, again South Pacific, the New Year begins with the appearance of the constellation on the eastern horizon. The Maoris of New Zealand likewise reckoned New Year from the Pleiades. But more important than any calendrical function is the fact that the Pleiades are devoutly *worshipped* throughout the whole of the South Seas.

In Australia the Aborigines (who are not South Sea Islanders or Polynesians) once again mark New Year from the eastern rising of this star group – at which point they, not at all unlike the Aztecs and the Blackfeet – hold elaborate religious ceremonies, in the belief that these will ensure an increase in food supplies in the coming year. The Aborigines believe not only that the Pleiades bring rain (so here too, as in South America, these are 'the mothers/sisters of those who are thirsty') but some even believe that *they* and *not* the sun generate the warmth of summer!

Away from the South Seas in Malaysia, Borneo, Java, Sumatra, the story is the same. On to Africa, where once again the Pleiades signal New Year among the Bushmen, Bantu, Masai,

Hottentots and many other tribes. It must be further emphasised that among many of the primitive peoples so far listed (as, interestingly enough, in the Bible itself, as we saw) only three star groups are named: the Pleiades, Orion and the Bear. Others name even fewer, the Masai recognising only the Pleiades, Orion's sword and Orion's belt. The Kikuyu name only the first.

What a truly remarkable story this is so far – and we have not yet even mentioned the Great Pyramid! Worldwide, various aspects of this tiny, faint constellation – its rising, its setting, its culmination – are not merely used as indicators of the New Year, or the start of spring, or the continuation of the world, but the constellation is *worshipped* as the provider of good things, a major controller of human destiny. It is the only star group, to repeat this once more, which every people knows of and every people respects.

Let us not in any sense pass over the European, Middle Eastern and Asian arenas. Agricultural writers in the classical world such as Virgil and Hesiod advised, respectively: 'Twice men gather the teeming produce; two are the seasons of harvest; either so soon as Taÿgete the Pleiad has shown her fair face to the earth, and spurned beneath her foot the despised streams of Ocean, or when she flees before the sign of the watery Fish, and descends from heaven – sadder maid – into the wintry waves': and 'Begin your harvest when the Pleiads come/To rising, and your ploughing when they set.'

Incidentally, we must vigorously discount any suggestion that the observation and worship of the Pleiades came about in the context of agriculture. Their role (as that of all the material in this book) is far older than that: which we understand when we realise that peoples who do not practise agriculture or animal husbandry at all – such as the Australian Aborigines, or the American Indians of Paraguay – nevertheless equally revere the Pleiades. The Paraguayan Indians, for their part, say that the Pleiades are 'an image of their ancestor'. We shall eventually see that they are not mistaken.

In ancient Egypt the Great Pyramid was so oriented that in 2170 BC, when the Pleiades were on the meridian at midnight, they could be viewed through the south passageway. So the Great Pyramid itself was built with the Pleiades in mind. In ancient India the Pleiades are named as the first or the chief of the asterisms (constellations) – possibly, it is thought, because three or four thousand years ago the rising of the Pleiades coincided with the vernal equinox (which it no longer does – see below). The Babylonian zodiac of eighteen asterisms also began with the Pleiades. In ancient China this star group was one of the four 'marker' constellations which divided the year into four equal sections – again perhaps because of its then connection with the vernal equinox. In China, further, we have good grounds for suspecting that Orion has taken over part of the earlier role of the Pleiades.[60]

Here I would like to add a speculation of my own concerning the European arena. In Europe in more recent times (and we have still to consider the fact that over long periods of time the various constellations gradually move forward in relation to the year) the Pleiades have been rising in May and setting towards the end of October. The two main witches' sabbaths are on 30 April and 31 October (May Eve and November Eve). Is it possible that the Great Sabbaths of the witches are connected, originally, with the rising and setting of the Pleiades? If so, we would have a definite link between witchcraft and antiquity – as Margaret Murray always argued.[133]

There is a further maverick item concerning the Pleiades. As already mentioned, this constellation consists of six readily discernible stars (although, as stated, only of fourth magnitude) and one considerably fainter. Particularly in Europe and Asia there are many different legends which 'account' for this situation. A typical story tells how one of the sisters lost her virginity, and in her shame hid her light from her companions. P.E. and G.D. Considine write as follows in this connection: 'Of the seven stars one is at present distinctly fainter than the other six, and there are many myths regarding this so-called lost Pleiad. In fact the myths occur in so many ancient literatures that there is a well-established theory that at one time all seven of the stars were of approximately the same brightness.'[35] B. Ernst and T.E. de Vries add: 'It is remarkable that so many nations speak of them as seven sisters [n.b.], although only six stars are clearly visible. All the legends therefore have a postscript to account for the missing seventh.'[54]

These are most interesting comments – for if correct they carry recognition of the constellation back beyond 5000 BP, since already from then on we begin to find the stories of the lost Pleiad. How much further back, on this evidence, we cannot say. But is it the case that other changes in other constellations might give us a clue to their 'birthdays' in human affairs? Is it possibly the case that once at least some star groups looked more like the shapes and figures whose names they carry than they do today – did the Great Bear once look more like a bear, or Orion more like a man? This possibility is considered again in a later chapter.

Giorgio de Santillana provides us with a rich vein of further evidence.[162] He begins with Samson of biblical legend, who as everyone knows slew a thousand Philistines with the jawbone of an ass (Judges 15:15). The Babylonian creator-hero Marduk, who was the Babylonian chief deity, performed *his* heroic deeds with the jaw-bone of a bull, which he used as a kind of boomerang. But that jaw-bone is in heaven – it is in fact the jaw of Taurus the Bull, specifically that part of Taurus the Greeks call the Hyades, a small, faint constellation. Hyades in Greek means 'watery' – and in the Bible we further read that 'God clave an hollow place that was in the jaw and there came water thereout, and when Samson had drunk his spirit came again and he revived' (Judges 15:19). Santillana in fact goes on to suggest that Samson, Marduk, Nimrod ('a mighty hunter before the Lord' – which might mean 'before Yahweh existed'), Gilgamesh (in Mesopotamia) and Orion are all one and the same figure. In the sky, Taurus is immediately adjacent and to the north of Orion, and a glance at the star map at once suggests that these two are confronting each other – and presumably in combat, that is, as hunter and hunted. (We note, incidentally, that the Pleiades, like the Hyades, are a further part of Taurus.) Many other commentators also suggest links between Marduk, Nimrod, Gilgamesh and Orion, but not with all the specifics which Santillana offers.

The 'heavenly jaw', Santillana tells us, is also identified by the Dyaks of Borneo, but he gives us no further information on that. But he does tell us that in South America 'the jaw of the tapir' is an aspect of Hunracán, the God of the Hurricane, and of course a great destroyer. In China, Orion is the War Lord Tsan, who is Master of the Autumn Hunt – once again a hunter. (We have to appreciate, incidentally, that the dawn rising of Orion, just like the dawn rising of the Pleiades, also heralds the spring; while the evening rising of Orion, just like the evening rising of the Pleiades, also signals the advent of autumn/winter.) However, the War Lord Tsan, as a hunter, uses a net. How interesting, then, that in Polynesia the constellation Orion is considered to be a huge snare for birds, while in Cambodia Orion is a trap for tigers. In Borneo it is a trap for pigs. But back to Polynesia for their fuller story. The Polynesians say that Orion is the snare which the creator-hero Maui used to hunt the sun-bird. And having caught the bird – with what did Maui beat it? Why, with the jawbone of Muri Ranga Vhenua 'his own respected grandmother'.

What a remarkable weave of 'coincidence' we see here. In every part of the world, including Africa, and including also Australia, if we are willing to agree that Wurrunna is Orion, the constellation Orion is seen either as a hunter (a hunter-warrior) or that with which you hunt. Is there any way, however, that we might consider these various legendary accounts to have been generated independently? Let us attempt such an explanation. First, the 'horns' of Taurus really do, for once, look like the horns of a bull – or the ears of an ass, or of a tapir. And if Taurus is an animal, then one might fairly readily consider a constellation which confronts it to be that of a hunter. In partial objection to this proposal we might however point out that the Australian Aborigines do not actually identify Wurrunna with Orion, nor have any concept of such a constellation, nor of Taurus, nor of any animal. The Aborigines merely identify the Pleiades as a group of girls, who are chased by a hunter. Then again, does Taurus look like a tiger (Cambodia), or a pig (Borneo) or a sun-bird (Polynesia)?

What of the idea, however, that Orion's evening rising signifies autumn, traditionally the time for hunting? Any aspect of hunting will therefore do to symbolise Orion, and any animal at all will do to symbolise his prey. Hence, perhaps, such stories arise independently around the world. Well, one must agree that there certainly are some possible grains of explanation along those lines. Of course, as it happens, most peoples do not reportedly use Orion to signify the onset of autumn – if they use anything at all, it is the Pleiades – but still.

Yet the deciding points for myself are these. (1) First, the recurring image of the jaw-bone, and its use as a weapon. I cannot personally accept that this motif could arise coincidentally or independently in so many parts of the world as an integral part of this material. (2) There is the original material with which we opened this chapter – the Pleiades as a group of hunted women. Here we see no objective way at all in which different peoples could independently produce such a fanciful story. In the light of hard evidence such as this (and there is much more of the same hard evidence to come in the remainder of the book) we are, I think, justified in ruling less emphatic evidence also in our favour.

In short, then, I find myself in absolute agreement with Santillana's general conclusion – though we have much more evidence to come – namely: 'Someone before history must have blocked the constellations out for reasons known to himself, and with such an authority that they were repeated without question substantially the same from Mexico to Africa and Polynesia – and have remained with us to this day.'

Santillana himself, incidentally, is a convinced diffusionist. He considers that some kind of migration carried these ideas around the world – but his earliest date for this event seems to be 8000 BP, which will not do at all. The idea that from some small area in the Middle East (the favourite starting point for most diffusionist theories) mankind set out into every nook and corner of the world, where they persuaded every single human group to accept their ideas – but without leaving any trace of this startling journey and events anywhere in legend, and without bequeathing any foreign loan-words anywhere at all (except, perhaps, Wurrunna – although as it happens Santillana does not seem to know that story) along with the alleged loan-ideas, really doesn't stand up. All *traditional* dissemination theories break down under such detailed reflection.

The sheer degree of veneration of the Pleiades world-wide, as well as the at least implied veneration of Orion, if not in religious ceremony as such, then in terms of enshrinement as hunter-hero-warrior, must also seriously influence us. To labour the point somewhat, it is not just the fact that all peoples world-wide have chosen the Pleiades as *the* constellation which matters above all others; it is also the absolute *fervour* with which they have done so.

For there are, after all, any number of celestial mechanisms which primitive peoples could have elected to use as the marker of the New Year. They could have done what we do (well, almost do!), that is, take the day after the shortest day as New Year's day. (In actual fact we take the eleventh day after the shortest day, which happens to be 21 December.) The shortest day is easily determined, especially in countries with clear skies, by studying the length of shadow cast by any fixed object. Or if a spring start were wanted, the vernal equinox could have been selected. The cyclic behaviour of any number of stars and constellations would do also, and ones that are far brighter than the Pleiades – *these* are actually very difficult to see at all when low on the horizon. (But of course the whole business of using primarily the stars is itself a little suspect among peoples who were allegedly first and foremost sun worshippers – like the Aztecs, the Incas and the ancient Egyptians. Actually, as we shall see, the sun-worshipping card has been dramatically, and one has to say deliberately, over-played by modern historians.) But then – the second point above – having all allegedly independently selected this quite unlikely candidate, the Pleiades, everyone goes completely overboard about it. They say, variously, it is the image of our ancestors, that it has a marvellous symmetry, they use the same word for 'year' and 'Pleiades' (what word were they using for 'year' before?), they say it is responsible for the summer heat and the rain, they use it as a metaphor for the power of Almighty God, it signals whether the world is to end or not, the Great Pyramid is aligned in deference to it, and so on.

However, the mystery here is even deeper than it looks at first sight. For unknown to the peoples of historical times – otherwise, for instance, the Great Pyramid and many other major temples and monuments of that period would not have been aligned with star groups – and due to a phenomenon know as the precession of the equinoxes, the activity of the constellations over long periods of time gradually moves forward through the earth's year. The constellations move forward approximately one month every 2000 years. Thus the first morning rising of the Pleiades currently occurs in May. Two thousand years ago that same rising occurred in April. Two thousand years before that it occurred in March. In fact, about 4000 years back that rising more or less coincided with the vernal equinox – and this particular coincidence, it is often suggested, is why the Babylonians and the ancient Indians chose it as the first or chief asterism. But go back another two thousand years still, and the Pleiades rises in February – and so is no indicator of anything particular at all.

Therefore, we are necessarily expected to suppose that no more than 4000 years ago, all over the world and simultaneously, mankind noticed that the morning rising of the Pleiades coincided with the vernal equinox, or less precisely with the more-or-less beginning of spring. And this realisation excited everyone so much that they all, without exception, set up elaborate religious rituals in respect of it, and also wove stories around this star group and the constellations immediately adjacent to it. By an amazing coincidence these stories often involved describing the Pleiades as a group of maidens – but we've been through all that. And remember, these events must (on the basis of normal explanation, that is) have happened simultaneously all around the world not more than 4000 years ago – because prior to that the risings and settings of the Pleiades and of Orion signified nothing in particular.

I myself find the above account unacceptable, even supposing there were not all the other evidence of the present book. Instead I now propose the following possible explanation of events. While, certainly, a critic might point out that this is at best only a hypothesis – nevertheless no one can deny that it is extremely neat, quite remarkably neat. An amazing 'coincidence' perhaps.

The point has already been made that the constellations in terms of our obervations of their habits move gradually forward through the year. But after a considerable time – about 26,000 years – they in fact arrive back at their point of departure, that is, back in the month they were observed in all that time ago. If we track back 26,000 years from our present date, we find the Pleiades and Orion rising in the spring months – just as they do at the moment. Or go back instead from the time when Babylon and India made the Pleiades chief of the asterisms, and where its morning rising coincided with the vernal equinox, why then we have (—4000 years) + (—26,000 years) = —30,000 years. And as it just so happens, 30,000 years ago was the point when Cro-Magnon overran and destroyed Neanderthal. At that precise time Neanderthal – as I believe, expert in all the phenomena of the heavens – would have been logging and worshipping the Pleiades and Orion as the heralds of spring.

I will go further into the details of this possible situation in later chapters – but I think, in short, that Cro-Magnon took over all the 'magic' and ritual of Neanderthal for his own. But he took it over without any real understanding of most of it, and also with certain appropriate changes to suit his own world view, his own existing social structure, his own biological imperatives. He took over essentially empty forms, while losing the priceless content. So he at least saw the Pleiades (and Orion) only as gods/goddesses who made the spring, who made the world go on.

As further time subsequently passed, of course, the two constellations in question moved forward into summer, and no longer marked the spring. And meanwhile too Cro-Magnon (or rather the mixed Cro-Magnon/Neanderthal population) was now coping with the renewed onset of ice-age conditions in all of Europe, Asia and North America – and so with not too much time for philosophical analysis or scientific innovation. Nevertheless, through all those dark millennia, those many thousands of years, mankind did not lose the imagery and the stories and (in that sense) the knowledge the encounter with Neanderthal had bequeathed. Certainly all of this became gradually altered, gradually more garbled, losing further of even such meaning as it had once had. But survive, and still recognisably, it did everywhere.

Yet *could* that happen? Could a word-of-mouth tradition, unsupported by writing or any other form of hard record, persist recognisably over tens of thousands of years? Well, on that particular point, thanks to Robert Temple and others, we have some very hard evidence indeed (see notably Chapter 7). Quite conclusive evidence, in fact.

Then, around 10,000 years ago, with the final withdrawal of the ice caps, modern history effectively begins. Mankind recovers, fairly rapidly in fact, from the millennia of climatic oppression. In the northern hemisphere by 5000 BP we have the beginnings of ancient Sumeria, Babylon, Egypt, Crete. From this point on the old legends do now also everywhere become overlaid and intermingled with more modern and more sophisticated ideas. But once again, they survive. Still enough of the old core material is retained, and some of it remains recognisable – just.

And now we really do have a genuine coincidence. Purely coincidentally, around 4000 BP, by when astronomy is becoming a flourishing science in many parts of the world, the star groups resume the same positions they last occupied at the fall of Neanderthal man (although they are not necessarily the same shape – that is a different point). And suddenly the astronomers 'understand' the hints, the 'real' meaning of the old legends and rituals! (Yet still and all, they have no idea how old these are, nor do they understand such matters as the precession of the equinox.) In this renaissance – and I think that is a fair word – these new seekers and thinkers now re-discover something of what ancient legend had always taught. Such realisation is then, of course, a tremendous spur to astronomy, astrology, religion, magical practice and much else of a desirable or undesirable nature.

One of the proofs of the position argued here is that different civilisations stick different bits of the old accounts in different places in their new philosophies. Nevertheless, the correspondences between the various new philosophies in respect of their loading of old material remain greater than can be accounted for by chance, as we have already begun to see. In Chapter 14 we shall, for example, be making some detailed comparisons between European, Babylonian, Chinese and Central American cosmologies and astronomies, even submitting some of these to straightforward statistical comparison and evaluation.

Meanwhile, back to the other 'Ms'.

5 Three Ms: (2) The Dancing Maze

In 1922 W.H. Matthews published his book *Mazes and Labyrinths*. Like Robert Briffault's *Mothers* and J.G. Frazer's *Golden Bough*, Matthews' work is important not least because it is in touch, as a then still living concern, with a wealth of books and accounts written in the nineteenth century and earlier – prior to what we might call the 'final solution' of the twentieth century, the imposition of the current tidy, orthodox view of human development on our schools and universities.

Apart from its general wealth of information, which we draw on, *Mazes and Labyrinths* gives us one particular and very salutary lesson. Discussion of this particular item leads us into the central topic of the present chapter.

On the wall of an old Indian building in Arizona was said to have been found the drawing of what is usually called a Cretan labyrinth, due to this figure's supposed origin in Minoan Crete. In 1761 a Spaniard had questioned the Pina Indians about this labyrinth – did they have any information on it? In response one Indian drew a labyrinth for him in the sand (see *Figure 2*), saying that this was the ground plan or design for a 'building' which had once existed. The Spaniard, fortunately, preserved a copy of the sand drawing in his notes.

At the beginning of the present century, J.W. Fewkes, Chief of the Bureau of American Ethnology, attempted to investigate this matter. He showed an old Pina Indian the Spaniard's drawing from 1761, and asked if such a building had ever to his knowledge existed. The Indian replied no, but the design was one commonly employed in a children's game called *Tcuhiki*, or the House of Tcuhu, involving the movement of pebbles along a series of holes in the sand (presumably following the curves of the whorl). Tcuhu is a mythical hero, who is supposed to have made the spiral hole through which the Pina Indians came up from the underworld.

This is an absolutely thrilling account – in the light of the further material of this chapter – and one which, fortunately, we can accept totally at face value. Fewkes, Matthews, and those others involved, necessarily had to settle for the explanation that the labyrinth design had been introduced to the Indians by the early Spanish invaders – who themselves knew it very well from the floors of their own Catholic churches and cathedrals where, indeed, it served not only for penitential purposes, but as the basis for a children's game; both during the tedious church services (and often to the annoyance of the adults present) but also more legitimately in the fields, where such mazes were cut in turf or marked out with rocks or stones. Matthews, whose instinctive feelings about mazes are very strong, adds wistfully:

> *If it could be shown that these Indian childrens' games were associated with the labyrinth figure in those regions before the date of the Spanish invasion of Mexico we should be forced to conclude either that, by an extraordinary coincidence, the figure became evolved independently in the Old World and the New,* or that in both it had a common origin of astounding antiquity. *(emphasis added)*

What a thousand pities that Matthews never knew that the same Cretan labyrinth was a sacred symbol of Mother Earth among the Hopi Indians, and that the Indians of Peru had laid out two giant versions of it on the Nasca plain more than 1500 years earlier.

Figure 2 shows, variously, the sand design recorded by the inquiring Spaniard in 1761, the sacred symbol of the Hopi Indians, one of two specifically labyrinth designs on the Nasca plain (there are in all five spiral designs,) the Cretan labyrinth

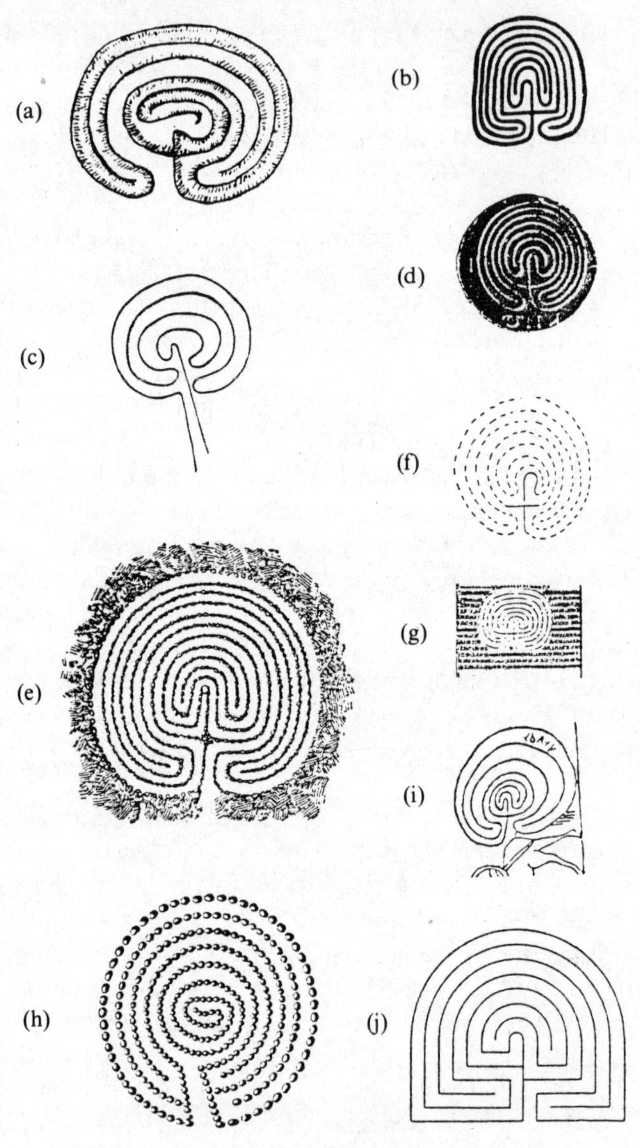

Figure 2

(a) North American Indian labyrinth from an eighteenth century Spanish manuscript. (b) Sacred symbol of the Hopi Indians. (c) Design from Nasca plain, Peru. (d) Cretan labyrinth (coin design, Cnossos). (e) Stone labyrinth from Gothland, north Europe. (f) Rock carving, Cornwall, England. (g) Labyrinth from Rajasthan, India. (h) Stone labyrinth from Finland. (i) Etruscan vase representation of the Trojan 'Troy Game'. (j) A Welsh *Caerdroia* ('city of turnings').

(usually, though incorrectly, held to be the original model of which all others are copies), a stone labyrinth in Gothland, a rock carving from Cornwall, England, a design from Rajasthan, India, a stone circle from Finland, a reproduction on an Etruscan vase of the 'Troy Game', and a Welsh *Caerdroia.*

How easily the Pina Indian evidence could have been dismissed by orthodoxy, had it been our only evidence for American labyrinths: we have been very fortunate in the truth here.

There exists, further, a paleolithic carving of a spiral maze on a mammoth bone, from Siberia.[155] This is not of the same standardised or advanced design as the labyrinths shown in *Figure 2.* It is a simple, but nevertheless seven-fold spiral leading into a central point. Importantly also (see below) the entrance to this spiral is by means of an initial left-hand turn.

It is, then, absolutely clear that the 'Cretan' labyrinth design (and leaving aside the mammoth bone) is at least 20,000 years old, since otherwise we could not find it extant both in the pre-Columbian Americas and in Crete. How disgraceful it is, first, that academic orthodoxy has as usual made no move whatsoever to come to terms with the implications of this evidence. How sad too that so many otherwise progressive writers also show a complete loss of nerve when faced with these implications. So, unlike Matthews, but like many others, Francis Hitching writes by way of 'explanation': '... since it is possible to find an identical maze pattern emerging in places as far separated in time and distance as, say, a rock in Tintagel, Cornwall, a coin design in Crete, and a symbol for the Earth Mother among the Hopi Indians of Arizona, some powerful unconscious drive must be at work'. Much use is also made by writers of the term 'archetype' in attempts to avoid the obvious truth – that we are dealing with a dissemination from some common ancient source.

It had better be said here and now that the idea of such detailed, parallel designs occurring throughout the world as a result of unconscious drive is absolute balderdash. The various writers concerned appear also, in particular, not to have the slightest idea what an archetype is and can actually achieve. In a later chapter we shall attempt to define the concept and discuss what is and what is not possible in archetypal terms.

But let us take a moment here to be quite clear about the objection. One is not at all saying that the experience of being lost in some naturally occurring maze-like terrain, or in an actual man-made maze of some kind, does not powerfully remind us of the purely mental experience we have all had of trying to find our way out of some emotional problem or relationship, or of grappling with some complex reality-task (at work, say) where repeated failure overwhelms us with weariness or panic. It very much does – of course it does. In turn, these mental feelings of twisting, turning, repeatedly losing one's way, or of winding up back where one started from, may be given concrete form in the deliberate drawing, or building, of a physical maze – such concretisation of inner experience is almost a commonplace of artistic expression. But we are speaking *here* not just of maze-like structures in general, but of a very, very precise and detailed design. We only have to glance at the various items of *Figure 2* to realise that we are dealing with one, specific model. Think of it this way – if we asked ten architects to design a swimming pool, would we get ten identical models? Of course not. So to say this again – the degree of agreement in our maze designs *absolutely could not be achieved through the medium of common unconscious impulse*. Any more than stars can look like hunted maidens!

Further proof regarding the common origin of these mazes comes from consideration of other surrounding evidence. But before moving to that, perhaps we should first define more precisely the artefact under discussion.

As regards the terminology used in respect of the phenomenon, there are two words in common use, maze and labyrinth. These are used interchangeably. It would be very convenient if the two terms applied specifically to what are in fact two different sub-categories, but they do not. The two categories are (1) the maze which requires to be solved, which sets out to trick, so that one easily loses one's way in it: indeed, once lost therein, the chances of finding the way out again either by chance or strategy are remote. The second category is (2) the maze which does not set out to trick or trap at all! One *cannot* in fact get lost in it. There is a (usually) long, winding path to the centre, where one turns into, or reverses into, a similar, or the same long, winding path that leads out again.

This second category of maze, perhaps surprisingly, irritates and upsets some commentators; or perhaps on reflection, not so surprisingly, for its unobvious mystery is actually far more threatening, both psychologically and historically, than the deliberate challenge of the first. Thus, referring to Welsh examples of the second type of maze, one researcher, P. Roberts, expressed dissatisfaction on these grounds – 'because there are no means of losing the way into the citadel, the supposed way continuing regularly through all its winding, unbroken, *which could scarcely have been the design of the inventor*' (emphasis added).[128]

No, such inevitability was *precisely* the intention and design of the original inventors. It is in fact the other kind of maze, the puzzle maze, which is the 'wrong', intrusive, Johnny-come-lately, meddlesome form (and representing intellect as opposed to intuition, method as opposed to ritual, conscious as opposed to unconscious*). As suggested earlier, it would be extremely useful if the term maze were reserved exclusively for this puzzle form, and labyrinth for the ritual artefact. But unfortunately that is not the case. However, what is very much the case is that our concern in the present book, and this chapter specifically, is only and solely with the ritual maze, to which both terms, maze and labyrinth, must be understood henceforth to refer.

Regarding the structure of our ritual labyrinth, Francis Hitching tells us that it very often consists of a spiral of seven turns – 'a twin seven-coil spiral'. This claim can be instantly checked from the designs on offer in *Figure 2.* Starting at the top of each figure, count the number of coils or tunnels to the centre. Most have seven, including the Cretan, Cornish, Rajasthan, Hopi Indian and Finnish designs, the Welsh *Caerdroia*, and the Etruscan Troy Game. (Seven, incidentally, as we shall see, is always a moon number.) The fact that there are seven coils more frequently than there are any other number is of course further strong evidence for a common-point origin of this widespread design. The significance and distribution of the number seven is nevertheless also a separate phenomenon in its own right.

The Pina Indians spoke of the maze as the basis of a children's

* Interestingly, from a psychological standpoint, the puzzle maze is usually composed of straight lines and right angles (as in the case of the giant mazes built by Egyptian pharaohs), while the ritual maze is habitually round and cursive. Among the other matters mentioned above, we are also speaking here respectively of masculine versus feminine, and Cro-Magnon versus Neanderthal.[63,69]

game. As so often, such apparently unimportant and incidental comments are full of instruction. Pliny (in his *Natural History*) makes a similar throw-away comment, that we should not compare the Egyptian and other labyrinths 'with what we see traced in our mosaic pavements *or to the mazes formed in the fields for the entertainment of children*' (italics added). Then we have the hundreds of stone labyrinths found throughout Scandinavia (as a rule near the sea or on islands), the building units ranging in size from small pebbles, to stones about the size of a head, through to large blocks requiring the combined strength of several men to lift. In Finland these mazes are said to have been used for children's games – 'where a girl stood at the centre, while the boys raced for her along the winding paths'. The possible implication of some orgiastic or sexual initiation rite is not at all misplaced here. For in Britain, at Hillbury labyrinth, the 'youths and maidens' of the town used to congregate there on Good Friday and indulge in boisterous celebrations 'the origins of which are unknown'. Here again, in all probability, are the faint traces of a once orgiastic spring rite; and if this claim seems extravagant now, like many others it will not do so by the end of the book. Still on the subject of young people, shepherd lads in Wales, up to the nineteenth century, would cut a labyrinth in the turf (a *Caerdroia*) to play a ritualised game called 'the walls of Troy', which involved the idea that the city of Troy was defended by seven walls. (It was the 'pointlessness' of this maze game to which Roberts objected.) Then, as already mentioned, the labyrinths in churches throughout Europe, as well as those found in the surrounding fields, are said specifically to have engaged the play of children.

Apart from these links with children and young people, there are strong connections too with ancient sacred mysteries. Let us by no means overlook, for a start, that the labyrinth of the Hopi is for them a very important sacred symbol; nor the strong religious/ritualistic background of the Nasca images; and that for the Pina Indians the spiral maze is the path leading from the underworld. In Britain, then, a spiral maze formerly existed at Asenby in Yorkshire, in a hollow at the top of a hillock called the Fairies' Hill. Local people would tread this maze, and then kneel at the centre 'to hear the fairies singing'. There will be a good deal more to say about fairies, but for the moment we might just recall the common belief that the fairy folk danced in circles in the moonlight, and that the penalty for being caught watching them do so was death. A general point, which all observers admit, is that these European mazes are as a rule not in places where they are likely to be stumbled on casually, and are 'liable to escape the notice of all but the intentional seeker' – a slight further hint, therefore, of a mystery aspect.

More impressive at this stage of our argument however will be Glastonbury Tor, an extremely significant mystical site. As Mary Williams writes: 'No part of the British Isles is so important and therefore so deserving of preservation as the Glastonbury area, the meeting place to an extraordinary degree of Christian and pre-Christian legend.'[205] Very recent research has revealed 'a large and massively cut maze surrounding the steep summit' of the Tor itself. It is to Glastonbury that Joseph of Arimathea is said to have brought the Holy Grail (usually held to be the cup which Christ used at the Last Supper). We have then, whatever else, a firm link here with King Arthur and his knights. It is also widely believed that at Glastonbury Joseph of Arimathea founded the first church in Britain, and perhaps in all Christendom. It would of course be a commonplace political step, repeated often enough throughout history, to found a new order on the most important site of the old.

This is the correct point to discuss Spiral Castle. First, revolving islands (we recall here that many of the Scandinavian mazes were located on islands) and castles with revolving wheels at the entrance are common in Celtic legend – one of them is the Welsh Caer Sidi (or Caer Sidin), which means literally the castle of the wheel. Prince Elfin (or his bard, who is probably himself), as we are told in the riddle of Gwion, was imprisoned in Caer Sidi, with the Thirteen Prison Locks.[78] (These thirteen locks are without doubt the 13 × 28 months of the moon year, making 364 days, and Elfin was released on the 365th day, making up the full year, i.e., the 'year and a day' of legend and fairy story.) Caer Sidi is also the Castle of Arianrhod, the Lady of the Silver Wheel (see Chapter 6). When Celtic warriors said 'our king has gone to Spiral Castle' they meant that the king was dead – and here we connect directly with our present theme. For Spiral Castle was also the name applied to the great New Grange burial mound in Ireland (also further called the Fortress of Magic or Fairydom). New Grange is a flat-topped, round barrow about a quarter of a mile in circumference, and 50ft high. It is constructed from without of some 50,000 tons of heaped stones, although the total stonework used is some 180,000 tons. Originally the finished mound was entirely covered with white quartz pebbles (the chief colour of the moon or White Goddess). It was also originally surrounded by twelve great stones at the south end, weighing between 8 and 10 tons apiece. (These twelve stones plus the barrow itself would of course make up the traditional Druidic coven of thirteen.) The ground plan of the inner barrow is in the shape of a Celtic cross. In front of the doorway is a broad slab covered with spirals. 'These spirals are double ones: follow the lines with your finger from outside to inside and when you reach the centre, there is the head of another spiral coiled in the reverse direction to take you out again.'*[78]

So there we are – once more squarely, or rather roundly – back with the Cretan labyrinth.

One further very significant feature of New Grange, however, is that on only one day a year, that of the winter solstice, are the sun's rays low enough to penetrate the interior at midday (a remarkable piece of engineering). So Spiral Castle is not only the place of the dead king. It is the place of the dead Sun. The point is extremely important, and one on which Graves also is in no doubt: 'The sacred king, then, is a Sun-King and returns at death to the Universal Mother, the White Moon Goddess.'[78] The King goes, that is to say, to Spiral Castle.

Here it is appropriate to turn to an examination of the Cretan labyrinth itself, and its own very strong mystical connections, for though in no sense the starting point of the story of the labyrinth (as is incorrectly believed) it and the legends which surround it are nevertheless an important focal point.

This particular story begins around 8000 BP, when settlers first colonised the island of Crete. From then on, on the site of the city of Cnossos, are found neolithic deposits 'of great thickness' that lead in an unbroken sequence into the so-called palace era of around 4000 BP. The culminating era of the great structures associated with King Minos, the Cretan labyrinth, the Minotaur and Theseus begins around 3500 BP. In the earlier neolithic

* Graves' imagery here very much recalls the labyrinth as often shown in ancient Egypt and India: two snakes coiled about each other, head to head at the centre.

period, however, are found many terra-cotta images of a goddess 'with exuberant thighs and breasts'.[179] These are cousin to the older 'stone Venuses' found in many areas (see Chapter 10) and are considered, like them, to be images of Mother Earth – but the Mother Earth card, like the Sun card, has once again been greatly overplayed by historians, as we shall see. In the palaces of later Cnossos, as in all the legendary tales associated with them, we find reference only to the moon. On those grounds alone we would argue that the earlier figures are also hers.

The story of Cnossos and its Minoan civilisation was brought to a sudden end by violent earthquake. There is therefore no direct historical record of its objective nature, but only the legends concerning it which circulated in later Greece. Recent archaeology of the present century has however revealed its architectural magnificence.

The ruler of Minoan Crete was King Minos, though the name almost certainly refers to an hereditary office and many different individuals, as with 'Pharaoh'. Minos is said to be the son of Europa, a moon goddess, and Zeus – he having seduced Europa in the guise of a three-coloured bull. The three colours are those of the lunar deity, but bulls in any case always represent the moon: these are all matters for a chapter specifically concerning the moon. Minos in any case is married to the moon goddess Pasiphaë, and their daughter Ariadne is also a moon goddess (and moreover, as Graves tells us, identical with the Celtic Arianrhod). Already we see that from all points of view Cnossos is the Court of the Moon, but there is much more evidence still.

At Cnossos was allegedly located the famous Cretan labyrinth, the image of which appears so prolifically on Cretan coins of the period, as do also, however, swastikas and the heads of bulls. 'Allegedly' because excavation has revealed no trace whatsoever of such a structure, only a meandering, swastika-like red (n.b.) motif on a white (n.b.) background on the walls of the palace. I myself think the reason for the non-discovery of the labyrinth is because this was no permanent structure in stone, much less underground as many assume, but one built of bushes or trees, and quite deliberately left open to the (night) sky. Even rings of large, free-standing boulders would of course vanish without trace in violent earthquake.

The story goes that the labyrinth was built, at the suggestion of the oracle, to form the prison of an offspring born to Pasiphaë following her perverted love affair with a bull (perhaps a father-in-law fixation!). This offspring was the Minotaur, a creature with the head of a bull and the body of a man. Anyone entering the labyrinth was killed by the Minotaur. Meantime, a son of Minos had been unlawfully slain in Attica, and as a penance Minos demanded of the Athenians that they send him a tribute of seven youths and seven maidens every nine years (seven and nine, we note, both being moon numbers). These young people were then thrust into the labyrinth, taken by the Minotaur and killed. On the occasion of the third tribute, Theseus offered himself voluntarily as one of the party.*

As is well known, prior to his entry into the labyrinth, Theseus was provided with a ball of thread by Ariadne (and a sword) so that he could find his way out again after killing the Minotaur, which he duly did. The legend as it comes down to us is however, I suggest, seriously misleading in one respect. For the Cretan labyrinth was emphatically *not* a puzzle maze, as is altogether clearly shown in the numerous coin designs of Crete, and all the versions of this maze throughout subsequent classical Greece and Rome. Theseus therefore needed no 'clue' (the word means, literally, a thread) to escape from the labyrinth – all he needed was to be told by Ariadne that the 'maze' consisted of one path in and one path out. No, the clue, in both senses of the term, is telling us something quite different – namely that the maze dancers laid down a cord as they went in, and gathered it up again as they danced out. The cord laying and gathering was a symbolic and ritual act, the evidence for which, and whose explanation, must largely wait for the next chapter. However, the original rope dance may have been replaced later by one in which the dancers held hands, before and behind, so forming a linked procession and a symbolic rope. This arrangement can be seen, for example, in the farandole of Provence, which, interestingly enough, involves dancing 'a great variety of spirals'. (None the less, from evidence we shall look at in later chapters, there is little doubt that the original method of killing the human sacrificial victims

* There are many points we should constantly be fastening on here – but to do so would turn the narrative itself into a labyrinth (which, however, it is). The 'sacrifice who goes willingly', for instance, is a very important theme indeed. It figures centrally, of course, in the story of Christ himself.

involved strangulation with a cord.)

That dancing was quite certainly involved in the maze ritual we know from more than one source. For example, Homer wrote: 'Daedalus in Cnossos once contrived/A dancing floor for fair-haired Ariadne', a reference, as scholars agree, to the labyrinth dance. More directly still, legend states that the subsequently fleeing Theseus and Ariadne, on the island of Delos, founded and performed the *Geranos* or crane dance, which was still performed (in actuality that is, not in legend) up till recent times. This ballet enacted the threading of the labyrinth and the associated rituals. The precise details of the dance are not known today, but Graves, quoting Plutarch, tells us that 'it was performed around a horned altar, and represented the circles that coiled and uncoiled in the labyrinth'. The horned altar, of course, represents the Minotaur – or rather that which the Minotaur also symbolised – and quite certainly actual human sacrifice was involved. We can be sure that on Minoan Crete, at least originally, seven young males and seven young females were sacrificed at an important rite every nine years in honour of the Moon Goddess, most probably on the altar at the heart of the labyrinth.

The historical thread of the maze dance is one we ourselves do well to follow. This dance certainly flourished in the city of Troy – not, I am sure, as a borrowing from Crete, but having there its own local genesis.* We have already seen the name 'Troy' inscribed on the labyrinth on the Etruscan vase (*Figure 2*). Matthews comments on 'the frequency with which the name Troy is associated with the idea of the labyrinth'. He continues: 'We find this association, for instance, in the case of the "Troy towns"

* There is much talk in all historical texts of customs being borrowed here or imposed there. While borrowings and enforced impositions of traditions have certainly sometimes occurred (in the contexts of religious conversion, war and conquest, and whatever) this aspect of affairs has been greatly over-emphasised – there is, in other words, in many cases a patently strained air of forcing the argument. It is much rather the case, I suggest, that similar customs have grown up around the world – or rather *survive* everywhere – because, as the present book is in the process of demonstrating, all cultures have brought the same seeds with them from one extremely ancient point of origin. Orthodox scholars (as we shall see further) have a strong vested interest in denying parallel generation in widely separated areas. For argument in favour of local dissemination in recent times is one important method used by orthodoxy in denying the genuine and extreme antiquity of the old ways we are examining.

of Somerton and Hillbury, the "Walls of Troy" of the Cumberland marshes and Appleby in Lincolnshire and the "*Caerdroia*" of the Welsh shepherds. In northern Europe we find it as "Troja" or in such combinations as "Trojeborg" or "Tröborg".'[128]

The *Caerdroia* of the Welsh shepherd may mean 'the walls of Troy' (*caer* meaning variously wall, fort, castle, citadel); or it may be a contraction of *caer y troian*, meaning 'the city of wanderings or turnings' (or of course the *castle* of wanderings or turnings, and so again Spiral Castle). The second case gives us a purely Welsh derivation for *Caerdroia*, one which is disputed however, and probably precisely for the reason suggested earlier, that the idea of greater and indigenous antiquity always constitutes the greater threat to orthodox, reductionist views. One would turn the whole argument on the objectors here, and far from agreeing that *Caerdroia* arises from the name of the city of Troy, propose rather that Troy derives it own name from the Indo-European word for 'to turn' (as in Welsh *troi*, modern German *drehen*, and our own word 'turn' itself). In other words, then, Troy itself would effectively mean the city 'of the labyrinth' or 'the turning dance'.

In at least indirect support of this view, the 'Troy Game' or the 'Troy Dance' was, according to Graves, 'a labyrinthine dance of Asia Minor' and was also performed in Rome by young noblemen (the 'young' may be significant here, see above) 'in honour of their Trojan origin'. Ceremonial parades called Troi or Troi-Aldei are also written of in thirteenth-century Germany, and the songs which accompanied them were called Troyerlais. Some one-time folk-dances of Serbia were called Trojanka and Trojanac. Unfortunately no details are recorded of how these dances were performed. In Britain, Graves further tells us, the Troy labyrinth dance survives as the Easter Maze dances of country villages – so we would have then a further link between the turf and stone mazes and spring/fertility rites – and he further himself connects the dances with the tradition of Spiral Castle, all of which is very satisfactory.

Many churches and cathedrals throughout Europe (particularly in France, Britain and Italy) have large Cretan mazes inlaid on their floors. Why should that be the case? The answer is a tribute to the great importance attaching to the maze among the general population well into historical times.* Many churches and cathedrals were actually built on the sites of former major labyrinths, for possibly purely political reasons – i.e., to make the churches more acceptable to the people. Even then, the mazes were too important simply to obliterate – they had to be actually incorporated into the physical fabric of the church. And not only that – they had to be *used*. Walking the maze on the church floor was a recognised act of penance, with suitable prayers and votaries offered at points *en route* by the penitent. Treading the maze thus was often known as taking 'a trip to Jerusalem' – for very wealthy penitents would sometimes make a real trip to the real Holy Land to atone for some major sin. The mazes in the churches were not danced, at least not by adults. That would have been too great and too dangerous a concession. On the contrary, the church with good reason frowned on dancing in general, and especially dancing on the Sabbath. We do in fact readily come to understand much of the nature of the Old Religion simply by reversing the edicts of the church – clearly dancing on the Sabbath was *exactly* what you did in the Old Religion, that is indeed why witches did it: bearing in mind also that the (Christian) Sabbath is in origin not a weekly but a monthly event, a festival held to celebrate the menstruation of the Moon Goddess (see Chapters 9 and 10).

There are a number of further points to make concerning the labyrinth.

The idea of giving Theseus a ball of thread was suggested to Ariadne by Daedalus, the engineer who built the labyrinth. After the departure of Theseus and Ariadne, Daedalus himself was thrown into the maze – but escaped by making himself a pair of wings out of old feathers. (The fact that he could fly out of the labyrinth does suggest that this was open to the sky.) So then Daedalus went into hiding, pursued by King Minos. Minos went

* It is really astonishing that conventional accounts could so readily swallow the view that the notion and the entrenched use of the maze could have spread throughout Europe (even into non-Romanised, non-Celtic Finland!) from an 'origin' in a fanciful Cretan legend, which does not even have a physical maze to its credit as far as archaeology is concerned. Well, everyone believes what they want to believe – as long as the evidence allows it. But sadly for orthodoxy, the evidence, as we have already seen even thus far, is that the 'Cretan' maze/labyrinth is at least 20,000 years old.

everywhere asking a riddle – namely, how could one pass a thread through an empty snail shell without breaking the shell? – knowing Daedalus would be unable to resist tackling the problem. Sure enough, Daedalus gave away his whereabouts by providing an adequate solution, which was to tie the thread to an ant, and let the ant enter the shell. The true significance of his ant-and-thread answer must wait for the next chapter. Here we can point out not simply that the snail and its shell, like all wet and watery creatures, belongs to the moon – but that in ancient Mexico the moon god, Tecciztecatl, is shown enclosed in a snail shell. The shell itself, of course, is a spiral labyrinth. If we needed it then, here is one further identification of the Cretan labyrinth with the moon – or for that matter, of all labyrinths with the moon.

The Minotaur at the heart of the labyrinth in Crete has special significances for which we need other contexts. In particular, James Vogh has given us a remarkable insight into this creature (see Chapter 10). Not for a moment, however, need we doubt the grim realities of the Minotaur cult: 'At Cnossos a deposit of children's bones with clear knife marks has been unearthed pointing, as it seems, to the cannibalistic feast of some minotaur.'[19]

The word 'labyrinth' itself is commonly said to derive from the word 'labrys', meaning a two-headed axe. The symbol of the two-headed axe is certainly found everywhere in Crete, and on altars where it is combined with bull horns (which themselves are found on all sides, both in naturalistic and highly stylised forms). On the Mycenaean mainland also, the archaeologist Schliemann discovered in a grave an ox-head in gold plate, with a double axe between the upright horns. There are, however, problems with the words labyrinth and labrys which many, though not all, philologists are inclined to gloss over. First, the suffix *-inthos* (*labyrinthos*) is invariably applied only to words of pre-Greek origin. Second, the word labrys reverses the 'yr' of labyrinth into 'ry', which is not a particularly easy change to accept philologically. I am inclined myself to think that labyrinth is actually another surviving Neanderthal word (the name for what was, as we have already begun to demonstrate, their central religious structure) and labrys a later barbaric corruption of it. However, be that as it may, my own view again is that the two-headed axe is certainly a stylised female vagina(!), as is then also the derivative two-headed god, Janus, who looks both ways, back into the old year and forward into the new. The moon, divided into two halves of light and dark, the likewise so divided yin-yang symbol of ancient China, and so forth, I take to be further variations of the same basic symbology. Interesting, and I think relevant reports come from two mediaeval Spanish writers,[29] and from Margaret Murray.[134] These tell us that witches danced in couples joined back to back with interlocking hands or arms. In this position they spun around shaking and tossing their heads in frenzy. In general terms, in this whole context, we probably also have a further oblique reference to the labyrinth with its two paths, one leading in and one leading out, so to speak, 'back to back'.

Early and mediaeval alchemists were also preoccupied with the labyrinth – which they usually called the Labyrinth of Solomon – and we shall want to look at their views. It is in fact most curious how, all over Europe, similar such names were given locally to mazes and labyrinths – the Ruins of Jerusalem, the City of Nineveh, the Walls of Jericho, the Walls of Troy. Suddenly the image springs to mind of Joshua with seven priests marching seven times around the walls of the city of Jericho. Or perhaps they danced. It seems, as the Arabs say, *koolshi wahed*, it is all one.

It would be excellent if it were the case that entry into the labyrinth always involved an initial turn to the left. It does, for instance, in the Pina Indian, Rajasthan, Cretan and Cornwall designs (*Figure 2*), and the mammoth bone carving. I would say that of all the instances I have examined about fifty per cent involve an entry turn to the left – which is, however, still remarkable, given that turning left is the instinctive move of the left-hander, while nevertheless only some ten per cent of Europeans are in fact left-handed. (That turning movements are indeed instinctive we see from the following experiment. If a left-handed person is blindfolded and asked to walk across a field in a straight line, he veers to the left. A right-handed person in the same situation veers to the right.) My own view is that entry into the labyrinth was, originally, always a left-hand turn – partly because I consider that Neanderthal man was left-handed – but also, very importantly, for the reasons given at the end of the next chapter.

Finally, do we have any evidence of mazes in Africa? The short answer is no – but we have some 'evidence' from W.H. Matthews which, like his intuitive grasp of the importance of the Pina Indian sand drawing, one is inclined to take very seriously. Matthews came across an old review of a book titled *Some Zulu Customs and Folklore*, by L.H. Samuelson, published in 1912. According to the review, the book contained a description of mazes made on the ground by Zulus. Matthews' efforts to obtain a copy of the book were in vain – the British Museum had no copy, nor the Folk Lore Society or any other library. A strange set of circumstances. We are left with the tantalising possibility that African tribespeople in recent times also possessed a faint memory of the labyrinth. Here we were too late – but, fortunately, enough of the story of our real history survives.

6 Three Ms: (3) The Spinning Moon

It is a fortunate circumstance for present purposes that from our point of view on earth the moon appears to have no spinning motion, i.e., does not seem to revolve about its own axis. On the contrary, it appears locked solid towards us, presenting always the self-same side to the earth. This circumstance is fortunate, for otherwise there would certainly be those who would want to equate any perceived spinning movement of the moon to the movement of a bobbin, or the turn of a spinning wheel.

The proper explanation of the 'spinning moon' is indeed a very different one, and will enable us to solve many hitherto considered impenetrable mysteries. But before proceeding, let us emphasise that we are dealing here, once more, with a universal stratum of material of great antiquity. Again we cheerfully invite (or rather defy) orthodoxy to produce an explanation of the material's world-wide provenance and intensity, other than that of dissemination from a once central and totally authoritative source.

As opener, Robert Briffault tells us that world-wide 'one of the activities most commonly ascribed to the moon is that of spinning and weaving', and proceeds to a series of instances. He reports that in ancient Egypt, for example, the moon goddess Neith was held to have invented weaving – her symbol is the shuttle. The

Navaho Indians of far away North America likewise call the moon 'the Ancient Spinstress' and say that she sits at a loom for ever weaving a girdle. In similar vein, the Iroquois say that an old woman lives in the moon, eternally weaving a forehead strap – which once a month is unravelled by a cat, so that the woman must weave till the end of time. (Here, perhaps, is a parallel with Greek Penelope, who unpicked her own weaving secretly each night, so that she might never complete and so not have to marry.) In China the moon was said to supply the threads which bind marriages. In Sumatra the moon is said to spin cotton. In Mexico, before a woman embroiders, she should stroke a serpent – and serpents, as we see in a later chapter, always and universally represent the moon. Jewish women were recommended to do their spinning and weaving by moonlight, while in Germany precisely the opposite counsel applied – on no account was spinning to be done by the light of the moon. The moon as spinstress is also found in 'innumerable' European fairy-tales. There are several German and Slavonic stories where a woman who is guilty of breaking the Sabbath by working at her loom on that day is changed into the moon. The Walloons in Belgium, who are possibly Celts, say (just like the Navaho and the Iroquois) that the moon is the Eternal Spinstress (it is interesting how often the concept 'eternal' recurs). The Kashubs of Poland say that they see Mother Eve sitting spinning in the moon.

Precisely similar associations are found in cultures which do not actually spin (so no turning bobbins or spinning wheels there in any case) but who weave and make cloth with raffia, the fibres and sheets of the prepared inner bark of trees, the filaments of palm leaves and so forth. Thus among the Potowatomi North American Indians the moon is a basket maker, while in Polynesia the moon's favourite occupation is making bark-cloth.

Of further note is that always and everywere in the world all activities connected with the spinning, weaving, dyeing and fashioning of cloth were conducted exclusively by women. There are in fact strong hints of once powerful religious connections here. Among North American Indians the processes involved were surrounded with all manner of ceremonial rites, producing a kind of secret society from which men were excluded. The Dyaks of Sarawak say weaving is dependent on 'the Great Female Spirit'. Among Maori women initiation into the art of plaiting and mat-making was a religious ceremony. The workshop itself was consecrated, and no work proceeded when a man was present. Above all to mention, perhaps, is that there is *never* any sense of inferiority connected with this exclusively female domain – quite the contrary in fact. In Polynesia, for example, the royal princesses spent most of their time at the art of weaving – and it was a strong point of honour for the queen to be the finest cloth-maker in the land.

Very similar elements of the involvement of the highest in the land, of mysticism and of an exclusive female preserve are found also in classical Greek legend. The goddess Athene (who however is not identified as a moon goddess, although her symbol is the owl, a night bird), a daughter of Zeus, was the patroness of spinners, weavers and embroiderers. She considered herself to be the most gifted of weavers. She had heard, however, of the great weaving skill of Arachne, the daughter of a humble artisan. Athena then challenged Arachne to a weaving competition – and lost. In a towering rage at the perfection of Arachne's work, and her own defeat, Athena tore Arachne's tapestry to pieces. (Most interestingly, what Arachne perhaps wove was a thirteen-division zodiac – a matter we shall be considering in detail in Chapter 10). In despair at this outcome, Arachne hanged herself. But Athena now took pity, and saved Arachne by turning her into a spider hanging from a thread (which is said to be why spiders indulge in this behaviour). In other versions of the story, Athena strikes the triumphant Arachne with her shuttle in hatred – but once again turning her into a spider.

Before proceeding further we need to address the central question, *why* should spinning and weaving be associated with the moon? We have just had a very dim and distorted clue – but the first part of the answer is in any case on full view, in the primitive world that is, for there the moon *is* a spider. Such must also have been the case in old Europe – that is, long before ancient Greece – as we shall see, but the direct understanding has there long been lost. We have only coded fragments.

So the Pawnees of North America actually call the moon the Spiderwoman. The Paresi of Central Brazil likewise identify the moon as a spider. The Indians of the Banks Islands in Canada say the companion of the moon god, and his associate in the creation of mankind, is a spider. In far-off Borneo, the moon deity is said to have created the world by assuming the form of a spider and spinning a web. Among the Nias of Indonesia the soul of the moon is a spider. In the Loyalty Islands of Melanesia the spider and the worm are the representatives of the power that sends rain – and all water, again, always signifies the moon (see later chapters).

In Europe, as already indicated, similar elements and connections can with patience also be identified. In this respect we shall be drawing, among others, on the work of James Vogh. Vogh, unfortunately for him but fortunately for us, was not aware of the open situation prevailing in the primitive world, or the work of Robert Briffault. He was obliged therefore to discover the moon-as-spider connection in the European arena by sheer detective work. His work, however, is our gain.

For the moment, returning to Briffault, we take a tack apparently away from spiders and threads, but which nevertheless will lead us back to them in due course.

Unlikely as it seems at first hearing, a further world-wide symbol for the moon is the square cross, that is, the upright cross with all arms of equal length, usually known as the Greek cross, or the crux quadrata. (Vogh actually considers this cross to be a stylised spider, and it is true the cross is also found on the back of spider amulets in American Indian burial mounds – but there is, I think, a much more dramatic explanation.) Once again this phenomenon, of cross as moon, is fully public in the primitive world. The Polynesians, who regularly use the crux quadrata to represent the moon, say that its four arms are her four limbs, which she formerly extended so as to rule both day and night. At the present time, they say, she has retracted those limbs, and rules only the night. The Maoris of New Zealand, who are Polynesians, habitually wore a neck amulet of the square cross, of the four outstretched arms. The statues of Easter Island, again in Polynesia, are likewise marked with this cross. On another continent, the Luiseño Indians of California, North America, also represent the Great Mother with her limbs extended in the form of a cross. They say that her four limbs represent the four points of the compass, or the four winds.

In Mexico the crux quadrata is especially associated with Quetzalcoatl, the plumed serpent (n.b.), who controls some aspects of the weather. The same cross appeared prominently on the shrines of the Great Goddess in China, and is likewise found throughout Tibet and western Asia ('the cross is an alternative symbol of the moon in western Asia generally' – Briffault), including Sumeria, Assyria, and among the Semitic/Hamitic peoples. It is seen, strikingly, in Egyptian portraits of the moon god who wears it as a neck pendant.

Is it not a truly remarkable circumstance that we find the square cross, in both cases representing the moon (an unlikely enough choice of symbol, heaven knows), worn as a pendant about the neck of the Egyptian moon god and that of the Maori warrior?

Robert Graves tells us that 'the square cross . . . has from time immemorial represented the full extent of sovereignty'. (All commentators, incidentally, agree that the cross, in its various forms, has universal pre-Christian distribution; and is almost invariably regarded as possessing deep religious and magical significance, in the large majority of cases connected with nature worship – while Briffault, concurring, insists this in turn is almost invariably primitive cosmic lunar religion.) Graves continues: 'This cross was a prime symbol in Minoan Crete, either alone or enclosed in a circle, reserved for the Moon Goddess and her royal son, King Minos.' As we already saw in Chapter 5, the palace of Minos is hardly anything *but* the Court of the Moon. Yet, in a way, it makes a greater impact still when we learn that the square cross symbolised the moon among the Bushmen and Hottentots of South Africa. There pregnant women in particular kept a wooden square cross over their beds.*

Back now to North America, where we find conclusive evidence of the spider-moon-cross equation, in the form of numerous designs found in Indian burial mounds. Three of these are shown in *Figure 3*. These, as we see, are readily identifiable naturalistic spiders, on whose backs appears the square cross – or sometimes a swastika. Consideration of the swastika is postponed for later in the chapter, where it leads to important conclusions.

* Those who attempt to explain away or rationalise such remarkable and of course pre-Christian parallels often appeal to the concept of the (Jungian) archetype. As it happens, I would myself be prepared to accept a possible archetypal significance for the fourfold mandala in general and perhaps also for some aspects of menstruation. But there is no way whatsoever we can appeal to archetypes for an explanation of, for instance, the seven maidens of the Pleiades, or the Spinning Moon of the present discussion.

Figure 3
Spider and cross designs from North American Indian burial mounds.

For the moment we return to threads and spiders, specifically in Europe.

Very many of the most important goddesses (not gods, note) of the European pantheon have a clear connection with spinning and weaving. The Greek Athena has already been mentioned. Then there is Persephone, the daughter of Demeter (and it is the cult of Demeter and Persephone which is involved in the great Eleusinian mystery rites) who is also, Graves tells us, the third or death aspect of the Moon Goddess. Persephone was abducted by Pluto, the god of the underworld. However, Zeus, her father, was able to come to an understanding with Pluto whereby Persephone was allowed to come back for two-thirds of the year, only spending one-third in the underworld. (Here is a clear reference to the death and rebirth of the year.) When in Hades Persephone was occupied with weaving the shrouds of the dead. Artemis and Aphrodite (both moon goddesses) and the Nymphs were also spinstresses. In northern mythology Freia/Frija/Frigga/Frigg ('the horned goddess who is avowedly the moon' – Briffault), Holde and Bertha are all spinstresses. Expremely important are the three Norns of northern mythology and the three Fates of Rome and Greece (the Parcae, Moirai). In the classical scheme these three (the 'three' of course alerts us to the fact that we are really talking about the triune Moon Goddess – and in any case at Sparta, and elsewhere, one of the Fates was specified as Persephone) control the destinies of all mortals: one spins the thread of our lives, the second fashions it, the third cuts it at the moment of death. We can hardly imagine processes more important to mankind – so the high estate of this material cannot be disputed. All our European metaphors concerning the weave of destiny, the tapestry of life and so on are said to derive from this source (although the fact is that both derive from far older roots).

James Vogh has further explored the wider ramifications and influence of threads and cords. He draws attention to the *sutra*, a cord worn by high-ranking Hindus, and quotes the *Upanishads*: 'By Vayu, the inner controller, as by a thread, O Gautama, are this world, the other world, and all beings held together.' Sutra (as in *Karma Sutra*, and so on) is the same word as 'sew'. Vogh goes on to speak of the *cinctura* of the Franciscans, the cord which binds them to their holy work, the *llatu*, a cord said to protect the life of the Inca emperor, and the Celtic *torc* (torque). The *torc*, worn by all the moon-worshipping Celts, was a neck collar in gold, silver or iron, depending on what one could afford, fashioned to resemble twisted cords. All these, I agree with Vogh, are undoubtedly derivatives of the spider's thread. One of the two possible derivations of the word religion itself is from *religāre*, meaning to bind up, to bind together – so religion is 'that which binds'. (The second possible derivation is from *relegere* meaning to go through again in reading or thought.) Vogh could also have mentioned the leather *tifilin* worn by all orthodox Jews at prayer, and he very much should have mentioned all the following items.

First, far back in time, we have the cord the ancient shamans and medicine men wore, which is often depicted in cave paintings. This was tied below the knee or on the thigh. It is, undoubtedly, the origin of the garter worn by the leader of the witches' coven in France as a sign of rank; also of the garter which, throughout Europe, the new bride threw into the wedding crowd, and was considered to have magical and luck-bringing properties. In France, the bride's garter was ceremonially removed by one of the pages, then cut up in pieces and distributed among, or even sold to, the congregants. There is also a legend which connects King Arthur with the garter. According to Northumberland folklore, King Arthur and Guinevere sleep in a cave under the castle of Sewingshields – of course the name of the castle itself is of considerable relevance – waiting to be reawakened. The story runs that a farmer once found his way into this cave by accident. Near the entrance he saw a stone sword, a garter and a horn. He took up the sword and cut the garter, but his nerve failed when he saw the sleepers beginning to wake. As he ran from the cave he heard King Arthur say: 'O woe befall the evil day/that ever the witless wight was born/who took the sword, the garter cut/but never blew the bugle horn.'[134]

This knightly connection is continued in respect of the Templars. At the trials of the Templars, after their universal arrest in 1307, one of the charges laid against them was that they surrounded or touched the head of their idols with small cords, which they wore around themselves next to the shirt or flesh. When the Templar order was originally founded, only nine knights were admitted, and despite pleas no more were admitted for another nine years. (Nine is one of the numbers of the moon, for it is three times three.) The arrests of the long-suspected Templars were made simultaneously throughout France on Friday, which of course is Freija's day – the 13th – the most unlucky day in our calendar. Did the authorities believe that on that day the Templars would be very much occupied with something – precisely as when the Arabs launched the six-day war on Israel on Yom Kippur, the Jews' holiest day? The Templars wore a white mantle – just as the Druid priests had – and took for their emblem a red cross on a white background (two of the moon's colours), choosing the eight-pointed Maltese cross, which may indeed by a stylised spider. In case this idea seems extravagant, *Figure 4* shows four 'Maltese' crosses from Indian Central America, bearing the spider cross/swastika. (The fourth design suggests lightning, always a symbol of the moon – see Chapters 7 and 10.) The seal of the Knights Templar in Britain has a Maltese cross standing on a crescent moon. During the 200 years of their existence before the trials the Templars were suspected of being sorcerers, adepts, magicians, alchemists and sexual deviants. One purpose of their secret ceremonies was said to be to make the land germinate and the trees grow. The Templars (and this matter links directly with the material of the previous chapter) were also said to be guardians of the Holy Grail. Finally, they had close connections with the Gnostic sect of the Cathars, who were also alleged to wear a sacred cord of some kind.[5]

Of still greater interest is the founding of the Most Noble Order of the Garter in Britain, some forty years after the demise of the Templars.

The Garter Order was founded by King Edward III in 1348. It was then, and is today, considered the highest British civil and military honour obtainable. However, the earliest records of the

Figure 4
Splayed eight-point 'Maltese' crosses from Indian Central America, bearing also square cross, swastika and lightning motifs.

founding of the Order were destroyed by fire (whether accidentally or otherwise) so that the only accounts available are those of (a) speculation and (b) popular legend. As it happens, popular legend is far more useful from our point of view than any official statement! One speculation is that Edward III wished to revive the traditions of King Arthur and the Knights of the Round Table. (I would rather put it that Edward was continuing a tradition of which the Round Table was itself a continuation.) Another proposal is that Richard I, while in difficult battle against Cyprus and Acre, and inspired by the valour of St George, tied a leather thong or garter around the legs of certain of his knights (perhaps not the first thing one would think of doing) so that they might be reminded of the honour of their enterprise. The most common account, however, the popular account, is that while dancing with Edward, Joan of Kent (the Duchess of Salisbury) dropped her garter. The King picked this up, and placed it on his own leg, saying '*honi soit qui mal y pense*' (shame to him who thinks ill). Thereupon he formed two groups of knights, who were to wear garters.* The first consisted of himself

* The Knights of the Order of the Holy Spirit in France – 'whoever is of the highest quality in the kingdom' – also wore a blue garter (the *cordon bleu*). This Catholic order, which like the Order of the Garter became the most illustrious order of chivalry in the kingdom, was founded by Henri III in Paris in 1578. These French knights too, as well as a garter, wore a collar just as do the Garter knights – see above. But the wearing of the garter in France must strike us as even more strange – for, as mentioned earlier, the head of a witch coven there wore a garter to indicate his or her rank, and the witch trials had by then been in progress for some 200 years. From the collar worn by the French knights hung an eight-point cross (the Templar cross) bearing the *fleur-de-lis* design of three (n.b.) petals or leaves. One commentator tells us that an emblem similar to the *fleur-de-lis* 'is found from the earliest times in many parts of the world', and does not always symbolise a flower – including in ancient Egypt and the Far East. In India the device seems to symbolise the trident of the Hindu god Shiva. A single red (n.b.) *fleur-de-lis* is the coat of arms of the city of Florence in Italy.

and twelve companions, the second of the Prince of Wales and twelve companions. So we have two 'covens' of thirteen. If this association with witchcraft seems absurd, let us note (with Margaret Murray) that the robe which each knight wore was embroidered with 168 garters. Together with the actual garter worn on the leg, the total is 169 – or 13 times 13. Moreover, the garter was worn on the *left* leg, below the knee. One would certainly have expected both the left (given its world-wide bad press and occult connections – see Chapter 12) and the number thirteen to have been avoided. The witchcraft trials and burnings were by this time (1348) getting into their full stride throughout Europe – just to be seen dancing anticlockwise round a church, the natural movement for a left-hander of course, was a burning offence. My own view is that Margaret Murray was absolutely right in her belief that by picking up the garter and placing it on his own leg (whether that incident really occurred, or whether it is but a metaphor) Edward was placing the countess of Salisbury, now revealed as a witch, under his own personal protection. (As we shall show and as did Murray, there is good evidence of the widespread involvement of highly placed individuals, both churchmen and laity, in all aspects of witchcraft.) Also significant in this story, for myself, is the mention of dancing – for dancing is as firmly identified with witchcraft, and fairies, as is riding broomsticks and moonbeams (and connected, ultimately, with maze dancing, fertility dancing, and orgiastic ceremony).

Matters do not end here, however. The Countess of Salisbury subsequently married the Prince of Wales (the leader of the second 'coven' of Garter knights), known as the Black Prince. It is said that he was called such from his alleged habit of wearing black armour in battle – but historians say 'this is only a story'. So much the better! The Black Prince, along with the red square Cross of St George (representing the moon, as we saw earlier) on a white background – which the Order adopted as its flag – gives us the three colours of the Moon Goddess. The Black Prince's own emblem was three ostrich plumes, so here we seem to have another reference to the triune Moon Goddess. But we are still not done. The companions of the Order also wear a collar, which consists of many knotted cords with tassels joining small insignia – something very like a *torc* in fact. And we are still not done. The full insignia of the Order shows at the centre St George killing the dragon. The dragon, however, as all commentators agree, is a stylised and embroidered snake (see Chapter 10), so once again the moon. Admittedly St George is shown killing it – but we will discuss that matter elsewhere.

Yet we are still not done. It occurred to me that St George himself might bear looking into. To my surprise, it was hard to find anything more than one-line passing references – often not even that. Eventually I found the information sought, and the probable reason for its non-ready availability, in MacCulloch's *The Mythology of All Races.*[120] It seems that today's famous personage of St George was, at the English Synod of 1222, classed as a saint only of the second rank;[144] and he is today the Patron Saint of England *only* because he was plucked from obscurity to become the Patron Saint of the Order of the Garter.

The person who was later to become St George was born at Lydda (modern Ludd) in Palestine in AD 270. In adult life he was a Roman officer, and a Christian. When the Emperor Diocletian began persecuting the Christians, St George resigned his commission and urged the Emperor to accept Christ. For this action he was put to death. But he came to life again! Once again – and many more times subsequently – he was put to death, but always sprang to life again. He was only finally killed when his bones were ground in a mill and winnowed into the fields. Clearly, we are speaking here about the dying and resurrected god, the dying and resurrected year. The story of St George is actually the story of the principal Sumerian god of corn-and-vegetation, Tammuz. The sister of Tammuz is Ishtar the moon goddess. The noble deed of Tammuz, for which he was executed, was to urge the king to worship the seven planets and the twelve (or as we shall argue later, the thirteen) signs of the zodiac. But as often as the king killed him, Tammuz came to life again – until the king ground his bones in a mill and scattered them. Tammuz, incidentally, was also worshipped in Babylon, Syria, Canaan, Phoenicia and among the Jews. His festival is known as the Festival of Weeping Women (n.b.).

The legend of St George was widely taken up in the Middle East, and was far more written about by Islamic writers than by Christian commentators – perhaps for the fairly obvious reasons indicated. The contributor of the entry in *The Mythology of All Races*, Dr S.H. Langdon, notes dryly that no western reference article on St George (apart from his own) makes any reference to the numerous Arab sources on St George.[120]

There is a further circumstance of note (and, incidentally, we are not wandering from the central point of this chapter: for we are always talking about the moon, the spider and the feminine). During the fourteenth and fifteenth centuries – in other words right from its outset – companion *ladies* were regularly admitted to the Order of the Garter (Dames de la Fraternité de St Georges). 'Nothing is known today of the form of admitting them to the Order' (are we surprised?), but portraits of some of these ladies show them wearing the garter on the left arm. Why were ladies admitted to this very exclusive male Order at all – was it for the usual reason that men and women habitually seek each other's company?

There is one further cord we should mention. And that is the umbilical cord which connects the unborn and newly-born baby to its mother. This cord consists of two veins plaited about a central artery – so there are *three* strands in all (not unlike a *torc*, of course). At birth, momentarily, the baby hangs suspended by a thread from its mother.

At this point we should come back to the swastika, and to what I believe is the true explanation and ultimate origin of all the material we are considering. There are two forms of the swastika, the one which faces left (the *sauvastika*) and the one which faces right (the *svastika*). The fact that Sanskrit has two different names for the two symbols emphasises that they are not, originally at any rate, identical or interchangeable. The swastika symbol is first found on permanent record in Asia about 5000 years BP. Thereafter it is found widely also throughout the Middle East and Europe. It became a favourite symbol on ancient Mesopotamian coinage (and Cretan coinage, as we noted in Chapter 5), and also in early Christian and Byzantine art. It is further widely found in Polynesia and in North and South America, but only occasionally in Africa. In Australia it is unknown. At the present day it is the most widely used and auspicious symbol of the Hindus, Jainists and Buddhists. Always and everywhere throughout its history it appears to have been a religious symbol, and clearly one of considerable importance.

It is intriguing, to say the least, to find this sign in use throughout Europe, Asia, America and the Pacific – once again, world-wide. Indeed, the Spaniards arriving in South America were 'astonished' to find it in use.

In early historical times in Asia the left-facing swastika, the *sauvastika*, had, though not absolutely or always, the reputation of being ill-omened; while the right-facing swastika, the *svastika*, is definitely auspicious. Partly due to the manner of its use in the Indo-European arena, majority opinion is that the swastika generally, but certainly the right-facing version, is a solar symbol. It was for this reason, and on the suggestion of a nationalistic poet (Guido von List) that all anti-semitic organisations adopt the right-handed swastika for their symbol, that Hitler chose this as the emblem of the Nazi party. (Curiously enough he nevertheless happened to pick on the three colours of the moon for his flag – a black swastika in a white circle on a red background.) However, is it perhaps the case that the left-hand swastika represents the moon? This is the opinion of Robert Graves, and my own also. (Perhaps Guido von List likewise realised that the Jews are the people of the moon – see Chapter 10.) Usefully in this connection, we not only find left-facing swastikas in the Americas, but that they are there also *not* considered to be unlucky. *Figure 5* shows one of the symbols of the Navaho Indians, a stylised left-hand swastika, whose arms are formed by the gods of wind and rain. (The mention of rain, as usual, alerts us to the presence or influence of the moon.)

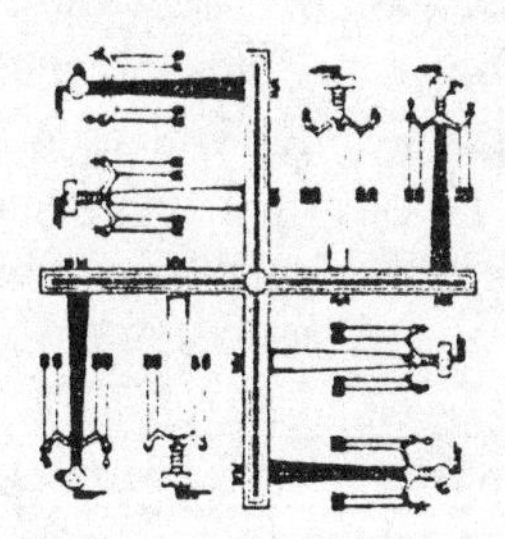

Figure 5
Navaho Indian stylised left-facing swastika, incorporating the gods of wind and rain.

But how does the swastika actually arise, how does it come to exist? As Robert Graves mentioned earlier, and as is widely known, the square cross is often found contained in a circle, probably more often even than it is found freestanding, thus ⊕ .

This symbol, which, incidentally, also forms the centrepiece of the Celtic cross, is often said by primitive peoples to represent the moon and her four arms. One could even suppose it to be a stylised representation of the four quarters of the moon. However, if we take the symbol and make four small breaks or erasures in the containing circle at different points, we can easily produce both 卍 and 卐. Such cursive or running swastikas are in fact quite commonly found (see *Figure 3* above). It could be that artists and engravers hit upon this running form of the cross in the circle as a way of indicating the *movement* of the celestial body or bodies through the sky. The sun 'runs' to the right – that is, if, in the northern hemisphere we face the sun (which is in the south) with our backs to the north. Then in the course of the day the sun moves from our left towards our right (from the east to the west). Does the moon, then, move from our right to our left?

Remarkably enough, the moon really does actually *rise* in the *west* and *set* in the *east*: so having precisely the opposite motion to that of the sun, that is, from the *right* towards the *left*. But nevertheless, *due to an optical illusion*, it nevertheless appears to the observer on earth as if the moon is following the same path as the sun, i.e. from east to west, from left to right.

Let us be clear what we are saying at this point about the movement of the moon. It is, of course, true that the sun's (apparent) movement from east to west is itself an optical illusion – the sun does not move at all, it is we who move around the sun. But the moon *really does* move around the earth from west to east, even though the casual viewer sees it, by optical illusion, moving east to west. To say this just once again, despite all discounting of all optical illusion, the moon demonstrably (see below), and really does, move from west to east across the face of our planet.

This account, that the moon, despite appearances, travels right to left, is not an easy proposition to accept, or even once accepted, to visualise. For we are speaking in all of three bodies (moon, earth, sun) changing their positions relative one to another, even though only two of them, the earth and the moon, are actually moving.

Optical illusion notwithstanding, there are nevertheless various observations one can make which lead to an understanding of the true nature of the moon's motion. One of these is quite clear, and was certainly noticed by every moon-watcher since study began. It is that the moon, during its monthly cycle, rises later each succeeding evening (or day), on average some fifty minutes later. In other words (and in round figures) the moon is taking twenty-five hours to complete the twenty-four-hour cycle. Or in other words again, it is *moving backwards.* It is continuously, so to speak, falling into the east.

It may well be that Neanderthal indeed used this and still other observations to determine the true motion of the moon in respect of the earth; and those who would wish to say 'nonsense' at the idea of Neanderthal man even realising that the earth was a planet floating in space, or a revolving body floating in space, or that the sun was really a fixed, unmoving point (despite optical appearances), should first read Chapters 10 and 16.

However, let us set these more sophisticated matters aside for the moment, and say only this: that Neanderthal observed – what? – that the moon abandoned the east more reluctantly each succeeding evening; and that the east is of course on our left when we face south (observing the sun or the moon). Not only this, but that on each succeeding evening (or day) during the monthly cycle the moon rose a little further to the left along the line of the horizon. And one further point. The observed light on the moon's surface begins at its right edge (with the new moon), moves across towards the left of the disc until the moon is full, and then gradually departs, still towards the left. *All* these readily observed actions and phases of the moon, then, proceed from the right towards the left. Above all, perhaps, the moon is born, flowers and dies in a leftward motion. (This is why, for example, in India the right side of the goddess Kali is that of benefactress and mother, the left side that of blackness, death and destruction.)

The reasons advanced in the previous paragraph do, by themselves, provide ample reason for a regard of the moon as a leftward-oriented principle. But the daunting possibility, for orthodoxy, still remains that the ancients understood the true, reversed, leftward movement of the moon about the earth.

We asked earlier, how might the running swastika arise; and also why its running motion to the left might perhaps represent the moon, its motion to the right perhaps represent the sun? We have already given answers to those questions that are both adequate and fully correct – as far as they go. Yet they are, I believe, only the later outgrowth of a situation far older still and yet more basic. That basic situation which we now describe also finally explains for us the origin and meaning of the labyrinth.

We also earlier asked and answered the question, why does the moon spin – answer, because the moon is a spider. But *why* is the moon a spider? After all, is that not a ridiculous and very unlikely choice for a symbol – even though that *was* the actual choice the ancients made? For the spider is small, earthbound, often dark or drab in colouring, most species operate by day and not by night – whereas the moon is gloriously radiant, sails free in the night sky, is large, and so on. How could anyone even associate the two together, let alone merge them? There was of course the little matter of the baby hanging by a three-fold thread from its mother – but no, it is still all ridiculous, isn't it?

We are by no means done with the spider and the moon yet – but here in conclusion is presented evidence which shows beyond any reasonable doubt why the spider is the moon, why the two are one.

When a spider builds its web it first sets up one or two foundation lines of thread outlining the space it has chosen. Then it sets up a number of straight radial lines of thread connected to a centre. This will be the centre of the finished web. Then from the centre the spider begins to spin an *anti-clockwise* or left-handed spiral (see *Figure 6*). This thread is not sticky. When the spider reaches the outer edge defined by its foundation lines, it turns and begins to spin a *clockwise* or right-handed spiral back towards the centre. This is now a sticky thread. But as it goes, the spider gathers up and discards (or sometimes eats) the original thread.

Here, surely, we see the maze, and what the maze and the maze dance symbolise. Here, surely, we have Theseus and his dancers treading the labyrinth, still more the Daedalus 'ant' and its thread following the spiral of the snail shell. The maze, the labyrinth of the Minotaur, is a stylised spider's web. The maze dance represents and mimics the 'dance' of the spider – with one probable but understandable difference. The spider goes from the centre of the web to the edge, then returns to the centre. The human maze dance however probably went from the outer edge to the centre, and then back out to the edge again. If so, this is a simple matter of logistics – for if the dancers copied the spider exactly, they would end their dance at the centre, and then be

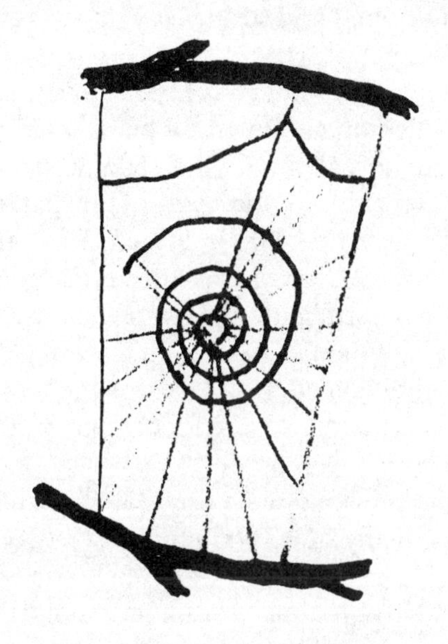

Figure 6
Initial left-handed or anti-clockwise spiral, out from centre, constructed by spider when building web. On the return journey from the outer edge the spider constructs a similar but now clockwise or right-hand spiral to the centre, meanwhile gathering up the initial anti-clockwise thread.

obliged to walk rather anticlimactically out. Or, however, from the centre they might have a straight *underground* tunnel as a means of exit, or even as a means of entry of course; for the maze itself was in all probability, as already said, open to the sky, in particular the night sky. (Such a tunnel might be the explanation of the straight lines on some of the spiral rock carvings of Chapter 7, although there is another possible explanation for those too.)

One view of the Minotaur, then, is as the spider which often sits at the centre of its web waiting for prey. (But the bull/cow is itself in any case always the 'hornéd moon'.) Or sometimes the spider will sit hidden under a leaf, with one long signal thread running to the centre of the web, to alert it to any vibration caused by a trapped insect. (Here would be another possible reason for the straight lines on the rock carvings of Chapter 7.) Could we go so far as to imagine that the priestesses had some version of the spider's signal cord attached to their altar, tugged at the moment of execution? But bound and strangled with a cord the victim no doubt was (see chapter 13).

Almost certainly there would have been a space at the centre of the maze where ceremonials of various kinds could take place – in particular a stone, horned altar where human sacrifice could be made, and whatever else. For the *centre* of the spider's web is even more special than we have so far indicated. This particular detail is not shown in *Figure 6*, for the sake of simplicity. But when the spider first creates the straight radial lines, it attaches them, at the centre, to a very tight, anticlockwise little spiral of thread. Once the radials are tightly joined to that centre, the spider is then free to begin the more widely-spaced polygon of the first anti-clockwise spiral of the web proper.*

Note, from the previous sentence, that the spider's web is a polygon – that is, many short, straight lines (between the radials) angled inwards to form a spiral, not the continuously curved line of the true circle. Now, I think, we can understand the symbolism of the swastika, both cursive and straight, and the square cross enclosed in a circle. These, I suggest, particularly the former, are stylised versions not, as James Vogh proposed, of the spider itself, but *of the centre of its web.*

The spider and the moon will concern us still further. But one more poetic image in conclusion. Ariadne, the moon goddess who helped Theseus with the thread, is also the Celtic moon goddess Arianrhod. Arianrhod is known as 'the Lady of the Silver Wheel'. Her title is usually held to be a reference not just to Spiral Castle but also to the disc of the moon. These are, of course, apposite. But is her title perhaps rather a reference to the spider's web, heavy with dew in the morning mist?

* The full, step-by-step construction of the web, including foundation lines, the tight central anti-clockwise spiral, the first, wider anti-clockwise spiral to the edge, and the return clockwise spiral to the centre, are shown in detail in many popular reference works – e.g. *Collier's Encylopedia*, London, 1985 and *The World Book Encyclopedia*, London, 1986.

7 Aboriginal World

This chapter is concerned with aboriginal peoples world-wide, but in particular with the Aborigines of Australia. The general term 'aboriginal' is applied to those peoples everywhere who inhabit areas in which they alone constitute, and have always constituted, the sole human population. They have not, in other words, supplanted any preceding people. Prior to the coming of the aboriginals concerned the land had been empty of human beings.

Such peoples are important to us in the present book for more than one reason, but first because they have not taken over or absorbed the ideas or practices of any previous human population – something which has repeatedly occurred in Europe, the Middle East, Asia and parts of Africa. Whatever ideas aboriginal people currently have are their own. They were either brought with them when they first arrived as migrants, or have evolved entirely from new in the present location.

For our present purposes, aboriginal peoples can be divided into two sub-groups. There are those who have gone on to evolve very complex civilisations in historical time, such as the Incas, Aztecs and Mayas of Central and South America. In these cases we face similar problems to those we confront in the Old World in our attempts to identify the fragments and nuggets of the truly ancient wisdom (which is our concern), for in both instances we have to deal with an extensive overlay of recently evolved thought and practice.

In our second subgroup of aboriginals we have peoples who, for one reason or another (a general inhospitability of climate for example) have changed and evolved little in past millennia – who have sometimes in fact *de*volved from a previously higher level. Or even if not quite that, all these groups have nevertheless been in the process of gradually losing old traditions and ancient practices through long-term attrition or decay. Examples of this second type of aboriginal are the Australian Aborigines, many of the tribes of South America, and those of the Malay Peninsula, the Philippines, New Guinea, Melanesia and Micronesia. With these we find, as before, only residues of what once was – but at least this is not hidden under or within later superstructures. Sometimes, however, in one particular set of circumstances we find almost nothing at all, as is the case for instance in Micronesia. That set of circumstances is after contact with modern Europeans or Asiatics. For all too often such contact – and the contact itself need not have been in any sense hostile, though often it was – totally disrupts the existing tribal/cultural life and abruptly shears through the long strand of verbal tradition that has held since the beginning of time. Once broken, the link is gone forever. In the absence of written records, if at any point one generation fails to speak to the next, the verbal treasures are lost, and not all the brilliance of the twentieth century can bring them back. What do we know today, for example, of the mass of Druidic lore, which it took the novice priest a lifetime to learn by heart?

The worst of all possibilities is when we find nothing. The second worst is when we find almost nothing – but that is not such a bad second worst after all. With even small fragments, and with patience, we can manage a great deal.

Overall here we have almost an experimental arrangement. We have (a) multilayered, complex civilisations, such as those of Europe and Asia (b) complex civilisations that have nevertheless grown from only one continuous tradition, such as those of Central and South America (and, yes, Minoan Crete) and (c) cultures which likewise derive from one continuous tradition, but which have no complex civilisational overlay. Parallels which we are able to demonstrate among all three types cannot therefore be argued away on the grounds of multilayering, as a side-effect of complex civilisation, or as a side-effect of lack of it! No, the similarities and parallels shown in this book exist and persist despite the, in principle, major distorting factor of the differing social histories involved.

Both subcategories of aboriginal peoples, aside from facts and legends, give us also something further of great value – namely the style, the flavour, of actual Neanderthal life.

In Chapter 4 we had already a description of the festival of the culmination of the Pleiades among the Aztecs at the end of a fifty-two-year 'great period'. This festival was, first, one in which the whole nation was directly involved – in the extinguishing and rekindling of the fires, for example. But more than any purely numerical participation, one had the total involvement of heart and mind of all. They all *really did* think that the world might be about to come to an end. Imagine too the long hours – days in some cases – before the arrival of the runners with the new fire, to say that all was well once more, than humankind had been paroled not for ever – oh, no – but only for a further fifty-two years, pending good religious behaviour. (Or perhaps instead of news a great shout, spreading like a joyous wave from the festival centre out across the whole land.) This idea that the world is allowed to continue *only* because of unremitting, unbroken religious effort – and even that might not suffice – we meet again and again, also among the Australian Aborigines. We ourselves have no such degree of involvement in the religions of our own historical time, except perhaps occasionally in quite exceptional circumstances, such as those of the Black Death.

The Aztec ceremony no doubt gained much from its setting among impressive temples and other stone artefacts, wonderfully wrought, coloured, ornamented. Yet, as we see now, such effect can also well be achieved without any permanent artifice or artefact of any kind. The Australian Aboriginal ceremonies here described are, I would suggest, but a pale reflection of what Neanderthal himself achieved in this respect. Both these two accounts are from R.H. Mathews, writing at the end of the nineteenth century.

The Wiradthuri cut a groove several inches wide and deep to mark a rough circle measuring 86 by 77 feet. They cleared the bushes and grass within the circle and stood upright at the centre a pole 8 feet high and topped with bushes and emu feathers. From the south-west side a path ran for 368 yards. After 150 yards it entered thick scrub and after another 25 yards came to the gallery.

The first object was a hole symbolising the place at which a woman sits for her first menstrual flow. Next came a figure of the All-Father's wife outlined by a groove cut in the ground. The same technique had been used for an emu figure, near which were shown emu tracks, the tracks of a giant man and a screen of the kind behind which hunters lie in wait for emus to come to water. Then came a bower bird's playhouse containing such objects as small bones and pieces of broken crockery and glass. Further along the path strips of bark had been cut spirally from a tree to signify that it had been struck by lightning.

Two hundred and thirty-three yards from the circular ground a sacred fire burned day and night. Two men stood watch with dogs to give the alarm should anyone approach. . . . To one side of the fire and parallel to the path lay a moulded figure of a giant man almost twenty-two feet long. This was the All-Father. He had tripped while chasing an emu he has speared, and was depicted sprawling face down with arms outstretched. Nearby were prints of a giant hand. The All-Father had lain in wait at the screen further back on the path. A model of an eagle-hawk's nest had been placed twenty-two feet above the ground in a tree a short distance further on. Images of sun and moon were cut into the bole of the same tree, and from its foot extended a snake fifty-nine feet long, the tail of which twisted about a sapling. Near here one of the All-Father's sons was outlined on the ground.

One hundred and twenty yards on from the sacred fire a rectangular space spanned the path. At each corner a mound had been raised to about two feet. Weapons had been thrust into their sides. Two seats made from uprooted saplings, whose roots were turned upwards, stood within the rectangle, one to each side of the path. The seats were stained with blood drawn from the gums and beneath the tongue.

In addition to the objects described up to thirty characters were cut into the ground, fifty-nine trees were marked, mostly with straight or spiral lines but sometimes with naturalistic figures of lizards, fish and other creatures, and two or three dozen models of birds' nests were fastened to trees.[127]

In this account, the trees marked with a zig-zag to show they have been struck by lightning are very important. They are an aspect of Aborigine ritual – not the only aspect of course – which will enable us to link that ritual firmly with Druidic practice in Celtic Europe.

In one of the early initiation ceremonies (and we should not forget that these are mounted almost continuously from age fourteen to twenty-five) the adolescent boy will have one or both of his upper front incisors knocked out by the medicine man. This will again prove a very significant custom for us, but here we can note that 'Aborigines share with Eskimos the distinction of having the best human teeth in the world'.[1] So the youngster, agreeing in any case to be disfigured for life, is offering one of his finest attributes. (A sacrifice is useless, of course, unless it is the sacrifice of something worthwhile and prized. J.G. Frazer tells of an African tribe, where every single day of the year one of its finest warriors was sacrificed. This incalculable loss was borne year after year after year.) Such is also the case in the circumcision rite. Not only is the foreskin removed (with a stone knife) but the penis is slit open underneath from base to tip. As Bettelheim and others before him have commented, when such a slit penis is held up against the stomach it resembles a vagina.[13] (But I would add that it represents specifically the menstruating vagina.) At other ceremonies, incidentally, girls also have parts of their sex organs removed (a practice common of course also in Africa and other parts of the world). The elder males present eat portions of the foreskin and so forth, and drink some of the blood.

The second account of Aboriginal ceremony is shorter, but contains a most exciting piece of information indeed.

The Kamilaroi used to prepare two circular enclosures. The larger, about seventy feet in diameter, had a pole nine feet high in the centre with a bunch of emu's feathers tied on the top. In the smaller circle, two young trees were fixed in the ground with their roots in the air. The two circles were connected by a path. On either side of the path a number of figures are drawn on the ground or modelled in clay. The largest, which is fifteen feet in height, is that of the Supreme Being, Baiani. A couple represent the mythical Ancestors, and a group of twelve human figures stands for the young men who were with Baiani in his first camp. Other figures represent animals and nests. The novices are not allowed to look at these images, which will be destroyed at the end of the ceremony. . . . The whole represents the first camp of Baiani on Earth, and the people who were there with him at that time. This is the first creation.[126]

We notice that this intricate and quite substantial structure, whose creation has involved many man-hours of effort, is destroyed after use. Here is a totally opposite attitude to our own, which strives for permanence. For the Aborigine (and as, I suggest, for Neanderthal) the idea of permanent religious structures was abhorrent, and possibly actually blasphemous.

The very exciting information in this second account is that the Supreme Being, Baiani, when he first came to Earth at the time of Creation, was accompanied by twelve companions. So Baiani and his twelve together make up a coven of thirteen. We shall have occasion to discuss many other such 'founding' groups of thirteen (Romulus and his twelve shepherds, Arthur and his twelve knights, Christ and his twelve disciples, and so on). And since this note has been struck, let us take our next two examples of 'Neanderthal' ceremony not from aboriginal sources, but from multilayered Europe. For in any case we must never forget, when discussing one particular part of the world or one particular period of historical time, that we are nevertheless *always* speaking of the same set of originating events and one all-driving historical imperative. Here, then, is Robert Graves.

The manner of Hercules' death can be reconstructed from a variety of legends, folk customs and other religious survivals. At mid-summer, at the end of a half-year reign, Hercules is made drunk with mead and led into the middle of a circle of twelve stones arranged round an oak, in front of which stands an altar-stone; the oak has been lopped until it is T-shaped.

He is bound to it with willow thongs in the 'five-fold bond' which joins, neck and ankles together, beaten by his comrades till he faints, then flayed, blinded, castrated, impaled with a mistletoe stake, and finally hacked into joints on the altar-stone. His blood is caught in a basin and used for sprinkling the whole tribe to make them vigorous and fruitful. The joints are roasted at twin fires of oak-loppings, kindled with sacred fire preserved from a lightning-blasted oak or made by twirling an alder or cornel-wood fire drill in an oak log. The trunk is then uprooted and split into faggots which are added to the flames. The twelve merry-men rush in a wild figure-of-eight dance around the fires, singing ecstatically and tearing at the flesh with their teeth. The bloody remains are burnt in the fire, all except the genitals and the head. These are put into an alder-wood boat and floated down a river to an islet; though the head is sometimes cured with smoke and preserved for oracular use. His tanist succeeds him and reigns for the remainder of the year, when he is sacrificially killed by a new Hercules... This Hercules is the leader of his people in war and hunting and his twelve chieftains are pledged to respect his authority.[78]

These are to us absolutely horrifying events. Yet we must realise that by those concerned, including the victim, they were nonetheless accepted as completely necessary. When one of one's own people was sacrificed (as opposed to a captive) he or she went willingly, for the sake of the people, and the glory to come in the afterworld. (How very like the Christ story this is.) The Aztecs in some cases actually reared individuals especially to act as sacrificial victims, and these always understood their position. Yet when the moment came a young girl would go joyfully to her fate (decked with flowers) even though she was to be roasted to death over a slow fire.

There is a great deal we could pick up on in Graves' account, but that would take us too far away from the present chapter.* Instead let us emphasise the sheer determination, and the hard reality, of the rituals described. Our subject matter is no jolly

* But we note the Hercules plus the twelve merry-men, and Hercules plus the twelve chieftains, both equal thirteen, as do further the twelve stones plus central altar; and that Moses also sacrificed at just such a thirteen-stone arrangement – Exodus 24, *4–6*.

schoolboy adventure story, no charming schoolgirl fairy-tale, elements with which a variety of present-day apologists are (for a variety of reasons) only too anxious to sugar the true pill. Here, on the contrary, is the Roman historian Lucan describing a Celtic sacrificial grove in Gaul: '... whose interlacing boughs enclosed a space of darkness and cold shade ... gods were worshipped there with savage rites, the altars were heaped with hideous offerings, and every tree was sprinkled with human gore'. Tacitus wrote that the Druids in Anglesey 'drench their altars in the blood of prisoners'.*

Our last example of the life-style in question is purely ritualistic. But it does convey again the great power and spectacle of these ancient ceremonies. Those involved are the Apinagos Indians of Brazil.

> *The Indians danced in two long ranks which faced each other, the women on one side the men on the other. Between the two ranks of dancers blazed a great fire. The men were painted in brilliant colours, and for the most part wore white or red skull caps made of maize-flour and resin.... Opposite them the women, naked and unpainted, stood in a single rank, their bodies bent slightly forward, their knees pressed together, their arms swinging in measured time, now forward, now backward.... A remarkable figure in the dance was a personage painted scarlet all over, who held in his hand a rattle composed of a gourd full of pebbles. From time to time*

* The traditions still live on. For example, while the Red Ochre Men of Chapter 2 can only operate secretly, operate they do. Sometimes long splinters of wood or bamboo are thrust through the skin in the vicinity of vital organs – these leave little external trace, but gradually produce death. When recently a woman was found guilty of transgressing the rituals, she was executed thus. She was laid flat on the ground, her breasts pushed aside, and one of the Ochre Men knelt on her chest, breaking the ribs and driving them into her lungs. She was then released, and died after some weeks of pain, without speaking of the matter. (This came to light only after a post mortem.) In present-day India, a child was recently sacrificed in Delhi to propitiate the fertility gods. This is no isolated incident. 'Sacrifice of human lives is fairly common in rural areas of India. According to a recent survey nearly a hundred people are sacrificed every year to propitiate the gods. Nearly eighty per cent of the victims are children. In the backward states there are temples where human sacrifice is regularly practised. The sacrifices are generally carried out to invoke the rain gods in drought-prone areas, or by individuals as a part of fertility rites to bear children.' (*Guardian*, 9 August 1979)

he leaped across the great fire. . . . Then he would run rapidly in front of the women, stopping now and then before one or other and performing a series of strange gambols, while he shook his rattle violently. . . . The dance lasted for hours. When a woman was tired out she withdrew and her place was taken by another; but the same men danced all night. Towards midnight the moon attained the zenith and flooded the scene with her bright rays.[59]

This was a fertility rite, and we are not surprised to learn that the scarlet figure represented the moon.

Turning again now to the Australian Aborigines, as we saw in Chapter 3, the earliest traces of Aboriginal occupation of Australia go back 40,000 years. This people has been present there in strength for at least the past 25,000. The *Britannica* article on Aborigines gives a figure at the end of the eighteenth century of 300,000 individuals comprising some 500 tribes, each with its own recognised territory and distinct language or dialect. A.A. Abbie however gives a conservative estimate of 630 Aborigine languages in 1964 – so one of these statements must be seriously adrift. But our concern here is not with any particular number of languages, only with the fact that there are a great many. The number of Aborigines in existence in Australia today is also not our direct concern, which would include in any case many with mixed blood. What is important however is that, though the old tribal life has been very largely destroyed, much of the legendary material and former practice is on record.

While the Aborigines, until recently politicised, appeared to have no sense of themselves as one overall people, and while immigration may have taken the form of two, or even three major waves, nonetheless the evidence is in favour of all Aboriginal cultural material having had a once common-source origin.

Kenneth Maddock writes as follows:

We come now to a belief of which it was pointed out by Radcliffe-Brown that certain elements are so widely distributed in Australia that they might 'very possibly be practically universal' and form a conception 'characteristic of Australia as a whole and not of any one part or stratum of it'. The 'more essential' elements are that the rainbow is conceived to be a huge serpent, which perennially inhabits deep, permanent waters, and is associated with rain and rain-making and with the iridescence of quartz crystals and mother-of-pearl, the former substance being connected especially with magicians and the latter with religious cults. Radcliffe-Brown opined that the Rainbow Serpent is the most important Australian representation of the creative and destructive forces of nature, more particularly those evinced in rain and water. . . . He (the Serpent) is credited with the dual role of shaping nature and instituting culture.[121]

The Rainbow Serpent or Rainbow Snake is important to our argument not just as a binding symbol among the various tribal groups, but as a major link between Aboriginal belief and practice and other religions around the world. Nevertheless, the Aboriginal legacy is a very fragmented one. It does look very much as if we are dealing with only remnants of a once great whole. Logic and precise statement (even for religion!) are notable for their absence, so that R.B. Dixon feels able to state: 'Myths of the origin of the world are largely lacking in Australia.'[120] This is something of an overstatement – but we are certainly dealing with largely residual material.

The Rainbow Serpent, then, existed, or appeared, at the very beginning of the world. There is an implication that it somehow produced or led to all the other events of primal times, but no precise statements to that effect are made, and there is absolutely no hint of the mechanism(s) involved, if that were the case. The Rainbow Snake may have come from below ground before appearing in the sky, but even if not, he nevertheless spends much of his time below ground where he is chiefly concerned with subterranean water. Here, I would suggest, we have a firm link first with the Great Plumed Serpent of the Swazi in Africa, who likewise lives underground and guards subterranean resources, and also with India. There we find 'Shesha, the serpent endless, representative of the cosmic waters, who is the source of all waters'. And Jill Purce writes: 'The Great Serpent King of the underworld was one of the Nagas who embodied in Indian mythology the life energy, the powers of earth and water.' Above ground, the Australian Rainbow Serpent controls rain and all surface waters and floods. As we can therefore easily understand, since in many parts of Australia the life-giving aspects of water are not just of great but of paramount importance, the activities of the Rainbow Snake are second to none. Many commentators beside myself have noted the parallels between the Rainbow Snake and the Plumed Serpent Quetzal-coatl of the Aztecs and Mayas which, while not specifically concerned with rain, does control some aspects of weather (including hurricanes). Or perhaps an equally striking connection, after all, is with the Mexican rain-god, Tlaloc, who is represented by two snakes twisted together.

Two further important aspects of the Rainbow Serpent are its frequent association, throughout Aboriginal Australia, with the Ancestresses (see below) and with women and women's mysteries; in addition, the belief in many tribes that the medicine man draws his power from the Rainbow Snake.

Although the Rainbow Serpent is held to be primordial and endowed somehow with creative powers, there is no suggestion at all that it directly produced the other phenomena now described, or even that these were subsequent to the appearance of the Snake. In any case, all Aborigines also speak of the Dreaming or the Dreamtime. These names refer to the period that was in the beginning. At this time mythical beings, prominent among whom are the Ancestors and the Ancestresses, came out of the earth, shaped the land, brought various species into being, and established human life and culture. Afterwards they either sank back into the ground or mounted up into the sky. But in any case they live on eternally in spirit. (Perhaps the most interesting information on the beings of the Dreamtime is that they are said not to have been very different from humans today.) People alive now are in any case directly descended from the Ancestors, who in some sense reincarnate in us.

I am myself inclined to see the Dreamtime as a direct memory of the time when Neanderthal and Cro-Magnon merged. This view is supported, at least indirectly, by the fact that the Aborigines are physically the most Neanderthal-like people on earth today.

The spider appears not to play any significant role in Aborigine religion or mythology, nor is there any apparent moon-spider connection. The moon however figures in all important rites. (Incidentally, the Aborigine flag consists of a yellow circle on a split field of black and red. If we are willing to accept the yellow of the moon for the white of the moon, then we have here her three colours.) The moon's presence is indicated not only by naturalistic representations of her at the ceremonies, but by, for example, the zig-zag of lightning. For lightning is considered to be a moon phenomenon by the Aborigines, as by many other peoples world-wide, including the Celtic Druids. If this idea already seems strange, odder still is that many peoples also consider fire to be an attribute of the moon. The oddness yet prevalence of these ideas (which will be discussed in detail elsewhere) is one more piece of evidence we can summon to the cause of the common-origin hypothesis.

The spiral, very widely used both in Aborigine ritual and art, also indicates the moon. Once again, it must be stressed, this is also a world-wide symbolism and usage. (Mircea Eliade dates the use of a spiral to indicate the moon back to at least the last ice age, so a conservative 10,000 years, though I think it to be far older.) We are speaking now rather of the closed spiral than the maze spiral, although the two are certainly closely related. An Aborigine artist interviewed on British television (*South Bank Show*, 24 January 1988) said that the closed spiral in paintings also symbolised the men of the Dreamtime (the Ancestors/Ancestresses) while spirals with lines flowing from them indicate running water. Both these statements are perfectly acceptable in our framework. We recall here, however, that the Pina Indians of North America also connect the spiral (labyrinth) with their ancestors, saying this is the route by which they came up from the underworld. (The Ancestors of the Aborigines also, likewise, came up out of the earth.) We noted further (Chapter 4) that the Incas worshipped the Pleiades 'because of the symmetry of their shape'. Did the Pleiades perhaps once even more closely resemble the small spiral they somewhat do today? If so, we could also better understand why the Paraguayans say that the Pleiades are 'an image of their ancestors'. (But even if that is not the case, we nevertheless have three clear statements here specifically connecting the material we are considering with ancestors.)

Eliade and others have suggested that the spiral and the coiled snake are not unconnected, a symbolism which is again perfectly acceptable. I would like however to add a speculation of my own, that the closed spiral may derive from the image of a raindrop falling on still water. One sees a pond covered with such spirals during a rain shower – or can make such a spiral oneself by dropping in a pebble. This image may be the direct source of the artistic inspiration here – but of course all other associations and links nevertheless stand.

So now we can consider the so-called cup-markings or petroglyphs, found carved in rock throughout the world. Since rock carvings cannot be dated in the absence of other indicators, their precise age is unknown, but all commentators are agreed that they are paleolithic. There is no current explanation of their significance. A sample of these carvings – and it is but a small sample – is shown in *Figure 7*.

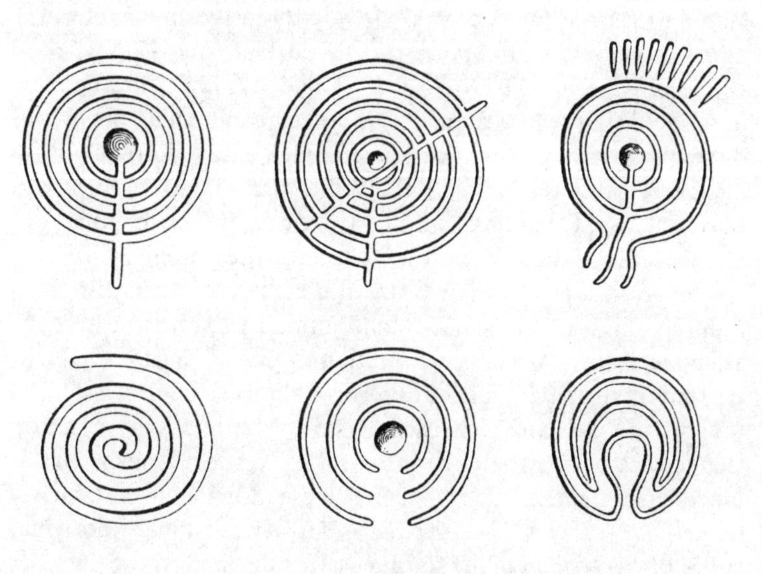

Figure 7
A small sample of 'cup-markings' or petroglyphs (rock carvings) found worldwide.

Garrick Mallery writes of them as follows.

The simplest form of rock inscriptions is almost ubiquitous. In Europe, Asia, Africa, America and Oceania, cup-like depressions are found, sometimes in rows, sometimes singly, sometimes surrounded by a ring or rings, but often quite plain.... Much stress is laid upon the fact that the characters are found in so many parts of the earth, with the implication that all the sculptors used them with the same significance, thus affording ground for the hypothesis that anciently one race of people penetrated all the regions designated.[122]

My own view (which is not Mallery's) is that these carvings do have one common origin and purpose. They are, I suggest, stylised versions of the spiral water-pattern, or of the spiral labyrinth, or perhaps on occasion a combination of both. As to the straight lines involved, which have otherwise puzzled everyone, they may be stylised (or just plain crude) indications of the spider's warning line, or the possible underground tunnels leading into the maze centre, already discussed in Chapter 6. I agree, however, with Mallery to this extent, that if these rock carvings were all the evidence one had available, it would be unwise to base an argument on them concerning the world dissemination of culture. But, given that we have so much other evidence, I think we can be allowed to draw these carvings into our brief also. One thing I would say is quite certain, that these are not just idle 'doodles', as at least some writers imply.

The Australian Aborigines are of great interest to us also from a purely physical and genetic standpoint. The Aborigine head, as all agree, is the closest approximation to that of Neanderthal that we find on the planet today. In terms of body structure, however, the picture is more confused. Many Aborigines have rather slender limbs, not at all like the very heavy, short limbs of classic Neanderthal, nor is the rib-cage of these individuals particularly barrel-like, as was Neanderthal's. However, some Aboriginal tribes (those mainly of the south-east) are distinctly more thick-set and appreciably closer to the classic Neanderthal body-type. Such wide differences between Aboriginal groups, incidentally, have led to the view that the Aborigines reached Australia in two, and perhaps three, distinct waves.

It is also the case that the slender-bodied Aborigines are not particularly endowed with body hair – certainly no more than Europeans – whereas on a number of grounds we suspect that Neanderthal may have been especially hairy-bodied. However, if, again, we consider particular tribes, especially those of the Murray River basin, we find very copious body hair. Tindale and Lindsay write: 'The Murrayians are among the hairiest people on earth and body-hair increases in length with age. Very old

Murrayian men become clad from neck to ankles in a great mat of white hair.' (This image actually reminds us very much of the red orang-utan; and many Aborigines are in fact red-haired, as we shall see.)

Of very great interest indeed is a condition found in all Aboriginal groups throughout Australia known as 'hairy pinna' – which, it should be noted, is also found in individuals in Sri Lanka, India and on the eastern borders of the Mediterranean. Those with this genetic factor produce a strong growth of hair around the edge of the ear.[1] Our interest here is that elves and goblins, and characters ranging from Puck to the mediaeval Devil, are said in legend and fairy-tale to have had large, hairy ears – animal ears in fact. (We must note that the phenomenon under discussion here is not the condition seen in some older European males, of tufts of hair growing from *within* the ear. What we are discussing is a marked growth of hair around the rim and edge of the ear, and in young men.)

Hair colour is also noteworthy. The hair of adult Aborigines is typically dark-brown to black. However, 'In most parts of the continent many people, particularly the young, have lighter brown or even reddish hair... blonde hair is present in some desert populations in the majority of children up to ten years of age.' Another source informs us: 'Aboriginal fair hair ranges from quite flaxen to a streaked tawny: occasionally it has a reddish-gold colour, flaxen is the rule in central Australia, while in the north a red tinge is decidedly commoner.' There will be occasion to discuss red hair in a wider and very significant context. Hair type, to conclude, ranges from completely straight to the very tightly curled, so much so that the latter may be confused at first sight with the frizzed curls of negro hair, which, however, it is not.

The extreme range of body and hair characteristics described has led some writers to suggest that in the Australian Aborigine we see a primal or parent population from which both Cro-Magnon and Neanderthal could have evolved. It can, however, be equally well argued that what we see in the Aborigine is, on the contrary, the *mixing* of the two varieties of man which the present book proposes. This second argument is actually a much more likely one – for we would not at all expect to find the range of variation observed here within one population, particularly within one contained population of human beings – very firmly contained, that is, within Australia. We do not in fact find such a broad range of characteristics in any other population anywhere else in the world.

In terms of its composition, then, I would suggest that the Aborigine population either received a more equally balanced ratio of Neanderthal and Cro-Magnon genes in the first place than occurred with other mixed populations; or that this group's very isolation subsequently saved the more obviously Neanderthaloid individuals from being selectively pressured and actually slaughtered, as I have no doubt happened in other arenas. We glimpse that process today in the Indian caste system, and saw it quite nakedly in Nazi Germany. As it just so happens, by reason of its distant, isolated location, Australia is generally noted for the 'living fossilisation' of biological types and situations that have not survived in other parts of the world.

Physical characteristics aside, we have had little difficulty in the book so far in demonstrating connections between Aboriginal and other cultures, arguing beyond doubt that the Australian Aborigines were once in close touch with the body of ancient knowledge which this book proposes. We have in this respect, however, two very important further areas still to consider: (1) the attitude of the Aborigines to women and (2) their attitude to menstruation. These are deferred for later chapters.

Before leaving specific consideration of aboriginal peoples, there remains one remarkable story from Micronesia to put on record. (I have to say that if I had been in the business of faking the evidence contained in this book, this mythical account is one that I would have forged.) We are very lucky to have it all for, as R.B. Dixon remarks, not just detailed myths of creation, but myths in general from Micronesia are rare. Contact with Europeans in this case had the result that 'much of the treasure which was once so abundant has now disappeared for ever'.[120]

This creation story tells us that in the beginning were only the sea and Areop-Enap, 'Ancient Spider', who floated above in endless space. One day Areop-Enap found a mussel tridacna shell. He managed to get it open and crept inside, where everything was dark. However, the roof was too low for comfort. Areop-Enap then searched around and found a small snail, which he asked to help him. For three days he slept with the snail under his arm, to give it strength. Then A-E searched again and found a larger snail. To this one he made the same request, and gave the same treatment. Now A-E asked the smaller snail to help him lift the roof of the mussel, which it did. At this point A-E made the small snail into the moon and placed it in the west. Taking the larger snail, he made this into the sun, and placed it in the east. The floor of the mussel now became the earth.

The salient features of this myth for present purposes are these: (1) the spider as original creator, (2) the use of a snail shell to make the moon, (3) the moon is made before the sun by the spider – i.e., moon things are older and of more concern to spiders, (4) the moon is placed in the west – and as we saw in the previous chapter, the moon *really does* rise in the west, even though by an optical illusion it appears to the casual observer to rise in the east, (5) the spider rests for three days – and it just so happens that the moon is absent from our skies for three days every month, being then in too close proximity to the sun to be seen. (I think that one central reason for the religious/magical association of the moon with the number three is on this account, but there is another important consideration also; see Chapter 10.)

What a remarkable catalogue of significant fragments this creation myth contains – fragments that we have already identified in other cultures world-wide.

We lost the Zulu mazes. But we have kept the Micronesian myth. Our luck is holding up. The moon is a snail shell in ancient Greece, in ancient Mexico and in ancient Micronesia. Who would have dreamt it?

A General Note on Verbal Tradition

A major premise of the present book is that verbal material, passed on purely by word-of-mouth from generation to generation, can survive recognisably for periods in excess of 20,000 years. More than just 'recognisably' in fact. For we propose also that not a few hard specifics have survived that treatment and that time span – such as the precise structural details of an ancient labyrinth design, such as the name Orion/Wurrunna, and stories of the mythical genesis of the Pleiades, which include a genuine observation of a major change in that constellation's appearance – and so on. Well, *is* all that possible? Isn't all this really just a wild hypothesis, which I 'underpin' by using a few lucky coincidences in a mass of data where apparent parallels will arise occasionally by chance? That comment is of course deliberately unfair to my arguments – for in fact we can show not just a few, but many 'coincidences', and in any case 'coincidences' of an order which pure chance cannot achieve (see on this point especially Chapter 14). But, still, I am using one, even if tenable, hypothesis (that seemingly widely separated cultures nevertheless contain identical components drawn originally from some central source) to support another hypothesis (that purely word of mouth traditions can survive intact the passage of tens of thousands of years). Clearly it would help the case considerably if I could demonstrate transmission of some very sizeable and indisputable items of hard information over a very long period – in particular, items that I had no hand whatsoever in collecting or interpreting!

Fortunately, exactly such an independent supportive brief is in existence, in Robert Temple's book *The Sirius Mystery*. Thanks mainly to Temple's investigative talents and formidable scholarship – although the first, triggering discovery was not his – we know today that an obscure African tribe, the Dogon, maintained until the 1940s a detailed, secret, accurate and purely verbal dossier of complex stellar information, originally put together by pre-dynastic Egyptians in 5000 BP and earlier.

The Dogon today are an unremarkable African tribe living in Mali, West Africa (the former French Sudan), and indistinguishable from their immediate neighbours, with whom they have obviously regularly intermarried. The evidence is that the Dogon originated in northern Libya where, however they are said to have been cousin to the pre-Hellenic population of Greece. It seems in fact likely that they themselves originally migrated from what is today Greece. Partly at least from that 'Greek' source, but perhaps also from some more direct Egypt-Libya connection, they obtained the knowledge they finally disclosed for the first time in the late 1940s to two French anthropologists, Marcel Griaule and Germaine Dieterlen. The first formal publication of this material, in French, occurred in 1950.[183]

The two anthropologists had been living with and studying the Dogon for several years. They had won the firm friendship and trust of the Dogon priests. After much agonising, and a special conference, these priests decided to tell Griaule and Dieterlen what they had never previously revealed to anyone else outside the priesthood – although, of course, the tribal religious rites had always incorporated aspects of the material.

This material is certainly staggering. It includes, for example, knowledge of such matters as the conjunction of Jupiter and Saturn every sixty years. Such an observation cannot be made in any one person's lifetime – discoveries of this kind can only be made in the context of continuous observation and record, a context which did exist in pre-dynastic Egypt. But the jewel in the crown of the material is the Dogon's precise knowledge that the star Sirius A is orbited by an invisible, collapsed, super-dense dwarf star, Sirius B, which has an elliptical orbit around Sirius A of fifty years! It is, among other things, the unlikely *detail* of this information which is so startling and so evidential – the notion of an elliptical orbit, for example, as opposed to a circular one.

What so puzzled Temple and others was how even the ancient Egyptians could have established such information. Sirius B is simply not visible by any normal means. Its existence, in modern astronomy, was not suspected until the middle of the nineteenth century, and the first photograph of it not achieved until 1970. Temple found himself forced to conclude (by much other evidence also) that the astronomical knowledge of the Egyptians had been conveyed to them by visitors from outer space – visitors, namely, from Sirius A.

I will comment briefly in a moment on this 'outer space' hypothesis – but let us first stress the importance of the informational events described for the purposes of this book.

Here we have absolute, unimpeachable proof that hard, complex scientific statements of fact have survived for over 5000 years by word-of-mouth tradition, in an otherwise untutored people, who above all possessed no form of writing. We must emphasise, incidentally, that no dissenting voices are raised concerning this aspect of Robert Temple's book, or Griaule and Dieterlen's earlier testimony. No one denies that the Dogon have preserved the knowledge in question through the period in question. There is more however. These peoples have wandered thousands of miles from their point of origin, and were *en route* for possibly hundreds or even thousands of years. During that time, and since, they intermixed with other peoples, to the point where they are indistinguishable physically from their neighbours. And *yet* the knowledge survived.

If such knowledge can survive for more than 5000 years under such clearly adverse conditions, then why not 10,000? Why not 20,000? Why not 25,000? In principle, there is no reason why not.

We do, also, have one other source of significant support, in Thor Heyerdahl's *The Kon-Tiki Expedition* and his massive study, *American Indians in the Pacific*. The Polynesians of the Pacific, Heyerdahl reports, have a verbal, historical record of their origins reaching back many hundreds and even sometimes thousands of years. This material is continuously updated. In each new generation individuals are selected to learn all the existing material by heart. The students are very carefully tutored, rehearsed and continually tested – and will one day become the senior historians themselves. Sometimes in the course of Polynesian history groups have left their original home islands (in their great canoes) and colonised other islands hundreds or thousands of miles distant. Clearly, the new history of these new colonies is from then on personal to them alone. But when Heyerdahl (and others) compared the earlier portions of the history of the new colonies with that of their original home islands, the earlier portions matched perfectly. There had been no loss or distortion of detail.

Here, certainly, we are speaking of hundreds rather than thousands of years of preservation, the isolated conditions involved are also favourable, and the material was not scientific. But again the *principle* is clear. Word-of-mouth tradition is effective and reliable. It manifestly works. There is no reason why it should not continue to work indefinitely.

Returning to Robert Temple's view that the ancient Egyptian knowledge of Sirius B, and much else besides, was given to them by space visitors from Sirius A, this is not a view I personally accept. As explained in an earlier book,[67] my own view is that the existence and nature of Sirius B could have been deduced by thoughtful observers, and a mixture of thought and chance, from the fact that Sirius A twinkles periodically. This phenomenon could suggest that an orbiting body is interposing itself between that star and the observer (which is indeed why it twinkles). It is also the case that Sirius A barely rises above the horizon, and so was actually said by the Egyptians to rise 'with difficulty'. Perhaps, then, it and its putative companion were very heavy?

The rising of Sirius A, in early Egypt, also coincided with the very hottest and driest part of the season, causing the spiritual 'heaviness' and depression which we know today are produced by a surfeit of positive ions. Sirius A is distinctly red when seen at the horizon, so that it seemed itself to be hot. Lastly, Sirius A is the brightest star in the sky. Might not 'brightest' also equal 'heaviest'?

(In all the foregoing, of course, we can equally well read 'Neanderthal' for 'Egyptian' – since, as we know, 26,000 years earlier stellar conditions had been identical – see Chapter 4.)

I do not claim that these arguments deal with all Temple's points – but they are at least a way of beginning to approach the knowledge or 'knowledge' shown by ancient Egyptians which does not involve an appeal to visitors from the stars. That the alleged visitors should just happen to come from a star which of itself gives us so much food for thought, which also happens to be the brightest star, and not from any of the millions of other anonymous stars in the galaxy – that I do find a rather suspicious coincidence. However, as said, I do not claim to have dismantled Temple's case completely, which is actually far more ramified than we have been able to discuss here.

One important error which I consider that Temple and many others make is to assume that ancient knowledge *begins*, that is, comes into existence, at the time it was written down, that is, after writing was invented. This is in no way necessarily the case. (On that view, for example, the Dogon's knowledge of Sirius B would 'begin' at the moment when Griaule and Dieterlen wrote it down!) On the contrary, I suggest that what happened when writing was invented was that some verbal historians and recorders, no doubt with considerable relief, seized the chance to set down in permanent form what had for so long been passed on by word of mouth. Naturally there was then a sudden apparent 'explosion' of knowledge (again, just as the Dogon knowledge 'exploded' into view in 1950). Then, of course, once in written form, knowledge could be circulated, inspected, collated, analysed and so forth in ways that are quite impossible with a verbal tradition. So, certainly, a genuine lift is also given to understanding, and to the then further development of the ancient knowledge. There *is* at that point a genuine secondary explosion, if you will.

However, the foregoing is not at all to say that everything which *could* have been written down with the invention of writing necessarily *was* written down, either then or later. Verbal tradition persisted where there was a strong wish not to risk communicating secret, or holy, or forbidden knowledge to those not entitled to it. *Or*, two further possibilities: (1) the written accounts of truly secret information were very carefully guarded and not generally circulated, (2) the accounts were written in code, and so were meaningful only to those who understood the code, the initiates. Here, I think, we have the answer to much of the apparent 'nonsense' of the mythical, mystical, kabbalistic and religious record.

James Vogh has, for example, succeeded admirably in cracking aspects of the Minotaur code, as we see in Chapter 10.

8 Shanidar

The matter of the present book, to use Professor Mary Williams's happy phrase, is 'the archaeology of ideas'. Though this discipline is not one you will find in the university prospectus, it has already its outstanding pioneers – Robert Graves, J.G. Frazer, Robert Briffault, Margaret Murray.

Where possible, of course, one does seek to match one's findings in this field of ideas with the physical artefacts and fossil remains of conventional archaeology and paleoarchaeology. The present chapter then, like Chapter 2, further demonstrates that the views of this book do not essentially violate (and are certainly not divorced from) the observed conventional archaeological record. Having said that, however, my own position is that where the archaeology of convention clashes with the archaeology of ideas, it is going to be the former which must give ground, not the latter.

In 1951 a Neanderthal cave-dwelling and burial site was discovered at Shanidar in northern Iraq. From then until 1960 the site was carefully investigated by archaeologists and other scientists working under the direction of Professor Ralph Solecki. As was eventually established, this site had been inhabited continuously from 100,000 BP to 40,000 BP, a total of 60,000 years. Excavation of the floor of this large cave yielded the remains of over thirty individuals from various periods. Most had been interred deliberately, but several had been unintentionally buried alive by falls of rock from the roof.[173]

Three of the sets of remains are of great significance for us. One of these, an accidental death, was that of a man who was nursing a week-old spear wound in his rib-cage at the time of the roof collapse. Clearly, then, this individual was being cared for by his fellows during his period of illness. A second individual, also buried accidentally, is of even greater interest. He was a man of about forty, which was then quite an advanced age – few lived to be so old. He was severely arthritic and blind in the left eye. This individual was, therefore, in no position to make a working contribution to the community, so that it seems clear he was being cared for and nourished out of simple concern. The third case, this time one of proper interment, is the most significant. Here soil analysis shows that the individual, an adult male, had been buried in a great mass of flowers, and that a subsequent burial feast had been held on the grave.

Some of the flowers involved were, from the point of our understanding at least, of purely decorative varieties. But others were herbs used still in the Shanidar neighbourhood today, and elsewhere, for medicinal purposes. These included yarrow or milfoil, applied to wounds ('yarrow' is from an Anglo-Saxon word meaning 'healer'), St Barnaby's thistle, groundsel (Anglo-Saxon 'pus-swallower'), joint-pine or woody horsetail, and hollyhock. From most parts of the hollyhock (roots, leaves, flowers, seeds) a great variety of medicines can be made, for toothache, for inflammation, against spasm, and as poultices.

Whether or not we accept that Neanderthal understood the herbal properties of these plants – though I have no doubt he did – what no one can set aside is the fact of the flower burial, and the burial feast. Myra Shackley tells us that evidence of burial feasts has been found also at other sites, although so far there are no other reports of flower burials; but, as Solecki points out, no one has been analysing soil samples in search of them.

The picture of Neanderthal that emerges from Shanidar, as from the mine workings and indeed also the burials mentioned in Chapter 2, is a very different one from that still purveyed by the standard textbooks. *These* vivid individuals are the people not even credited by orthodoxy with the power of speech!

Myra Shackley, mentioned above, is a lecturer in archaeology, progressive enough to have written a book not only on Neanderthal man which we draw on here[166] but another on surviving Neanderthals and the Yeti/Wild Man which we will consider elsewhere[167].*

It is what Shackley had to tell us of Neanderthal's relationship to the bear which is of greatest interest here. An analysis of the animal bones found at an important Neanderthal site at Erd in Hungary has shown that 90 per cent of these remains are those of bear. Some 5 per cent were those of horse, and the remaining 5 per cent comprised all other animals. Other sites, however, do not show this dramatic disproportion – so was this one somehow special? Further interesting facts to emerge are these. The frequencies of the various bones of the bear show that the whole bear carcase was brought to the site, whereas in the case of all other animals only parts of the carcase were brought back after killing. The manner in which the bear was then sectioned suggests that it was not cut up for eating (and bear meat is said not to taste good, in any case). So was this, in fact, a kind of factory or workshop for producing bear pelts? Well, we already have plenty of evidence for red ochre mines. Why not, then, pelt factories?

We have to understand here that a significant proportion of European Neanderthals lived for much of the time in conditions of extreme cold, in ice-age conditions in fact. They probably owed their survival to their warm clothing – which they skilfully cut, tailored, sewed, buttonholed and so on. It would seem that the fur they wore, above all, was that of the bear. We can say in fact without exaggeration, not just that Neanderthal's way of life, but his life *as such*, depended on this animal. Under those circumstances we can well understand the genesis of a cult-worship of the bear, for which there is conclusive evidence, and which we shall look at later.

There is, however, one piece of evidence which is too good to save.

At Drachenloch (which just happens to mean 'dragon's lair')

* For her courage in departing from the ossified views of her professional colleagues, Shackley has received the usual barbed-wire bouquets. An official of a major museum, another woman, remarked to me, with a sneer, that she would forgive Ms Shackley when she walked into the museum arm-in-arm with a Yeti.

one of the Neanderthal bear-hunter sites of the Swiss Alps, a bear altar has been discovered in a cave. A rectangular chest built of stones, and covered with a massive stone slab, contained the skulls of seven bears, arranged with their muzzles pointing towards the cave entrance. Deeper in the back of the cave were a further six bear skulls set in niches in the wall.[166]

Our apologies, conventional archaeology – all is forgiven! What sheer *joy* we have to feel at this find. For here we see, beyond any doubt whatsoever, that the number 7 and the number 13 were sacred to Neanderthal man (since 7 plus 6 equals 13). (Once again, had I been forging the evidence for the present book, this bear altar, with its seven and its thirteen, is an item that for certain I would have faked. It is so perfect.) But there is still more. We have not yet mentioned the age of the find. This altar is dated 75,000 BP[28]. The numbers seven and thirteen, therefore, have been sacred for at least 75,000 years.

The constellation of the Great Bear contains seven stars. We can hardly doubt that Neanderthal had already given it this name that almost unimaginable time ago. And so, in our own times, it is still called the Great Bear by ourselves, by the ancient Greeks, by the Romans, the Hindus, the Ainu, the North American Indians, tribes in Africa, and many others besides.

We come to these matters again in Chapter 10. Meanwhile we can proceed much heartened that the findings of conventional archaeology, in fact, offer us every support.

9 Blood on the Skirt

In this and the succeeding chapter we are faced even more pressingly with a problem we otherwise face in all chapters – that we should be producing not one chapter, but an entire book, on the subject matter concerned. We also face a further problem in these two chapters – how to write about a single subject as if it were two – how to divide, for the purpose of reasonable exposition, matters which are in fact inextricably bound up one with the other. Nominally, this first chapter is concerned with menstruation, nominally the second is about the moon. But menstruation *is* the moon and the moon *is* menstruation. As Briffault remarks, simply: '... all peoples of the world refer to menstruation as the moon', including ourselves of course, for menstruation and moon are the same word. In France then (as among German peasants) menstruation is *le moment de la lune*. In African tribes the word for moon and menstruation is one and the same (among the Mandingo, *corro*; among the Susus, *kaikai*; in the Congo, *ngonde*). The Aborigines of the Torres Straits, like the Asian Indians, use the same term for moon and menstrual blood. The Maoris call it 'moon sickness', and so on.

All the considerations here will become clear as we proceed. In this chapter, however, we are principally concerned with two main matters. One is the world-wide attitude to menstruation in historical times, which itself falls into two subsections, namely, the attitude to (a) menstruation in general (b) a girl's first menstrual flow – that is, the onset of puberty in females. The second main concern is the demonstration that magic and magical powers were once the exclusive property of women (as shorthand for magic, read menstruation) but were taken from them by men. One of our sources in this regard, and most interestingly, is the Dogon tribe in Central Africa, whom we met already in Chapter 7, and whose legendary material is demonstrably completely reliable. The Dogon say that 'men stole the sacred skirt, stained with sacred menstrual blood... and established dominion'.[168]

Much of the material we will be citing is drawn from older texts of the nineteenth century and earlier. For as a *living* tradition, much of the theory and practice of our subject matter is either on the verge of final extinction or has already gone. This situation, however, in no way detracts from the importance of our subject. We can say that the present, rapid disappearance of the traditions is like the final running out of what was once a great amount of bathwater. Rational orthodoxy is delighted to see the back of such 'nonsense' – and humanitarians also must be thankful for the disappearance of so much cruel practice. But unfortunately for orthodoxy, even though the bathwater is gone, the baby very much remains.

Nor is it at all the case that, because much of our original source material today derives from authors themselves long dead, those sources cannot be trusted. Recent surveys do confirm the earlier ones, albeit in paler form – as with George Devereux, reporting on menstruation attitudes and rites among the Californian Indians. For when we compare Devereux's findings, in 1950,[43] with those of A.L. Kroeber[107] who studied the same groups in 1925, we find notable reduction, e.g. in the length of time reported for the duration of taboos and in the severity of treatment of the menstruant. In the remarkably brief space of twenty-five years (admittedly encompassing that giant social earthquake, World War II, that huge bulldozer of social change) much had altered. Devereux's and Kroeber's findings will be discussed at the end of the sequence which follows.

We take, first, attitudes to menstruation in general. Here we draw mainly on J.G. Frazer's *Golden Bough*, but also on present-day authors such as Shuttle and Redgrove. Briffault, very surprisingly, has no comment at all on menstrual rites, still less therefore on their origins or significance.

Perhaps the best way to present this material is in the form of notes made during research, with the salient points arising discussed subsequently. The spare, almost telegrammatic form of the notes actually far better highlights the horror and strangeness of the events involved than any more lingering or discursive presentation – and more compellingly urges on us the question: but, *why*?

So, among South Australian Aborigines a menstruating woman must live away from the camp. From her seclusion she must call out a warning if a man or boy approaches, otherwise she will receive a beating. If a boy were to see the blood his strength would fail prematurely, and he would turn grey. The menstruating woman may not eat fish or go near water – otherwise there will be no fish for anybody. Sometimes the woman smears her face with red ochre during menstruation – in other tribes the entire head and the upper part of the body are painted red. In some tribes the menstruating woman – henceforth referred to as MW – must not gather any kind of food at all, otherwise the supply will fail. If the MW touches food, and this is eaten by anyone else, they will become weak and ill. In New South Wales and Queensland, if MW walks on a path used by males, or touches male possessions, she suffers the death penalty. She must keep at least half a mile from the camp. On some Torres Straits islands, once again, if MW eats fish, or turtle eggs, both will vanish for all. She may not walk on the beach below high water mark.

In Sumatra and New Guinea also MW must live in a special hut away from others. She must not cook food. Must not approach crops, or these will fail.

In South Africa the Bushmen say that the glance of MW will freeze a man in any position he happens to be in, or turn him into a talking tree. (Shuttle and Redgrove, and others, comment on the parallel here with Medusa's powers.) Therefore MW is strictly secluded. Other South African tribes say that cattle will die if MW drinks any milk. Cattle will also die if they step over a drop of her blood on the ground. Therefore MW must use her own roundabout paths. 'These MW tracks can be seen in every Kaffir village' (Frazer's vocabulary). Central African tribes also believe that MW drinking milk harms cattle. Among Baganda, if MW touches husband's weapons he will be killed in his next battle. MW can also cause a well to dry up. In East Africa warriors may not eat anything touched by MW, otherwise they lose their virility and physical strength. Central Africa: if a man has intercourse with MW he will become sick and die. MW may not add salt to food. In West Africa MW may not cook for her husband, lie on his bed or sit on his chair – otherwise he will die. In some tribes there are separate huts for MW – if she appears elsewhere then there is punishment or a fine, e.g. a goat or sheep, whose blood is then used ritually. She must not approach a well.

Among the Dravidians of India, who exhibit intense dread of MW, all houses have two doors, one of which is only used by MW. She eats apart from rest of family. Among Kharwars MW may not enter a kitchen or a cowhouse for eight days, must not even touch cooking vessels. Must take ritual bath after eight days. Hindus: MW must seclude herself, may not drink milk, not milk cows, not walk on common paths, not walk beside flowering plants, not observe the stars and planets, may not touch fire. Parsees: MW secluded in separate lodge. Since the Parsees worship fire, MW may not even look at a lighted taper. Must take a ritual bath after menstruation. In province of Annam MW must not touch food which is to be preserved by salting, and may not attend any religious ceremony.

Among the North American Indians, every living thing which MW steps on will die. If a man walks where she has walked, his legs will immediately swell up. MW often kept in special huts four to five days. Ritual cleansing bath follows. In Central America must leave village for seven to eight days, may neither cook nor handle food. Afterwards ritual bath in river. In many tribes everything touched by MW becomes ritually unclean. So MW must have own fire, own furniture, etc. in own lodges. If objects touched by MW are touched by others, then disease. All weapons (spears, arrows, etc.) are rendered useless if touched by MW. Some tribes impose the death penalty for infringements of rules by MW.

All these attitudes and customs are widespread among American Indians. Ritual cleansing following menstruation is a firm rule, usually in running water. There is illness if a man goes near MW. Cheyenne: a man who sleeps with MW will be injured in next battle. Ruth Benedict tells us that for the Kwakiutl 'menstrual blood was polluting to a degree hardly excelled in the world'.[11] And Frazer remarks that for most tribes hardly any other being was the object of so much dread as MW. Sometimes MW had to wear an opaque veil of leather for several days following her period, so that no man might look on her. Chippeways: MW must live in a hut made of branches, also wear a long hood which covers head and breast. Must drink only through a hollow bone, not touch water direct. If MW approaches lakes or streams, fish will fail. Eskimos and Lapps also have this belief. Similar practices and attitudes among South American tribes. If anyone drank from same cup as MW he would die. MW must eat from banana leaves and dispose of them in solitary spot. If a cow found and ate them it would waste away and die.

An Australian Aborigine who discovered that his menstruating wife had lain on his blanket, killed her, and died of terror himself a fortnight later.

The situation described in the above notes is not at all confined to 'primitive' or aboriginal peoples. The Jewish Talmud states that if MW passes between two men at the start of her period, she thereby kills one of them. The Arabs say that the shadow of MW causes flowers to wither and trees to perish, and even renders snakes immobile. We do well, then, to note the extensive and virulent comment made on menstruation in 'advanced' religions.

Thus an entire section of the Jewish Talmud, the *Seder Tohoroth I* (the *Book of Cleanness*), totalling 509 pages, is devoted to the observances and taboos connected with menstruation. We glance only at one or two of the chapter summaries. Chapter 1: describes the factors that determine the length of the periods of uncleanness in various classes of women, particularly with reference to the retroactive effect of uncleanness. Chapter 2: states the tests which establish the beginning of the menstrual period and indicates which colours of discharge are clean and which are unclean. Chapter 4: is concerned with the conditions of uncleanness of non-Jewish women, such as Samaritans, Sadduceans and idolators, and of women in protracted labour. Chapters 8–9: indicate the tests to be applied to decide whether a stain is that of menstrual blood or of some other matter; describe the symptoms of the approach of the menstrual period; and deal finally with the condition of uncleanness of the corpse of a menstruant.

As among 'primitive' peoples, after her period a Jewish woman must take a ritual cleansing bath at a special baths supervised by the Rabbinate. At one time sexual intercourse with a woman was forbidden for seven days from the start of the period. Later the prohibition was extended to fourteen days.

The Persian law-giver, Zoroaster, inspired by the supreme being Ahura Mazda, has this to say:

> *The menstrual flow is the work of Ahriman or the devil. As long as it lasts a woman is unclean and possessed of a demon; she must be kept confined, apart from the faithful whom her touch would defile, and from the fire which her very look would injure; she is not allowed to eat as much as she wishes, as the strength she might acquire would accrue to the fiends. Her food is not given her from hand to hand, but is passed to her from a distance, in a long leaden spoon.*
> (*The Zend-Avesta*, trans. J. Darmetester, Oxford, 1880)

Similarly again, the 'wisdom' of Manu, the Hindu law-giver, inspired by the creator Brahman: 'If a man approaches a menstruating woman his wisdom, energy, eye-sight and vitality will utterly perish. But if he avoids her in that time, all these functions will increase.'

What of Europe itself, and more especially, perhaps, recent Europe? Pliny gives a whole chapter of his *Natural History* to the subject of menstruating women, listing the great harm they can do – but, most interestingly, reporting also the good they can effect, witch-like. Here, I think, we have a dim memory of the time when the woman's 'curse' was once a blessing; and we should also bear in mind that blood, bless and blossom are all one and the same word. So, according to Pliny, MW can rid a field of pests by walking around it naked before sunrise, calm a storm at sea by exposing her genitals, and cure boils, hydrophobia and barrenness. On the bad side, however, her touch will blast vines and other plants, fade purple cloth or, conversely, blacken linen, tarnish copper, cause bees to desert the hive, and produce abortions in mares. Also, in present-day Europe, in country areas, the following beliefs are still held concerning MW. She can cause buds to wither and blight crops, turn wine to vinegar, cause mirrors to dim and razors to lose their sharpness, rust iron and corrode brass, turn milk sour, spoil well water, kill bees, cause mares to miscarry, and raise storms at sea. Here, then, in our own world and times, we have very distinct echoes of the still more virulent views of aboriginal peoples.

We will defer detailed consideration of parallels worldwide in respect of menstruation until we have considered the situation concerning the pubertal girl and her first menstrual flow. Ominously, Graves tells us that the baleful moon-dew used by the witches of Thessaly was a girl's first menstrual blood, taken during an eclipse of the moon.[78] And indeed the horrors surrounding the situation of the pubertal girl themselves eclipse all we have seen so far.

We revert to information assembled by J.G. Frazer. It should be emphasised here, so strange and unlikely does some of the information seem, that this has been gathered by reputable missionaries and anthropologists, and confirmed by more than one source. Frazer assures us of two things: one, that the seclusion of girls at puberty is (or was) practised worldwide; two, that the reason for the seclusion is the fear of the first menstrual blood. The notes which follow are extensive – but we very much need to display the full ramifications of the situation. Otherwise, when we start to question the origin of menstrual taboo, we shall be fobbed off with some vague reference to archetypes, dark psychoanalytic mutterings, or empty sociology.

Among the negroes of Loango in Africa, then, girls at puberty are confined to huts. They must not touch the ground with any part of their bare body. They may not be seen by men. The girl's head must be covered by a blanket, for if the sun's rays were to touch her head she would become a living skeleton. She must stay in the hut for a fortnight. Neither she or the girls who attend her must drink milk, otherwise the cattle will die.

Among the Akamba of East Africa, a pubertal girl – henceforth referred to as PG – must not walk on the usual routes, for a spot of her first menstrual blood on the path would cause barrenness in the partners of any man who touched it. The Baganda: PG must not handle food, she is fed by other girls. In tribes of (former) Tanganyika PG is secluded for at least a month. She must not see the sun, or touch the ground. She must undergo endurance tests and torture, e.g. wear a collar of thorns, live in darkness, eat poor food. In other Central African tribes PG is secluded for six days in a hut and must wrap her face in a calico cloth. On the seventh day she is ritually immersed in a stream for purification. Both PG and MW must not use salt.

Other African tribes: PG must live in a darkened house with a few companions. Among Wafiomi she lives in a special screened apartment for a year during the hours of daylight. She must not herself touch food, is fed by other women. In the case of members of the royal family, the seclusion lasts for three months, in a dark hut. PG must not be spoken to meanwhile, female slaves communicate with her by signs. The Barotse – PG must not be seen by men or touched by sun. South-east Africa: PG secluded for a month. If she stirs outside, must wear a dirty greasy cloth over her face. If a man were to look on such a girl, he would be struck blind (so again, the Medusa aspect). PG must plunge every day in the river, return home wet, no fire.

Kaffirs (Frazer's term) of South Africa – length of PG seclusion varies inversely with rank of father. Must not have milk during seclusion. At termination, PG rubs herself all over with red ochre. All objects she has touched must be buried in a secret place. Basutos – PG must cover head, wear a mask made of straw, and plaster her body with mud, so as to be hidden from the gaze of men. Congo tribes: PG undergoes two/three months seclusion. Her hair is shaved off, and she is smeared every day with red dye. If these ceremonies were not performed PG would be barren or produce monsters, the rain would cease to fall, and crops, hunting and fishing fail. (Frazer assures us that these particular views were held very seriously indeed.)

In Indonesia, New Guinea, New Ireland and associated areas PG is kept for *at least four or five years* (my italics) in a small cage made of broad leaves sewn together. Has only room to sit or lie in a crouched position. Is in continual darkness, and not allowed to touch the ground. Several of these cages would be crammed into a house some 25 ft long, and as wide. The atmosphere of the house, still more of the cages, was hot and stifling. In the cages themselves no light and little air. These were 7 ft high, tapering to a point after 4ft, and 12ft in circumference. Their bamboo floors were 3ft from the ground. PG allowed out of cage once a day to bathe in a wooden dish inside the hut. Other tribes similarly kept PG in structures the size of hen coops, sometimes for weeks, sometimes months, night and day, lying doubled up since no room to stretch out or move. Under these regimes the girls became fat and pale. British New Guinea: PG two or three years indoors in raised house, never allowed to descend to ground, no sun allowed to enter house. Other tribes limited incarceration to only five/six weeks.

(So almost unbelievable are some of these details that it must be emphasised again that they are all attested to by many reputable missionaries and clergymen.)

In Borneo, PG could be shut up in a special room in the house for as long as seven years. Not allowed to leave this room on any pretext whatsoever. Body growth became stunted, skin a pale, waxy colour. At the end of the incarceration a slave would be killed, and the girl smeared all over with his blood.

In the Torres Straits PG lived in a circle of bushes in a dark corner of the house for three months. Only her head visible, covered with a cap. Sun may not shine on her. May not handle food or feed herself, fed by other women. No man, including father, may see her, otherwise severe accidents. After three months carried, so that feet do not touch ground, to ritual bath.

North Australia: four/six months seclusion in a special hut, no sunlight, no man may see her. May not eat anything that lives in salt water, otherwise a snake will kill her. Among many tribes is buried up to hips for several days in sand. May not touch herself with her hands, must scratch self only with a piece of wood. Other tribes cover PG with sand or soil, then build a hut over her. Must scratch self with mussel shell. May not eat turtle or fish, otherwise tribe would catch none. In Yam and Tutu islands PG again must not touch self with hands, no turtle to eat, etc. Severely beaten during her one-month seclusion. Subsequently ritual salt-water bath.

Among North American Indians PG secluded from family and community for varying periods. In that time forbidden to see world or sun. In some tribes head and body covered with a blanket. Often only eat when fed by someone. Maidu Indians: PG shut in small hut for several days. No meat or fish, not allowed to feed self. A stick to scratch head, must not touch self with fingers. Afterwards ritual bath for purification. In various other tribes: no meat, blindfolded for nine days/live in secluded, distant booth, no animal food; death for any person to touch or even approach her; death will ensue if PG looks at a man in first two days (an interesting parallel with the Talmudic view); during this time PG hides in woods; then confined for further twenty days to small hut, with covered face.

Vancouver Islands: for several days PG lives in a cage of mats within house, where she must only sit in a crouched position. Sun and fire not to be looked at – otherwise PG disgraced for life. May not touch her hair with her hands, only scratch with bone or comb. After these days no fresh food, especially salmon, for eight months. In that time must always eat alone, using special cups and dish.

Queen Charlotte Islands: PG behind a screen for twenty days. For six months must wear a cloak or hood of cedar bark reaching below breasts. Other tribes: only allowed to eat black cod *for four years* (my italics) otherwise fish would disappear – PG may not look at the sea, or at a fire, for forty days; not walk below high-tide mark for a year, otherwise tide would not come in.

Tlingit and Koloch: PG must live in a hut or cage completely blocked except for a small opening. No fire, no exercise, no associates: a dark and filthy abode. Many could only drink through a hollow bone. Obliged to wear a hat with long flaps all round: for the gaze of PG would pollute the sky, and her look would destroy all luck, and 'turn things to stone'.

(In some of these cases regarding PG we are told that she would be carried from her place of confinement twice a day for voiding urine and excrement. In other, perhaps shorter, confinements it would seem that no such provision was made – in which case the conditions of confinement would be quite appalling.)

In British Columbia: sometimes PG wore a large hat or hood of leather for two years to screen her face from the sun/PG not to touch food with own hands, a stick for scratching head; wore a skull cap with a fringe of shells, and a bone hanging before the eyes/drank through a hollow swan's bone. In another tribe, PG lived in a conical hut of branches, within this a pit in which she must squat on her heels all day. Face painted red each day. Wore a heavy blanket over body, and a conical hat or cap of twigs. A tube of bone, so that lips do not touch water. These conditions for four months, but in earlier times a year. Other tribes also cover head of PG, and insist on bone scratchers. In one tribe PG wore a large robe painted red.

Here we can mention the already cited findings of Devereux and Kroeber among Californian Indians. There PG is buried up to her armpits, or up to her chin, in hot sand, for four days. She is allowed out for use of toilet, and renewal of hot sand or ash. Must use a scratching stick, otherwise skin would be spotted white, hair would become snarled and erect and stay that way for ever. When buried in the pit, PG wears a specially prepared willow bark skirt to absorb the menstrual discharges. No salt while in pit. From four to forty days no meat or fat. Hunting bows must be removed from premises. Ritual bath on fifth day, might be repeated every day for forty days. During all this time, and while ritually bathing, PG may not look into water or a mirror. No water must enter vagina – otherwise supernatural snakes will also enter and cause illness.

Among Alaskan Eskimos, PG confined to a small hut, must remain on hands and knees for six months. Then moved to a larger hut, where could kneel with a straight back for a further six months. During this time ritually unclean, so no social intercourse for a whole year. In other tribes less severe practices, e.g. forty days seclusion, wearing a hood.

Among the Indians of South America conditions imposed were even more desperate. PG sewn up in a hammock for two/three days, only a small hole to breathe, no food. Another tribe, PG similarly sewn in hammock, hoisted up to the roof for a month. Then another month halfway to floor. (Feeding and toilet arrangements are not described.) Among Paraguayan Indians, three days and nights in a hoisted hammock, minimum to eat and drink. Then could eat no flesh or fish for a year, could speak to nobody, must sit in a corner of the room with face turned to the wall. 'Many girls die or are injured for life in consequence of the hardships they endure at this time.'

In the Gran Chaco, PG lies covered with branches in a corner of the house 'for some time'. Must see no one, speak to no one, eat no flesh or fish. Upper Amazon: PG three months in a lonely hut. Rio de Janeiro (this account is from the sixteenth century): hair of PG is shaved off, and she is placed face down on a flat stone. Her back is scored with an animal tooth until the blood runs. Ashes are then rubbed into the wounds. Then she is bound hand and foot and slung in hammock, no food or drink for three days.

Guiana: PG endures hammock suspension for several days. Afterwards is beaten with rods, exposed to painful ant bites, and so on. During these tortures she must not cry out. Endures extended fasting, so that she becomes a living skeleton.

Brazil: PG starved for a month in a secluded hut. Then she is beaten by relatives and friends till she falls senseless or dead. If she recovers, however, the beating is repeated four times in all, at intervals of six hours. It is considered an insult to the parents if the girl is not beaten properly. Orinoco: hammock treatment and starvation. PG is also blindfolded and wears a bonnet. Thus prepared she is tied to a post. The old men of the tribe whip her with cords, sometimes knotted with sharp stones, till her back runs blood.

In Asian India, Hindu PG is kept in a darkened room for four days. No one may touch her. No salt to be eaten, and a restricted diet. Thereafter she is ritually bathed. The mat and other articles of furniture in the room are destroyed.

Rarhi Brahmas of Bengal: PG shut in darkened room for three days. Lives on rice and ghee. Tiyams of Malabar: PG in special room for four days. Must not touch any other person, or tree or plant. No salt, vegetarian food only. Kappitiyans of Madura: PG considered polluted for thirteen days, lives in corner of house or special temporary hut. Ritually bathed on thirteenth day. Hut then burned, pots shattered. Parivarams of Madura: PG spends sixteen days in a hut. Then hut burned and vessels smashed. If rain water were to get into such a vessel, the girl would be barren. Pulayars of Travancore – special hut for seven days. No one may approach PG's proximity. Singhalese: PG confined to a room for two weeks, not seen by any male. Is led out with face covered and is ritually bathed. If special hut, then burned down.

In Cambodia PG must stay in bed under a mosquito curtain for up to one hundred days – though in recent times five to twenty days is usually considered sufficient, in this very hot climate. However, general seclusion may last up to several years. The length of stay is inversely proportional to rank. During this time may not see any strange men, nor eat flesh or fish. Can go nowhere – except during eclipses of the sun (!) May not see the sun in all this time.

There are two features of this menstrual data which concern us centrally. One is the sheer *severity* of the treatment of menstruating women. The second is the remarkable parallels displayed in her treatment worldwide.

So obvious are these many parallels, in fact, that we need not take up too much time debating them. For example (1) the belief that the presence of a menstruating woman blights or kills crops, spoils fishing and hunting, harms livestock, spoils food, well water and milk and (2) the seclusion or exclusion of the menstruating woman from the rest of society. (It is true that in the – recent – European and Middle Eastern traditions MW does not undergo actual physical incarceration. But clearly, if she spoils crops, sours milk, drives bees from the hive and whatever, she is not going to be allowed near those activities, so there is exclusion. The Persian tradition specifically advocates feeding MW with a long spoon – and by the way, Persian is an Indo-European language. Again seclusion or exclusion is strongly implied here, as is the idea that MW should not touch her own food. We can, I think, fairly safely assume that the European/Middle Eastern taboos and treatments were once much stronger than we see them in historical time.) (3) the ritual cleansing following menstruation. It is important to emphasise that this *is* a ritual. Normal washing by itself will not do. Without the ritual aspect the woman remains unclean. It is true again that ritual cleansing is not specifically observed in historical Europe – but it is nevertheless clearly ordained in the Christian Bible, Leviticus 15:*19 et seq*., 'And if a woman have an issue and her issue in her flesh be blood, she shall be put apart [so seclusion *is* appropriate] seven days, and whosoever toucheth her shall be unclean . . . and on the eighth day . . . the priest shall make an atonement for her before the Lord for the issue of her uncleanness.'

We have a situation, then, of striking, and unexpected, parallels in this regard in widely separated parts of the world. When one says 'unexpected' one means that it is very hard indeed (and for myself, impossible) to imagine that such common practice could arise independently or fortuitously – which is what we must imagine if we are to accept the orthodox view of mankind's view of history. (Remember, too, that the effects said to be produced by MW do not actually exist in the first place – there is no *observation* of actual events here.) Moreover, our own argument can offer an explanation of these parallel attitudes and practices by reference to Neanderthal moon religion – the full details of which now increasingly emerge as we proceed into this second half of the book.

Why, then, in India, Africa and among the North and South American Indians should a menstruating woman be denied salt? Is this just another deprivation or punishment? No, there is far more to it than that. In this connection J.G. Frazer also tells us that a former Hindu custom decreed that on the first three nights of marriage there should be no sexual intercourse and no use of salt by the newly-weds. Further: 'For some reason which is not obvious primitive man in many parts of the world connects salt with sexual intercourse.'

Let us go at once to the heart of the matter and say that, for Neanderthal man, salt was both a holy and a magical substance. Salt comes from the sea (and salt deposits on land can also be readily understood to derive from times when the land was under sea). The sea and everything in it is sacred to the moon, and moves back and forth in homage to her. (One of the temples of the Moon Goddess Benten in Japan, of whom more later, was so constructed that the tide actually rose up into the lower part of the building.) Salt is also white, one of the three colours of the moon (and although all three are almost equally important, as we see in the next chapter, white is the moon's supreme colour). Moreover, salt is magical, for it stops food pickled in it from going bad – a process I am quite sure Neanderthal understood. Probably, also, salt was used by Neanderthal in the curing of skins for clothing. Finally, salt is clearly present in human blood (and all blood) the taste of which we may be quite sure Neanderthal knew well. What more, really, do we need to say? Next to red ochre, salt was probably the most sacred substance known to Neanderthal man.

What of the custom of not allowing a pubertal girl to touch the ground, which is observed in Africa, Indonesia and South America? This custom certainly goes back to the fact that the mistletoe, the plant most sacred to the moon, has no roots in the ground. Proper discussion of this important topic must again be deferred for Chapter 10. Here, however, it could be objected that, far from lifting the pubertal girl from the ground, the North American Indians and the Australian Aborigines actually bury her in it! We can make two immediate points here. One is that if the custom of not touching the ground exists in South America, it must also once have been part of the traditions of North America – unless one is prepared to say that the South American Indians (from one end of that continent to the other) thought up the practice for themselves, for whatever reason, in the last few thousand years. But very fortunately we have a better saver than that. Among the Arunda Aborigines of Australia the most sacred object of all was a pole, some 20 ft long, which was smeared all over completely with human blood. In the course of its cutting, preparation and transportation, on no account was it allowed to touch the ground, until it reached the holy spot where it was to be erected. So we see that the religious practice of 'not touching the ground' does survive among the Australian Aborigines – it is simply not (or no longer) applied to pubertal girls. In nearby Polynesia, too, the king must only touch royal ground. Otherwise he is carried everywhere.

We have other significant hints from other arenas.

For example, in medieval Germany, when witches were taken for trial or execution, it was said to be important not to let them touch the ground, otherwise they would be able to exercise their magical powers. In Laos, the chief of an elephant hunt was not allowed to touch the ground throughout the whole proceedings. In Greek legend, when Hercules fought Antaeus, the giant son of the Earth Goddess, Hercules found that every time he dashed the latter to the ground, Antaeus simply sprang up with renewed vigour. On this realisation, Hercules seized the giant and held him clear of the ground. As Antaeus now rapidly weakened, Hercules was able to crush him to death.

If I were myself obliged to account for the rationale behind the Australian and North American custom of burying the pubertal girl in the ground, I would use the analogy of 'earthing' an electrical system so that it discharges itself harmlessly. This analogy will not seem far-fetched after we consider the phenomenon of lightning in the next chapter. And indeed, why else do we use the phrase 'to earth' in connection with electricity? And why else, further, do we 'touch wood' to render evil harmless? (As the Arabs say, *koolshi wahed.*)

However, the 'inconsistency' of the matter we have just discussed does bring us on to the important issue of why some Neanderthal customs survive in some areas and peoples and not in others, and in different forms, and why then some are regarded favourably (e.g. dancing in the moonlight to encourage fertility, worshipping the Pleiades, the use of the number seven) while others (such as menstruation and the number thirteen) are regarded as anathema.

Here, I think, we must revert to our macro-scenario of the takeover of Neanderthal magic by Cro-Magnon. As in the well-documented religious takeovers and mergers of more recent historical times, three courses of action are possible in respect of every item. (1) You may adopt a particular custom or belief more or less as it stands, adding this to your own repertoire (as the Christian Church incorporated the cross and the maze, for example). (2) You may adopt a practice, while nevertheless somehow either (a) reversing its sign or (b) transforming or castrating it (for example (a) changing a goddess into a god, (b) permitting a traditional procession or ritual at a traditional time, but having it moved to a non-traditional location, or minus its usual climax). (3) You may – and this is then usually a rather desperate business – totally condemn, proscribe and outlaw the practice, full stop.

The circumstances of the Cro-Magnon takeover were rather special however, in that Cro-Magnon *very much wanted the amazing Neanderthal magic for himself*. The problem was how to get the magic (which we will describe in detail elsewhere) without falling into the power of, or under the spell of, the current holders, or of the actual spirits, powers and forces involved. That the situation was/is perceived as one of very real risk we see again and again in countless legendary descriptions. How do you manage to get the Nibelungen treasure? How do you get the Golden Fleece? How do you get the Princess away from the Dragon? How do you make a contract with the Devil that is not finally binding? How do you get the crock of gold from the leprechaun? How do you get safely into the Underworld and back, and so on and on. All these stories and many others are, I consider, actual accounts of how Cro-Magnon dealt – or rather tried to deal (for to get the Neanderthal magic, you really have to *be* Neanderthal) – with the magical dilemma. And we may as well make this next point, absolutely emphatically, here and now, that all legends, myths and fairy-tales are (a) not fiction, (b) not psychological or psychoanalytic projections – although, yes, they do have some inlaid or overlaid psychological content also – *they are statements of fact. They are all first and foremost, and essentially, historical accounts of actual events which once actually occurred.*

Now, certainly, the language used is perhaps a little colourful. And admittedly these accounts have sometimes got rather battered and altered over the course of tens of thousands of years (although I do not think the bearers of the legends who at last handed them over to the scribes in the dawn of our own modern times had lost the sense of them as history; that act of final castration was performed by our own 'thinkers'). But nevertheless, we do not refuse to study, say, an ancient vase because we find it in fragments; or a papyrus because it is only a torn, discoloured remnant, or because someone has taken that papyrus, turned it sideways and written something quite different across the original text. In such damaged and sorry condition the material of the archaeology of ideas also comes down to us. Far from despising or complaining about its condition we, like the physical archaeologist, must rejoice that it has come down to us at all.

However, reducing our focus below maximum aperture again for a while, let us look further at some of the detail of the menstrual data.

The menstrual woman is often placed in a special hut, or behind a screen, or buried, and must often in addition wear a blanket or other head/body covering. Clearly, a major purpose of these arrangements is so that she may not be seen and/or see, and we come to those aspects shortly.

In Indonesia, however, we are told that the menstruating girl is enclosed in a conical cage of leaves. Perhaps this design is to allow run-off of water – but on the other hand the cage itself is enclosed in a house. Some North American Indian tribes also build a conical hut of branches – in the open – but inside it the menstruating woman must wear a conical cap of twigs. In various other cases we are told that MW must wear 'a hood', 'a long hood', 'a cloak or hood', 'a hat or hood', or 'a head blanket'. In still other cases 'a skull cap', 'cloth over face', 'mask of straw', 'bonnet'. This covering of MW's head with what we can, I think not unreasonably, generalise as a pointed hood is no trivial item. For there exist, as we see in Chapter 13, both paleolithic and medieval European paintings which show ritual dancers, around what is, perhaps, a sacrificial central figure. Elves, fairies and witches also traditionally wear pointed hats or hoods, as does Puck (Robin Goodfellow); and so we shall also want to look at 'Robin Hood' in this connection. I think it no accident also that many religious orders of monks today wear hoods. And we draw into the discussion further the wig which the married, orthodox Jewish woman must wear all her life, keeping her head shaved: some of the menstruating women, too, had their heads shaved, before donning the hood, as do many monks. And, eventually, it may not seem too daring of us to include here even the crown of thorns worn by Christ.

What now of the universal belief in the power of the menstruating woman to turn milk sour, and the in many cases deliberate witholding of milk from her during her period? First, let us adduce here two cases not so far mentioned, beginning with that of the menstruating Gypsy woman. A Gypsy MW – even when fully dressed – must wash her hands after touching the upper part of her body before touching the lower half, and vice-versa. She may not even wear a continuous dress, but must have separate items of clothing above the waist and separate items below it. (And should she touch any kitchen item with her skirt, that item must be destroyed.) In the orthodox Jewish kitchen, permanently and for always, all utensils and cutlery which are used for any food containing milk must be kept rigidly apart from all utensils and cutlery used for any meat item. The Gypsy situation gives us the solution here. The breasts (which produce milk) must be kept separate from the blood-producing vagina. But what does this mean, why and how would such a view arise? The answer, I am certain, is (a) that menstruating women do not produce milk and (b) that breast-feeding mothers do not menstruate. Clearly, then, *the Goddess herself* had ordained that these functions be kept separate. (For the medical record, the non-menstruation of the breast-feeding mother, in the woman of today at any rate, persists for some six months. Under natural conditions and/or in the Neanderthal variety of man, the picture may not have been the same.) So here we do begin to see that at least some (and I would say probably all) of the 'nonsense' of the menstrual taboos has some kind of basis in some kind of fact – even if the view of the facts concerned may strike us as odd.

Covering up the menstruating woman has the dual function

and intention of hiding her from the sight of the world, and hiding the world from her sight. There is perhaps some confusion of reasoning here. On the one hand it is thought that MW's glance (or the sight of her) will cause the actual death of a man, freeze a man to permanent motionlessness, blind a man, freeze snakes, turn things to stone, damage fire, pollute the sky, and so on (the Medusa effect). On the other that the sun or sunlight will turn MW into a living skeleton or – or what? We are given no further details of what the sun will do. By far the main emphasis, therefore, is the other way about. It is MW who is *dangerous* – not really MW who is in danger. She is dangerous in three respects. The *sight* or look of her produces the effects just indicated. The *touch* of her can produce death and illness, makes food and cooking utensils poisonous, and robs weapons of their potency (a man died of terror because his menstruating wife touched his blanket). The *presence* of her can cause livestock to die, or abort, wither crops, spoil food and well water, drive away fish and game, even the sea itself, and raise storms.

(There remain puzzles in this exposition. Why, for example, is the menstruating woman not allowed to touch *herself*? One account tells us that should she do so, she will develop white spots, and her hair will snarl up permanently – but that is all we are told. It is interesting, however, that Medusa herself is said to have had hair which was a mass of writhing snakes, and girls with hair of snakes are also found in Chinese legend. Medusa, a very important topic, is discussed in detail in Chapter 10.)

Whatever else, we have a picture of the menstruating woman as a creature of immense potential powers – which will obviously be used unless she is closely secluded and guarded. She must also be deliberately weakened, physically by not being fed high-protein or high-vitamin foods, or in some cases not any food at all, by all kinds of physical hardship, including actual torture, by being deprived of light, air and exercise, the last by sometimes actually being bound. She must also be psychologically weakened – obviously by all of the foregoing – but also by being deprived of human company, in some cases not even being allowed to speak, by being regarded as anathema and knowing it. It is possible that the ban on touching herself, and not being touched directly by others, is 'merely' a potent psychological device, in a culture where, I suggest, touching and hugging played a more vital role in mental health and well-being even than they do in our own society.

World-wide we see a totally desperate fear of the menstruating woman (with close parallels in every geographical area) that we are unable to account for in any normal terms. How can this degree of fear have arisen, this quite grossly punitive reaction towards individuals who hold no position of power or influence under normal circumstances, and whose physical condition renders them even more vulnerable than usual? We might begin to offer a basis of explanation here if we could show that woman (but necessarily menstruating women in particular) did once indeed possess some or all of the stations of power. Fortunately such evidence exists. A major exponent of the position is Robert Briffault, but he is by no means the only one.

We saw at the beginning of this chapter a report from the Dogon tribe in Africa to the effect that men had seized power from women at some point in the past, specifically by stealing the sacred skirt stained with the sacred menstrual blood. We also saw in Chapter 6 not only that among many peoples all processes connected with the making of cloth had once been the exclusive preserve of women, but that its manufacture had also been a religious rite. In some instances, in Polynesia for example, the more high-ranking a woman, the more of her time she devoted to weaving. (Here we seem to have an echo of the fact that menstrual taboos are in some peoples more harshly applied to the woman of high rank than to commoners.) We also saw, in Pliny, hints that menstruating women *are*, allegedly, capable of calming storms as well as causing them, ridding crops of pests, and healing.

Among the Australian Aborigines we find statements which are remarkably parallel to that of the Dogon above. Mircea Eliade tells us that among the Aranda there is an admission that there was once a time when women had more to do with the sacred ceremonies than at present. As described by several tribes, the Ancestresses (see Chapter 7) 'are dignified and sometimes awe-inspiring figures who enjoyed unlimited freedom of decision and action. Frequently they were more powerful beings than their male associates, and the latter . . . lived in constant terror of their mysterious supernatural strength.' An Aborigine elder agrees: 'Our women have fallen from the estate of our great feminine ancestors. Why we do not know.'[51]

Even more intriguing, says Eliade, are the frequent traditions that in the beginning the ritual objects – the *tjurunga*, the bull-roarer, and so on – were created and owned by women. A specific Ganabuda myth tells that once the women had all the sacred things, while men had nothing. Shuttle and Redgrove appear to be quoting the same source (it is the Creation myth of the Aborigines of Arnhem Land): 'We have been stealing what belongs to women.... We have to trick them.... In the beginning we had nothing.... We took these things from women.' A.A. Abbie concurs: 'There are hints that the women and their ceremonies filled a much more important role in the past, but how far back in the past is unknown.'[1]

Eliade reports that similar myths relating how women once possessed the ritual objects and scenarios are found, notably, also in Melanesia and South America. Such legendary material, Eliade comments, has led some authors to consider that a similar primordial situation once existed world-wide.

On Australia again, Briffault considers there to be 'no doubt' that the patriarchal nature of Australian society, the dominance of the men and the debased condition of the women (see below) are of comparatively late origin. (Briffault, like many of the alternative thinkers we consider in this book, has no real way of putting dates on his views.) Quoting several sources for his authority, Briffault considers that there was formerly among Aborigines a social state in which women occupied a more influential or even dominant position: '... the tribal mother may even have been the virtual ruler or sacred chieftainess of the clan'.

Geoffrey Ashe offers hard evidence that Shamanism among the tribes of Siberia was once entirely the province of women. For the word for a female Shaman in many different tribes comes from one common root, e.g. *utagan, udagan, udakhan, utygan*; whereas the word for a male Shaman is a different one in all tribes. Moreover, the female word is almost certainly connected to the Mongolian word *Etugen*, which is one of the names of the Mongolian Earth Goddess. The Tartar word *utygan* also means a bear (see Chapters 8 and 10). Finally, the male Shaman today often dresses and behaves like a woman – but Ashe assures us that homosexuality is not involved.[4] (From Siberia too, of course, comes the mammoth-bone maze carving discussed in Chapter 5.)

Robert Briffault tells us that a basically similar situation exists among the Eskimos, and that all practitioners of the magical arts there were formerly females. At some point in time males usurped this female function.

We could continue to cite specific cases here, as Briffault does at length. There are, apparently, on Tierra del Fuego very detailed legends stating that in former times women ruled absolutely. There are stories of 'feminine terrorism' which, the Fuegians say, was terminated by a kind of revolution in which many of the women were killed, and after which men established a domination and a certain amount of terrorism of their own.

Here, however, we can do no real justice to the material which Briffault has collected in his three massive volumes, of some 600 pages apiece. In any case, I think we work best in the present instance by direct inference from the conditions prevalent in the last century, and still often observed in this. Nevertheless, we should in passing mention Briffault's legendary evidence that agriculture was first invented by women.

> *Thus among the Cherokee corn is said to have been discovered in the forest by the first woman. When she died she gave directions that her body should be dragged over the earth; wherever it touched the soil there sprang up an abundant crop. The traditions of the Cheyenne likewise ascribe the discovery of agriculture... to a woman. The Tupis of Brazil have a legend to the effect that a virgin conceived, and from the body of the babe to which she gave birth... grew the first plant of manioc. The Basutos of South Africa, and the natives of West Africa, likewise assign the invention of agriculture to the first woman.*[18]

In Chapter 10 strong evidence will be presented that the rain-making ceremony was formerly, world-wide, in the exclusive charge of women.

We should mention, too, Briffault's general view that at the beginning of recorded history we are still observing the last stages of a change from rule by priestesses to rule by priests, and from lunar worship to solar worship. Of much more direct interest to us here however, as mentioned, is the general treatment of women in very recent historical time. We draw first upon records concerning the Australian Aborigines – and if we seem to be concentrating on this particular people, that is because they are by far the most studied and written about of all aboriginals. However, we do have enough pieces of evidence from around the world to show that the Australians are not a special case and, on the contrary, are quite typical – despite the opening sentence below. These extracts are again from Briffault, who is drawing on a variety of sources.

> *Nowhere is it possible to meet with more miserable and degraded specimens of humanity than the women of Aboriginal Australia. The women are treated by the men with savage brutality. The poor creatures are in an abject state and are only treated with about the same consideration as the dogs which accompany them.... Blows over the head with a stick are the more common mode of correction, and spearing through the body for a slight offence. Few women will be found upon examination to be free from frightful scars upon the head or the marks of spear wounds about the body. Dr. Hewitt knew of women being cut almost to pieces.... The Queensland Aborigines chastise their wives by rubbing hot coals over their stomachs....*
>
> *The records of the Government Courts in Adelaide furnish numberless instances of male Aborigines being tried for murdering their* lubras. *The woman's life is of no account if her husband chooses to destroy it, and no one ever attempts to protect her or take her part under any circumstances....*[18]

As already said, such attitudes and treatments are not confined to male Australian Aborigines. Thus, when a New Caledonian chief acquired his first rifle, he ordered a row of women to be set up so that he could try it out. Another New Caledonian was told he could not become a Christian, because he kept two wives. The next day he reappeared to say that he was no longer in sin, because he had killed the second wife and eaten her. Similarly, a Fijian chief, lamenting the death of his son, said what a brave and fierce man he had been. 'If ever one of his wives disobeyed him, he killed and ate her on the spot.' The Bangala of the Congo were also commonly said to kill and eat disobedient wives. A chief of that tribe told a missionary (in 1887) that he had recently eaten seven of his wives, but had invited all their relatives to the feast so that there might be no family unpleasantness.

Among the Somalis, the bride began married life with a flogging from her husband, who waited for her in the bridal chamber, whip in hand. An exactly similar custom prevailed among the Sifon of Tibet.

The Hindu *Laws of Manu* state:

> *No act is to be done according to her own will by a young girl, a young woman, though she be in her own house. In her childhood a girl should be under the will of her father; in her youth under that of her husband; her husband being dead, under the will of her sons. A woman should never enjoy her own will. Though of bad conduct or debauched, or devoid of all good qualities, a husband must always be worshipped like a god by a good wife.*

So though they did not eat their wives, and stopped short of killing them (although let us not forget that other custom of *suttee*, requiring a wife to die on her husband's funeral pyre), the situation in India was not essentially or in psychological terms any different to that prevailing in the aboriginal world. And were matters any different either in Victorian Britain, or patriarchal Rome? Would not the Laws of Manu also have suited the Victorian husband ideally?

Well, enough of the details of the catalogue of these and earlier horrors. The question to which we must address ourselves is *why* women should, worldwide, be treated in this beyond-all-reason fashion. The answer must be, surely, because women once exercised a similar power and control over men.

For, in recorded time, we see women treated exactly (a) as throughout history victorious nations have treated the nations they conquered, (b) as oppressed classes within a society treat the ruling class once overthrown. In our second case we need look no further than the French Revolution or the Russian Revolution for examples. The appalling, even if in some sense deserved, treatment which the peasants visited on the aristocracy, in those two cases, are well enough documented.

The position seems absolutely plain. Women, in historical times, are treated by men exactly as the formerly oppressed always treat the former oppressor. Even if we had no actual evidence of women's former dominant status – though in fact we have – there would be, or rather is, every logic in assuming that former dominance on the basis of the circumstances described.

Cro-Magnon as such, of course, was never ruled by the Neanderthal people. But I think he was once, for a considerable time, and in considerable measure, ruled by Neanderthal magic. What, then, exactly happened?

Here, to an extent, one is necessarily playing guessing games. However, what is not a guess is that the replacement of Neanderthal man by Cro-Magnon man did not occur overnight. There was a period of probably several thousand years in which the two varieties of man lived in some kind of proximity. To understand what occurred in that time I think we can again look to the analogy of the North American Indians and the European invaders. What we see there (over a period of a few hundred years only) is a scenario of fierce pitched battles and continuous guerilla activity, interspersed, however, with brief intervals of peaceful co-existence, trading and territorial agreements. Such agreements only held briefly of course, broken more often on the white side than the Indian side, as the superior forces of the Europeans, driven by greed and the desire for acquisition and conquest, relentlessly advanced against, and finally overcame, the Red Man.

I would argue a not dissimilar scenario for the relentless advance of Cro-Magnon into the Neanderthal Near East and European arenas, but with at least one significant difference. Whereas the Red Man had only one thing his adversary wanted – territory – Neanderthal had two: territory – and magic. I believe that Neanderthal's religio-mysticism, with its convincing demonstrations of genuine 'occult' powers (and we will look at those elsewhere), called to something deep and dark in Cro-Magnon that had not yet found expression in his own culture and the conscious landscapes of his own psyche; just as still in our own present day, witchcraft, the Holy Grail, the world of Faërie and Atlantis call with undeniable siren voices to sober scholars and the sons and daughters of establishment – but with this difference – that the whole of Cro-Magnon society was involved.

Cro-Magnon would have come to know Neanderthal religion through initially secret (though dangerous) observation, and from actual demonstration when official delegations visited back and forth. No doubt Neanderthal deliberately used his psychological advantage in this area. There would have been times, too, when captured Neanderthals would have 'miraculously' treated and dressed Cro-Magnon wounds, and other ailments. There were other 'trifles' too, such as Neanderthal's undoubted ability to predict eclipses of the sun and moon (see Chapter 10).

The long-term result, and by whatever mechanisms we can envisage, was that Cro-Magnon was in large part converted to the Neanderthal religious world-view and practice. (Perhaps, first, Neanderthal woman converted and politicised Cro-Magnon woman – the modern phraseology being in no way out of place here.) But there were accommodations to be made to Cro-Magnon too, and no doubt also different balances were struck by different groups. One suspects the Moon Goddess often became a Moon God. The priestesses would also have operated under at least partial licence, being ultimately answerable to the king or chieftain – and not answerable wholly and solely to themselves, as under Neanderthal. No doubt, however, the balance of power over time shifted this way and that. The renewed onset of the ice age of course would have played very strongly into the hands of the priestesses – for this was the Moon's doing, and her anger. Probably then for some thousands of years the priestesses once again exercised full power.

The central dilemma for the Cro-Magnon male, both at the beginning and later, was always how to get control of Neanderthal magic without it getting control of him. This was a very real dilemma – and we again have direct statement of the considerable fear involved in many legends: males who came within the orbit of Circe were turned to swine; or lingered, unmanned, like Tannhäuser in the cave of the Lady Venus; or were turned to stone by Medusa; or like Celtic Bran or northern Rip van Winkel were otherwise entranced or changed. By no coincidence at all the many dangers described are almost exclusively portrayed as female! It was a long time before Cro-Magnon male (or rather by then the males of the mixed population described in earlier chapters) lost his fear sufficiently to move forward decisively on the central issues. The return of the ice-sheets had not helped matters at all. And initially, in any case, Cro-Magnon had been persuaded that Neanderthal magic could only be operated and administered by women. Yet as he gradually once again limited the power of the priestesses, and increasingly himself took over the actual rites, nothing further very terrible happened. The Moon did not step down from the sky and intervene – on the contrary – the ice-sheets now began to withdraw once again. With them went more of the male fear of feminine magic.

We are, in any case, as we shall briefly discuss in a later chapter, not dealing here with purely sociological matters. We are also dealing with innate biological drives and predispositions. The predisposition of Neanderthal was always towards a matriarchy and female deities. That of Cro-Magnon was always, basically, towards patriarchy and male deities. His step into Neanderthal, feminine religion was no more than a side-step. It was biologically inevitable that the Cro-Magnon male (for present-day males are some ninety per cent Cro-Magnon) would eventually seek to assert, or re-assert, full control for himself. We can say that, by instinct and construction, Cro-Magnon is a worshipper of the male principle and daylight rationality, and so of the Sun.[63–5, 69]

The final dénouement, in most areas (although events had their own local timetables in different locations) coincided roughly with the disappearance of the ice-sheets. During the 5000 or so years immediately preceding the beginning of our own historical times around 5000 BP, woman, and specifically magical-woman, finally lost the upper hand – was metaphorically dethroned, literally enslaved, and very literally punished. (The serpent/dragon had finally been conquered, and its strength now belonged to males; and so Pharoah wears the snake in his head-dress, and Arthur the dragon-winged helmet.) The more central an earlier religious element or cultural practice had previously been, the greater anathema it now became; the higher the previous status of individuals, the greater the fall and punishment.

It is clear that menstrual blood and all that was directly associated with it – childbirth, for instance – had been held, by Neanderthal himself, to be the very heart and bedrock of his (lunar) religion. Therefore the males of recent times held, and still hold, that the mere sight of menstrual blood can turn a boy prematurely grey, that one drop of it, stepped over, not even touched, will cause barrenness in people, and the death of cattle.

Although the fact has not so far been mentioned, aboriginals (and, for that matter, Jews) also regard the placental blood in which the new-born baby appears in the same category as menstrual blood. These are identical – and so the same taboos apply to a woman who has just had a child as to a woman who is menstruating. Although the new mother is not beaten or tortured, she is nevertheless unclean for a period of weeks or months, may be painted with red ochre, may be obliged to live in seclusion, and so on. Red ochre, then, today as in the past represents all blood, though for Neanderthal it had represented primarily menstrual blood. For him it was the birth-blood in which the Earth came bathed when the Moon gave birth to her. Strange as this next may seem at first, both water and fire are also equally attributes of the moon (see Chapter 10), hence MW may not touch water with her lips or touch or look at fire.

In the 'new order', therefore, many of the once central elements were entirely purged and anathematised – menstruation and menstrual blood, the important ceremony of 'coming to womanhood' (for just as male societies make a great fuss of the time when a boy becomes a man, so the matriarchal society had made a great fuss of the time when a girl became a woman), the number thirteen and the thirteen-month year. But other items were retained – the number seven, for example, and, in many societies, male circumcision (which both mimics the menstruation of the pubertal girl, and attempts to propitiate the moon). But here matters get a little complicated – for the ways of the moon religion also continued, *in secret,* at the very heart of the new sun dogmas, as we shall see, notably in Chapter 11.

Meanwhile, however, we need also the information of the next chapter.

10 Thirteen Moons

In every full year there are either thirteen full moons or thirteen new moons. There are never thirteen complete lunations, i.e., complete cycles of the moon. So every alternate year there is either a procession of twelve complete lunations followed by a new moon, or twelve complete lunations followed by a full moon.

Here, then, is a first reason which makes the number thirteen special, and which would, necessarily, have drawn Neanderthal's attention to that number – in each alternate year, thirteen new or thirteen full moons. Here, too, is a first example of the great variety in the moon's activities, of its personality, so different from the totally unvarying sun.

A lunation, the complete cycle of the moon from new to new, or full to full, takes 29.53 days. A normal human pregnancy, incidentally, lasts almost to the minute 9 × 29.53 days, so providing a further reason for 9 being a sacred moon number. We are not at all suggesting here, of course, that Neanderthal could handle decimals; but addition, multiplication and division of whole numbers were well within his capacity as we shall see.

A lunation, then, is the time interval between one new moon and the next. But there is also another form of lunar month, the sidereal lunar month. This is the time taken for the moon to reach again the same position relative to the background of stars in which you previously observed it. This sidereal month is 27.29 days in length, the actual return therefore occurring on the twenty-eighth day.

The ancient moon worshippers very wisely decided to use the 28-day sidereal month as their basis for sub-dividing the year, and not the 30-day lunation. For 28 × 13 (the number suggested, as we saw, by counting the new or full moons in alternate years) gives 364 days – one day short only of a full year. A *full* year then becomes 'a year and a day', the expression found so often in fairy-tale and legend.

The number 364 itself factorises beautifully – for example, 4 × 91 = 364. This is why, incidentally, the great Aztec pyramidal Temple of the Sun (yes, the Sun – see p.140) has four flights of ninety-one stairs, one on each side, leading to the platform top. The sacrificial altar itself probably symbolically represented the final 'and a day'. We shall look at factorised 364 in more detail later. The number 365, on the other hand, is completely hopeless, as indeed are the twelve months created when the old thirteen month year was castrated (or beheaded). (Thus we have the mess we operate with today – months of unequal length which do not work even then, since every four years we have to add in an extra day.)

The moon, to revert to the object itself, is so very much more like an organism than the sun. Like an organism it is born, grows, changes, diminishes, dies and is reborn – the moon worshippers, of course, being total believers in reincarnation, a belief which the moon both confirmed and probably in great part helped to create. Not only does the moon in many ways behave like an organism (it does, after all, also have a face on it – the sun has none) but is demonstrably closely linked to the rhythms both of organisms and of our planet. The moon draws the tides: and the moon directly governs the female menstrual cycle.

Before turning to the menstrual month, we treat here a very important subject, the question of why the number three is so significant in moon worship, why the very nature of the Goddess herself is triune or triple (Diana in the leavës green/Luna that so bright doth sheen/Persephone in Hell). It is a question whose answer, quite inexplicably, seems to have escaped everyone, even though the evidence is on full view. This matter also gives us further proof of the continuous astronomical tradition in

Neanderthal times.

One reason for the assignment of the number three to the Goddess is certainly the fact that for three days/nights of a lunation the moon disappears. It is, at this time, too close to the sun to be seen. Here, surely, is the reason why Hindu newly-weds abstain from sex and salt on the first three nights following the marriage.

There is a still more important three, however. The following are the words of Peter Lancaster Brown. Nevertheless, like everyone else, he seems totally oblivious of the relevance of these facts to an understanding of the nature of the Moon Goddess.

> *During total lunar eclipses the umbral shadow of the Earth assumes a coppery red tinge as it creeps across the face of the Full Moon. This is due to the refraction and absorption effects which occur when sunlight passes through the Earth's atmosphere. The colour is often highly variable in intensity, and in some eclipses it is of a very deep red. This phenomenon frequently invited dramatic comment and interpretation by ancient writers.* The Anglo-Saxon Chronicle *in AD 734 is typical and records: 'The Moon was as if it had been sprinkled with blood...' In 1044 Raoul Glaber, a French chronicler... wrote: 'In what manner it happened whether a prodigy brought to pass by the deity or by the intervention of some heavenly body remains unknown to the author of knowledge. For the Moon herself became like dark blood, only getting clear of it a little before dawn.'*
>
> *On more rare occasions the Moon may be blotted out completely by the Earth's shadow. This usually happens following a violent volcanic eruption on Earth when the Earth's atmosphere is choked with suspended debris, and sunlight normally refracted 'round' through the upper atmospheric layers is almost totally absorbed. These are the so-called 'black' lunar eclipses. Such an eclipse occurred on the night of 23rd January, AD 753 when according to one writer 'the Moon was covered with a horrid black shield'. A more contemporary 'black' eclipse occurred in December 1964 shortly after intense volcanic activity in the east Indies.*[111]

So the moon really does menstruate! From the above we also understand, for example, why the Babylonian festival of the Moon Goddess Ishtar's menstruation was held at full moon, whereas the evidence is that human women menstruate at new moon (see below).

How is it that no one even in classical Greek and Roman times, let alone our own scholars, realised that the above is the reason why Io, the Cow-Moon Goddess of the Ionians, was said to change her colour from white to rose and then to black? The heifer-calf born to Minos and Pasiphaë, Graves tells us, changed its colours in the same way three (of course, three) times a day. Clearly, the compartmentalisation that is the chief feature of our own hopeless education system was already well established in the classical world; literature pays no attention to science, and science none to literature. As it happens, however, this awful situation is here our total gain! For if in all of recorded time no one understands that the Moon Goddess has three colours because the moon herself has three, then Neanderthal must have done. It is, then, his teaching which has come down to us, a mute witness through all those millennia, and now at last speaks before the court.

The general or extended significance of the three colours are these. White is the colour of virginity, of the girl before menstruation and intercourse. Red is the colour of menstruation, of the deflowered virgin's first intercourse, of the new-born baby, of general sexual arousal (as in blushing, and so on) and (less relevantly here) of anger. Black is the colour of death; and truly devastating anger (so 'black with rage').

The Menstrual Month

As one ascends the animal scale the oestral cycle is increasingly replaced by a menstrual cycle. That is, instead of coming into season or oestrus once a year in the spring (or perhaps twice, in spring and autumn) the female animal increasingly develops the capacity of reproducing throughout the year; eggs are available for fertilisation more and more frequently. Unfertilised eggs are disposed of through vaginal discharge, and the quantity of the discharge, as well as the frequency, also increases as the animal scale is ascended. Among the higher primates (ape and man) the, as we then correctly term it, menstrual discharge is both frequent and copious, occurring approximately once a month. As most people know, menstruation and month are in origin the same word. Equally, both are the same word as moon.

In the case of apes and man something further and truly remarkable has happened: the menstrual cycle has become linked to the cycle of the moon. 'Remarkable' for two reasons: (1) because we have no idea at all why or how this should have occurred, (2) because the why and how are the subject of no debate whatsoever among orthodox scientists.

Many orthodox biologists indeed would dispute the very notion of any direct link between the two cycles, other than as a popular or primitive superstition – so that there is then nothing to debate. However, hard experimental evidence has recently emerged which establishes the said link beyond doubt. Neanderthal and moon worshippers generally not only believed there was a connection between the moon's cycle and human menstruation: they believed it correctly.

The average length of the menstrual cycle in women is often quoted as 28 or 29 days, numbers extremely close both to the length of a lunation and the sidereal lunar month. Aside from the fact that individual women can vary widely of that given mark – and there is some evidence that such variation is a product of modern life-styles – Louise Lacey cites evidence that the menstrual interval is longer for young girls and shorter for older women; and that individual variability also decreases with age. By age twenty-six, the average menstrual cycle is around 29 days.[110]

Very large-scale, recent statistical surveys of American urban women have shown a significant tendency for menstruation to occur at new moon, with ovulation and conception occurring at the full moon. The scientists concerned themselves suggest that these findings point to a primordial or prototypic situation, which was perhaps once universal.[168]

Could it perhaps be that Neanderthal women in particular (with Neanderthal's probable semi-nocturnal, if not wholly nocturnal life-style – see Chapter 17) all menstruated within one or two days of each other, if not indeed in precisely the same twenty-four-hour span? The impact of such a universal, synchronised menstruation would have been considerable, with a necessarily strong influence on calendrical perceptions and religious observance – and leading also to a particular situation which we shall discuss shortly.

We should first mention, however, another factor which would tend to produce universal same-day menstruation, especially in Neanderthal conditions. There is good evidence that women living together and/or in strong sympathy with each other begin after a time also to menstruate sympathetically. Their menstrual cycles become synchronised. This circumstance was known to the ancient Greeks, for instance, and is again confirmed today by recent studies.[168]

We have to mention also a number of experiments which demonstrate that women who have irregular or otherwise problematical periods can achieve regularity by sleeping with a light on in the bedroom during the fourteenth, fifteenth and sixteenth nights of the cycle. The clear inference is that the bedroom light is functioning as the moon – although we cannot altogether rule out some influence of suggestion. (In an altogether different experimental situation, for example, girls dramatically increased the size of their breasts over a matter of weeks in response purely to suggestion, without otherwise gaining weight.[204])

A very dramatic point, however, which all concerned seemed to have missed, is that if in primordial communities all women menstruated together, then they would also ovulate and conceive together, and so all give birth virtually simultaneously. Each month's births would cluster together in a period of only a few days. Using our own monthly terms, which are of course inappropriate, there would be a gap of some twenty-eight days between October children, November children, December children and so on. If, then, there *are* any genuine astrological differences between individuals born under different zodiac signs (and the evidence is that there are some) these would be magnified and concentrated by the clustering described. Is it under these conditions, then, that the 'astrological personalities' were first observed and described? (Astrologers could test this idea in principle. They should examine whether individuals conceived at full moon – it is not difficult to work out approximate time of conception, if the birth time is known – show the alleged zodiacal qualities strongly, and specifically more strongly, than those conceived away from the full moon. However, the caveats of the section 'The Thirteen Zodiac' below should also be taken into account.)

This is probably an appropriate point to record that many peoples consider the moon not only to be causally linked with menstruation, as we have seen, but to be the cause also of pregnancy itself, and that it is the true husband of women. (On the earlier point, Margaret Drabble, whose views have not so far been mentioned, also says that the commonest slang or popular expression for menstruation throughout the world languages is 'the moon';[45] and some peoples, like the Papuans, do state quite unequivocally that the moon causes menstruation.)

Thus, Eliade tells us that the Australian Aborigines believe the moon comes down to earth in the form of a Don Juan, makes women pregnant, and then deserts them. A similar myth, Eliade writes, is still current in India today. But many other peoples world-wide consider that the moon comes to women to impregnate them, not as a man but as a snake (Briffault). Shuttle and Redgrove also confirm that the 'other husband' is in many cultures referred to as the 'moon serpent'. Briffault further reports that both Asian Buddhists and New Zealand Maoris say that the moon is 'the real husband of women'. How interesting that peoples on these two distant continents should use precisely the same terminology. The inhabitants of Tierra del Fuego refer to the moon as 'the Lord of Women'. The Hindus, again, state that women are impregnated by the moon. Among Eskimos unmarried girls will not look at the moon for fear of becoming pregnant. Eskimo women also believe than an eclipse of the moon is fatal to an existing pregnancy. In Rome it was not only usual, but perfectly respectable, for girls to greet the new moon by rolling over on their backs and opening their legs to 'the symbol of Diana' in the hope that her rays would bring them 'the physical blessings of love', *inter alia*, pregnancy.

Moon Worship as the Primordial Religion

The further back in time we go, the more goddesses we find as opposed to gods, and the more priestesses as opposed to priests. This generalisation is not disputed by the academic establishment. To state that the further back in time we go, the more moon religion we find as opposed to sun religion is by no means so readily acceptable. Of course, if instead we said 'Earth Mother worship' then again we would find wide acceptance. However, we can in fact fairly readily show that Earth Mother religion is really moon religion; and also that the in any case over-trumpeted sun religions are in fact extremely shallow, and everywhere heavily in debt to an older, stronger moon worship.

On the subject of the Earth Mother as the Moon, Briffault, drawing on numerous texts and authorities (Bachofen: 'All Earth Mothers lead a double life, as Earth and Moon') is totally unequivocal: 'The moon and the earth are... identified in all primitive thought as aspects of the same thing' – in the Caribbean, central America, among the Maoris, among the Greeks, in the Middle East, in India ('the full moon is the earth') and China ('the moon and earth are both part of the feminine principle'). In these various accounts, further, whereas the moon is not always the earth, the earth is always the moon. Briffault himself contends that Mother Earth is never anywhere herself worshipped 'in any clear sense' as a goddess.

What I think occurred – and this has the clear support, in principle, of Briffault and others – is that because the moon was (universally) seen as the direct cause/producer of human fertility and babies, and by extension of fertility in the natural world as a whole, when agriculture came along, clearly it was the moon which actually produced the crop. Thus the Indians of Brazil state: '... the moon is the mother of all vegetation', the Mexican Indians 'the moon makes all things grow and multiply'. Eliade himself concludes that there is a clear connection between *all* gods/goddesses of fertility and the moon.[50] (One specific descendant of this situation, I suggest, is the 'horn of plenty', the cornucopia, of the classical world – the horn being never anything else but a symbol of the moon, see below.) Both Diana and Artemis are goddesses not only of the moon but of 'the teeming life of nature... of nature in general and fertility in particular'. J.G. Frazer, the author of the previous comment, goes on to confirm that the belief in the moon as the authoress of all growing and dying is found worldwide. The sacred spirits of trees (there will be more to say about trees) are 'everywhere' associated with the moon, not the sun. In India women (n.b.) would dance naked at night (n.b.) singing lewd songs to stimulate the crops.

Since Graves's *White Goddess* the influence of the moon at least in early European and Middle Eastern religions is more widely accepted than was previously so. However, some specifics will not come amiss. Islam, Israel, the ancient Greeks, the Celts and all other early cultures in this arena date the commencement of the month from the appearance of the new moon. In Hebrew the word for month, *chodesh*, means 'the newness of the new moon'. The very emblem of Islam today is still the crescent moon. What is perhaps of most interest for our purpose here is that new moon is the time when women naturally menstruate. Briffault and his sources are not in doubt that for all Semitic/Hamitic peoples the moon was originally the supreme deity. (Many of the moon elements have today been purged from Judaism and Mohammedanism – menstruation obviously, but much else besides. Briffault draws our attention to a remarkable passage in the Talmud, where the moon has a debate with Yahweh, the former bitterly complaining because her influence has now been so drastically curtailed. The debate ends with Yahweh saying: 'The Lord God said [to the people], make ye a sin-offering on my behalf, for I have caused the moon to become smaller.')

Nevertheless, and of course interestingly, the moon god of the Semites and Arabs was said to be 'the special deity and protector of women'. The name 'Chaldean' means 'moon worshippers' and the ancient town of Ur (whence Abraham) was named after their moon god. Prior to Mohammed 'the sole divinities of the Arabs were the male and female forms of the moon deity'. Mecca itself was originally the chief shrine of the moon, where popular local tradition relates that Abraham bought Mecca from the old woman of the moon. The black stone of Mecca is still the most sacred object in Islam – but this (as we might judge from its colour) is originally the altar and symbol of the Moon Goddess. Margaret Murray, quite independently of all this information, wonders whether the running step which pilgrims use when circling the black stone is a remnant of the round witches' dance (see Chapter 13). (Of course it is.) In Abyssinia, originally colonised by Arabs, the local religion today is the worship of trees, serpents and the moon. In ancient Babylon also, the national religion was moon worship. Ishtar, the Babylonian Moon Goddess, was horned, and indeed a cow. The portrayal of the moon goddess as a cow, and her horned husband (Tammuz in this case) as a bull, is in fact universal in the geographical areas in question. Eliade states, '... wherever the horns of oxen appear in iconography or as idols, they denote the presence of the Great Goddess of fertility, the moon'.[50] Briffault is even more emphatic.

> *But although the bull is a natural emblem of fertilising power, it appears, I think conclusively, that the primary ground for the equation and for the widespread identification of gods with bulls was the assimilation of the horned animal to the moon. In the great religions in which bull-gods are most prominent, the divine bull is either expressly identified with the moon, or is specially associated with those gods who are most unequivocally regarded as moon gods. The horns of cattle and the lunar crescent are interchangeable.*[18]

These statements (which Graves agrees fully in principle) unequivocally tell us that horned Osiris, in that alleged bastion of sun worship, ancient Egypt, is in fact a lunar deity. J.G. Frazer is in no doubt on this score (neither, again, is Graves) and produces a fascinating list of items in support. At the new moon of month Phamenoth, the beginning of spring, the Egyptians celebrated a festival called 'the entry of Osiris into the moon'. At another ceremony known as 'the burial of Osiris', the Egyptians made a crescent-shaped chest 'because the moon, when it approaches the sun, assumes the form of a crescent and vanishes'. Again, the bull (n.b.) Apis, which was held to be an image of the soul of Osiris, was born of a cow impregnated not in the common way, but by a divine influence emanating from the moon. A once-yearly ceremony, at one of the full moons, involved the sacrifice of pigs simultaneously to the moon and Osiris. In a hymn allegedly written by Isis to Osiris occur the lines, 'Thoth placeth thy soul in the bark Ma-at/In that name which is thine of GOD MOON.' Frazer gives further evidence of a similar kind. Graves, for his part, considers that the legend stating that the dead Osiris is found in thirteen parts (twelve plus his head) is a clear reference to the lunar year. The penis of Osiris, which had disappeared (a fourteenth part), Graves considers to represent the 'and a day' element of that lunar year, small but vital.

Another great sun religion, far away across the ocean, that of the Aztecs, is similarly riddled with moon elements. Still older, precursor elements, which we come to in a later section, show us that the moon here was formerly even stronger. Yet we have plenty of evidence even at the Aztec religion's height. We observe also that the number thirteen itself in America did not become anathema, as it did in Europe and the Middle East.

For in the Aztec religion 13 of the deities ruled over the 13 stations of the day, and 9 over the stations of the night. The total pantheon of deities, from which these officers were drawn, consisted of 9 gods and 9 goddesses.

The calendar had two divisions: (a) a ritualistic succession of days and (b) a solar calendar. These two were combined to make the cycle of the Great Year of 52 normal years, which we met already in Chapter 7. As we saw there, the number 52 can be factorised 4 × 13. Each day was distinguished by a combination of 1 to 20 names, combined with the numbers 1 to 13, yielding a 260-day period. This itself is also expressed as 20 weeks of 13 days each. The number 260 further factorises into 4 × 5 × 13 (and there are, as we see later, solid grounds for considering both 4 and 5 to be also moon numbers).

It is really absolutely astonishing that 'authorities' on these matters can write as follows: 'The significance [of these numbers]) may have been magical or possibly of an astronomical origin, as yet unexplained';[191] and 'the origin of the peculiar uses of the number thirteen is a puzzle without satisfactory solution'.[120] The two authors concerned are strong candidates for the wooden spoon award for academic obtuseness – but another author we shall meet later is still more deserving. For, clearly, the main import of the numbers is that they are principally multiples of the number thirteen – which is on full view in the thirteenth-month year of many ancient religions and cultures. It is on full view in the Celtic tradition, for example, and, as we know, has in fact been worshipped continuously in Europe for 75,000 years. Is one asking too much to expect 'authorities' on ancient civilisations to be aware of such matters and, more to the point, to apply the awareness?

We could pursue Central American matters here, but there is really little need. The god Tonacatecotl, for example, is said to preside over 'the thirteen causes'. The Toltecs speak of twelve heavens, plus the Earth, making thirteen heavens in all (a strong parallel with the Scandinavian view, see below). A stone medallion from the Mayan civilisation shows the central figure of Maya surrounded by twelve other figures or glyphs[140] – which may be a zodiac, and is certainly a coven, or perhaps the round dance (see Chapter 13). Zodiacs, as we understand the term, do not appear in central American cultures – but by great good fortune we have an earlier Mound Builder's thirteen-zodiac calendar from Arkansas (see below). We have indeed been very fortunate in this matter of single archaeological finds, which absolutely prevent the ideas we are proposing from the risk of being dismissed – quite unjustifiably of course – as mere speculation.

In up-front terms the moon plays a smaller role than the sun in Aztec religion. Yet, as already noted, the pyramidal Great Temple of the Sun has four flights of 91 steps, an emphatic nod in the direction of the lunar year. (There is also the interesting point that a pyramid has a total of thirteen sides and edges, counting the base, the only three-dimensional structure which has.) The moon as a specific object of worship, however, has two distinct aspects. On the one hand she is simply the consort of the sun. But in her other capacity, as Tlazoteotl, she is the power behind all witchcraft and magic. Burland, moreover, notes 'singular parallels between modern witchcraft and the ancient Mexican worship of the goddess Tlazoteotl'[23] (see Chapter 14). Here, clearly, in this second aspect of the Aztec Moon Goddess we have central elements of Neanderthal moon worship, which the distant ancestors of the Aztecs originally brought with them.

So there we have the much-vaunted religion of the sun, on two widely separated continents. In each case that religion is clearly little more than an outgrowth and an overgrowth of the much older, and still powerful, original moon worship.

There is an important word still to say on the true nature of Mother Earth as the Moon, concerning the 'stone Venuses' widely found in paleolithic times and here we shall also be able to award the coveted wooden spoon.

Moon Numbers

As ever, we could say far more on the items we are covering, all fascinating in their own right in any case, but we must be selective, and not simply for reasons of space. For our principal task always is to demonstrate (a) that very specific and detailed parallels can be observed world-wide in the particular subject matter under investigation, parallels that cannot be adequately explained by the action of chance or simply as the expression of common elements of general human psychology; (b) that the roots of the parallel situations reach far back into distant prehistory, and specifically not just to the time but to the culture of Neanderthal man.

We have already firmly identified 7 and 13 as highly significant moon numbers, and equally as centrally important in the religious observance of Neanderthal man. He was building shrines involving those numbers 75,000 years ago (see Chapter 8). The involvement specifically of the number seven in the spiral maze also goes back at least 20,000 years, and, in view of the Siberian mammoth-bone maze design (Chapter 5), probably much further. The Australian connection regarding the Pleiades legend (Chapter 4) gives another back-date of around 25,000 years for seven, and the Aborigines' report of the Supreme Being Baiani first coming to Earth along with twelve followers (Chapter 7) gives us another similar back-date for the number thirteen, in view of the close parallel here between Baiani's group and other such founding groups (see below): far too old for orthodoxy.

A critic might contend at this point that, well, perhaps as you say, the numbers 13 and 7 do have this rather surprisingly long history, and may indeed be connected with functions of the moon. But why couldn't each of the groups concerned have produced the numbers independently, for themselves? Then, of course, we point to associated physical artefacts such as maze designs and stone zodiacs (see below), as well as to extremely detailed legends such as that concerning the Pleiades, found alongside these numbers, and which could not conceivably be the result of accidental, independently generated parallel ideas.

I would now like to adduce some evidence which, though aspects of it have been commented on by earlier writers, has I think so far not been fully understood. First we must mention the importance of 'mid-points' to primitive peoples, for which there is much generally accepted evidence. The mid-point of the year (midsummer or midsummer's eve) is important, as are the mid-points of the two half-years, the spring and autumn equinoxes. Whatever else, these are important markers of the progress of the year, but their psychological-religious import is far greater. They are clear indicators of the cyclic nature of events (of the nature of nature, one would like to say), of return, departure and return again. Exactly so primitive man thought his own life departed and returned, in a probably endless cycle of reincarnation. By extension, and in their own right also, the mid-points of the day and night became important, midnight and midday.

Let us now consider the lower numbers simply in terms of their mid-points. For example, 4 is the mid-point between 1 and 7:

1 2 3 **4** 5 6 7

And 4 × 7 gives the 28 days of the lunar month.

Further, 7 just happens to be the mid-point between 1 and 13:

1 2 3 4 5 6 **7** 8 9 10 11 12 13

And 4 × 7 × 13 just happens to give us 364, the number of days in the lunar year.

That we need not doubt Neanderthal's ability to examine and handle numbers at this level we see at the end of this section.

The number four also has further recommendations regarding its significance. The naturally occurring midsummer's day, midwinter's day, plus the spring and summer equinoxes, equally naturally divide the year into four quarters. The moon symbol, the square cross within the circle (see Chapter 6), also produces four quarters, as does the moon herself. However, as we see from the Arkansas zodiac, it is possible to think of the moon as having five phases, so that five is also a possible lunar number. (That one has another pedigree also, however, in the five fingers on each hand, the five toes on each foot, and our five extremities – four limbs plus a head.)

We fully examined the moon attributes of the very important number three at the outset of this chapter. And as we have also seen, nine is important because pregnancy lasts nine lunations, but as well because it is 3 × 3. If we draw three rows of three dots, one row beneath the other, we then not only have rows of three, but columns of three, and diagonals of three – a magic square.

On the basis of these clear, inherently reasonable and by no means unsatisfying interrelationships of the lower numbers with each other, as also with observed natural events, there arises the 'study' of numerology – whether already in Neanderthal times or only in the historical period – which on the whole is not reasonable. In numerology one assigns all kinds of magical significance to number values, and by endless juggling with the numbers can achieve virtually any result one wants. This is not an activity which especially recommends itself, although sometimes numerologists did hit upon genuine mathematical relationships. However, as already mentioned, I am myself inclined to accept as both meaningful and important the fact that the pyramid has a total of thirteen edges and surfaces, if the base is also included. I think Neanderthal man observed the pyramidal shape in naturally occurring crystals – and all crystals belong to the moon of course, arising as they do from liquids – and that his perception and interpretation of this shape ultimately led to actual pyramid building in Egypt, China and America.

To what extent could Neanderthal actually calculate such matters as the interaction of the lunar and solar cycles, the periodicity of the planets and so forth? I think to a quite startling extent – and that through the use of the abacus device. Fortunately, we have hard evidence of this possibility. For it is the case that Tamil astronomers could accurately predict eclipses of the sun and moon, simply by manipulating groups of shells on the ground in front of them, and without written mathematical notation of any kind.[139] I believe that Neanderthal performed similar operations – hence, ultimately, the invention of the standard abacus in the more 'Neanderthal' of present-day ethnic groups – Japanese, Chinese and Asiatics generally, and including the Incas.[132]

Finally now the story of 'Neanderthal and the Seven Bears' deserves a section of its own.

Seven Bears

Anyone requiring a detailed account of the influence of the number seven in historical times need look no further than Geoffrey Ashe's *Ancient Wisdom*. No one can, in any case, fail to be aware of its effects in our own religion and culture. There are seven wonders of the world, seven seas, the seventh son of a seventh son has magical powers, Christ speaks seven times from the cross, there are seven heavens, seven colours in the rainbow, seven days in the week, seven ages of man, and so on and on. The number seven is employed significantly and anciently throughout Europe, the Middle East, India and Asia. Some of the references are striking in terms of our present subject matter; for example, the most solemn oath of the ancient Arabs was sworn on seven blood-smeared stones.[4]

More widespread still than the influence of seven is that of bear worship – but the two are really one and the same. It is entirely clear, as Ashe demonstrates, that a major significance of the number seven arises from the fact that the constellation of Ursa Major (the Great Bear) contains seven stars – a constellation which is not only easily found by the searching eye, but which also indicates the 'still centre of the heavens', that northern point in the sky around which all the stars appear to us to revolve, and around which the Great Bear also closely circles. We can, I think, be certain that Neanderthal himself so named this constellation 75,000 years ago, when he built altars of seven bear skulls. Therefore (and in any case) it is so called today by ourselves, by Hindus, by North American Indians, and many other peoples.

Bear cults flourish, or have flourished, around the full circle of the northern hemisphere, more vigorous as one proceeds north. The shamans of Siberia often wear a complete bear hide, the Ainus have protracted bear ceremonies and customs, as do the North American Indians. None of this material, incidentally, is in any doubt.

Eliade, however, takes us much further. He states that the bear is a lunar animal world-wide – not just in the northern hemisphere, but everywhere. He goes on to say that initiation ceremonies into manhood everywhere involve both the bear and the moon.[50] This is all excellent news from our point of view.

It does appear that Ashe has underestimated the extent and depth of influence of both the bear and the number seven. However, he is not wrong to insist that seven is a *major* force in the areas named above – where he is wrong is to suggest that the influence of seven elsewhere in the world is not important. My own hypothesis, in particular and in any case, does not require a strong presence of the number seven – it only requires its presence at all, although, yes, in connection with other matters important in their own right. For I need only show that seven was formerly important. I am, therefore, well content with the fact that in various Nigerian tribes when the ju-ju man attempts to restore the dead to life, he strikes the ground at the corpse's feet seven times, or the roof of the house seven times;[59] with the seven of the Hopi Indian maze; and with the worship of the seven-star Pleiades in South America and Australia. The importance of the Pleiades itself certainly, in part, derives from the fact that it, like the Great Bear, is composed of seven stars. Incidentally, without unfortunately giving full details, Ashe reports that a Jewish legend concerning the Pleiades involves a bear pursuing seven girls – just as in the Wyoming Indian legend (see Chapter 4). This is excellent further news concerning the antiquity and provenance of this particular legendary material.

The Moon and Earth as Planets

The possibility that Neanderthal understood the earth to be a planet is a notion that will prove useful in attempting to explain some of the finer points in his world/universe view (see Chapter 16). We have already seen statements in the present chapter that the moon and earth were anciently felt to be the same by some peoples, or at least to be aspects of each other. Since, then, the moon is a round object floating in space, might not the earth (her daughter) also be such an object? Certainly we do find in early historical times numerous statements to the effect that the earth is round and is a planet. Andrew Tomas gives a number of references on this score – two from China (3000 and 2000 BP), half a dozen from Greece (between 2500 and 2000 BP) and two from India (2500 BP). These may or may not be fragments of a much older understanding. Or else we may say that each of the peoples named reached this conclusion independently around the same time, which in this case is perfectly possible.

The Thirteen Zodiac

Ranking equal in excitement with the Neanderthal bear-skull altar is the carved stone zodiac of thirteen signs fashioned by the North American Mound Builder culture, and discovered in the Ouachita River, Hot Springs, Arkansas (see *Figure 8a*). The Mound Builders flourished around the time of Christ, all over the eastern half of North America, so this zodiac as an artefact is some 2000 years old. Its *tradition*, however, is at least 20,000 years old – for in Israel we find another thirteen-zodiac inlaid in the floor of an old synagogue. One could, perhaps, argue that the Mound Builders and the ancient Hebrews had independently conceived of a thirteen-zodiac, based on the lunar year, if both were moon worshippers. However, there is a clincher (aside from all our other evidence of course). Both zodiacs involve a spider.

Figure 8
(a) North American Indian Mound Builders Calendar Stone (2000 B.P.).

The Arkansas zodiac, which is carved on a boulder, consists of thirteen equal divisions. Above the zodiac itself appear five aspects of the moon – two quarters, two halves and a full moon. Clearly the statement is 'the moon rules this zodiac'. One of the zodiac signs is a spider, with a cross on its back, another is the head of a serpent. A third may be a lotus, as James Churchward claims, but the reproduction is a small one, so that it is hard to confirm that detail. However, certainly the design is an open, petalled flower. If indeed a lotus, then we have another very useful link with the mainland Orient. So although, then, neither the thirteen-zodiac, nor indeed any zodiac as we understand the term, is found in the later Aztec and Toltec cultures further south, we see that this did once form a part of Indian traditions.

When the Gnostic Jews built a fine synagogue at Beth Alpha in Palestine in AD 520, they set into the floor as a mosaic an elaborate zodiac (see *Figure 8b*). We will come to the many

(b) Zodiac from Beth Alpha Synagogue, Palestine (520 A.D.).

significant details of this artefact in a moment, but, as is fully acknowledged, the whole design is out of kilter. The original, balanced design has been altered – whether subsequently after completion of the full original, or at the last moment during construction when work was already largely completed, is hard to say. Orthodox archaeology, while commenting on the situation, has no explanation for the obvious alteration. As we see at Beth Alpha in its present form today, the zodiac has the standard twelve divisions and signs. But five of the sections are larger than the other seven, which are uniform; nor are the five larger sections uniform with each other. James Vogh has shown that by using the measurements obtained from the seven regular sections (which, as it happens, are all on the right side), and by inserting an extra division on the left among the irregular sections, we can create a perfectly balanced thirteen-division whole. There can be no doubt at all that Vogh is right in his idea. The sign which he chooses to insert is that of the spider goddess, Arachne.[194] As it happens, the place of its insertion is necessarily close to, and can be precisely if one wishes, where the spider occurs in the Arkansas Mound Builders' zodiac.

The centrepiece of the Beth Alpha zodiac is a goddess – clearly a goddess. This centrepiece gives us all the support we could require. The head-dress of the goddess is composed of thirteen items. Over her *left* shoulder (n.b.) appears not the new moon, but the crescent of the dying moon, against a background of stars. Directly from the body of the goddess (she has no arms) emerge a number of 'reins' leading to four 'horses' heads. Emerging from below the heads are eight feet. There are also two 'wheels' – so the whole may be a chariot. The 'horses' heads are rather odd-looking – they seem to have stylised horns in the middle of their foreheads, so are perhaps actually oxen. Vogh, in any case, thinks these heads also to be an afterthought or amendment (as indeed could be the two wheels). If we remove the heads, we find we have a goddess with eight legs – as, of course, does a spider. But even if we retain the heads, we still have eight legs. In this connection Vogh astutely notes that the mystical Odin/Wotan – which Graves and others fully identify also with Welsh Gwydion – rode a horse with eight legs, from which he seldom dismounted (a further European spider connection, therefore, to be added to those already noted in Chapter 6).

In the Arkansas and Beth Alpha zodiacs we seem to have two virtually identical statements. The first says: 'I am the moon, and this is my thirteen-zodiac, which includes my own special signs, the spider, marked with a cross, and the serpent.' The second says: 'I am the spider-moon, and this is my thirteen-zodiac.' In this second case we cannot definitely add the words 'which includes my own special sign, that of Arachne the spider', but this seems wholly likely, especially in view of Vogh's further research.

Vogh went looking for an actual constellation that could serve for that of Arachne the moon-spider in a thirteen-zodiac. There are both constraints on the choice that can be made, and hints towards it (for example, in the Druidic calendar), and Vogh ends up with the constellation Auriga, which happens to mean 'the charioteer'. Vogh takes this name to indicate a possible connection with Arachne's pseudonym 'the Lady of the Silver Wheel', but we could perhaps adduce also the goddess-charioteer of the Beth Alpha zodiac. Nor – and this is purely my own view – is it totally out of the question that 'Auriga' and 'Arachne' could be from the self-same root-word.

The constellation Auriga happens to lie between Taurus and Gemini. Since Taurus has horns, he necessarily must be a creature of the moon – but Vogh was thinking instead in terms of the Minotaur and its bull's head, which is from every point of view the moon's creature. Now comes his flash of remarkable inspiration. Could the name 'Minotaur' be a code word that was telling us something, if we were 'Gnostic' or knowing enough to spot it? Vogh reversed the elements of the name Minotaur – and found he had TAUR-O-MIN (Taurus precedes Gemini in the zodiac). Could this new word be telling us that the 'moon' lies between TAURus and geMINi? And that therefore the moon is the thirteenth sign and is Auriga/Arachne? I consider again that Vogh has to be right. (I would like to add that in Latin the written letter o itself could stand for the full moon – but that will not do for the Greek *ώ*. However, the Greek letter *ώ* was also pronounced in exactly the same way – by rounding the lips into an 'o' shape.)

Vogh's further views are more debatable. He considers that Arachne, in the story of her weaving duel with the goddess Athene, was working a thirteen-zodiac tapestry. But in fact we are told of thirty-six items in Arachne's tapestry. However Vogh, not at all unjustifiably, points to twelve of these as representing the signs of the conventional twelve-zodiac. (It would be quite usual and in order for a possible mystical coder deliberately to introduce irrelevant information in order to disguise the true meaning.) Vogh here takes Asterie, the starry one, to be the alleged thirteenth sign. But why not take Arachne *herself* as the thirteenth? I am indeed anxious to accept that Arachne's work did involve thirteen signs – because we are quite specifically told that Athene's tapestry contained twelve. And Athene, literally, 'knocks out' Arachne with her shuttle. So this legend could be saying that the twelve-zodiac has knocked out, or destroyed, or altered the thirteen-zodiac – which is perfectly correct. However, as said, the truth of the matter in this case must remain only a matter of opinion.

At any rate, the censored or castrated stone thirteen-zodiac of Beth Alpha is by itself solid proof of a general purge of the number thirteen. We have much evidence of that process from other sources. The Greek pantheon originally consisted of thirteen deities not twelve. The tribes of Israel once numbered thirteen, not twelve. The Sioux Indians, reckoning their year still by the moon, say it consists of twelve months – but also a 'lost' thirteenth.[176] In Teutonic mythology Asgard, the seat of the gods, is sometimes divided into twelve and sometimes into thirteen spheres – but the *Gulfaginning* confirms that there was once a golden age when there were twelve seats for the gods, plus one for the All-Father. (Both these last do sound very like the thirteen heavens of the Toltecs.)

Yet although generally purged, there are many significant references still to the former all-importance of the number thirteen. Jewish boys, after all, are still initiated into manhood at age thirteen (when they are 13 × 13 lunar months old) and orthodox Jewish thought considers there to be thirteen central qualities to God. There are thirteen Buddhas in the Asian/Indian pantheon. The number thirteen also figures centrally in the ceremonial rites of the North American Hopi Indians. The thirteen-month year was still observed in the English countryside, till at least the fourteenth century, as recorded in the *Ballad of Robin Hood and the Curtal Friar* (and it is indeed interesting to find here a connection with Robin Hood): 'But how many monthes be in the yeare?/There are thirteen I say.' The thirteenth card of the major arcana of the Tarot card pack is the card of Death *and* Rebirth. And so on.[67]

Lastly here comes the very important matter of *founding* or *leading* groups of thirteen. King Arthur heads a group of twelve knights, making of course a 12 + 1 = 13 coven. But a further point here seems to have been missed by all. These knights sit at a *round* table – is this not, in fact, another thirteen-zodiac? (It would be most interesting if astrologers were to examine the characters of the knights concerned – do their personalities conform to the traditional personalities of the zodiac?) We have already talked of the two covens of the Most Noble Order of the Garter (Chapter 6). To the full list here we can add; Roland and the Twelve Peers of France; Jacob and his Twelve Sons; Romulus and his Twelve Shepherds; Odysseus and his Twelve Companions; Hrolf and his

Twelve Berserks; Robin Hood and his Twelve Followers; the court Judge and his Twelve Jurors; Baiani and his Twelve Companions (see above, and Chapter 7). The most important one of all, perhaps, which seems to get overlooked by everyone – perhaps purely out of expediency by the authors concerned – is Christ and his Twelve Disciples. These last we shall be very much concerned with in the next chapter.

The Moon as Fire, Lightning, Water

It distinctly jars on our own particular set of prejudices and mental sets to hear fire and lightning listed as attributes of the moon, and still again to find fire bracketed with water. Yet the conceptual link is already clear from this section's title – for lightning produces fire, and lightning occurs in the proximity of thunderstorms (actual or threatening) and rain, being water, is of the Goddess . . . so it is all not quite as strange as our first thought judges it, and certainly in no way arbitrary. That other major source of natural fire, the volcanic eruption, is a phenomenon of flowing liquid (of rivers of fire). Is it so surprising, after all, that the Goddess can turn solid rock into water, when she has no trouble at all turning water into rocks and solids (ice, salt, crystals, gem-stones, snow)?

(These wonders are all acceptable as part of the breathtaking majesty and wonder and diversity and power of the moon. When she wills it, the mighty sea moves and turns, the very mountains change to liquid at her whim and briefly, joyfully released, flow downward eagerly to greet their sister sea. Can anyone be so blind as not to understand the depth and range of her power, these then so much greater, so far more diverse, than any feeble power of the forever captive sun?)

It was, of course, because fire is an attribute of the moon and not the sun – see also below – that in our own historical times fire, like salt, like water, like milk, must be shielded from the touch and gaze of menstruating woman.

The sacredness of (moon) fire was one of the elements of the Old Religion that more modern religions have retained and left unpurged. In several parts of the world fire is centrally used in rain-making ceremonies! The ritual extinguishing and relighting of fires is also a world-wide method of invoking general fertility and renewal. We observed this practice already, and notably, in the culminating Aztec festival of the fifty-two-year Great Period (Chapter 4). And, as Briffault tells us, most Christian countries observe the practice of extinguishing all fires and lights on the Saturday before Easter, prior to ritually rekindling them. (I have not seen this next precise statement anywhere, though it is certainly implied, but my own view in any case is that the ritual extinguishing and relighting of fire represents and mimics the death and rebirth of the sun *but as servant or sacrifice only* at the midwinter solstice – chapter 11.) The lighting of fires next to and the carrying of torches around, newly-sown fields is found all over the world, in Africa, Asia, North America, Europe. The custom of banning fire on particular holy days is found in the Near East, Asia, Africa and the Pacific.

Briffault is at pains to stress that the sacred fire of the Greeks and Romans, no less than that of Eskimos and other aboriginals, has no connection with solar worship. The idea that rituals connected with fire, and the tending of perpetual lights and fires (the former found in the Jewish synagogue to this day, for example) is a 'sure index' of the cult of the sun is, Briffault states, a widespread but total fallacy. The 'renewal of life' and the symbolic 'renewal of fire' is everywhere associated in primitive religions with the moon. The rites involved are 'far older' than those of any solar cult. And there are, in any case, specific legends among some peoples stating that fire comes from the moon.

Lastly here, Schliemann quotes several authorities suggesting that the swastika is the symbol of Indra in India, the god of rain, wind and *lightning*; and of Zeus, the classical god of sky, air, rain, wind and *lightning* – my italics – so giving us a further link with the material of earlier chapters.[163] And as noted in chapter 7, the Australian Aborigines use a zig-zag sign to indicate the moon. Some further information on the lightning-moon connection is still to come in the section 'The Moon and the Mistletoe' later in this chapter.

But here, importantly, we can give an explanation of the Medusa of classical legend, with her hair of writhing snakes, who could turn animate creatures to stone with her glance. Neanderthal, clearly, conceived and saw lightning as groups (or rivers) of snakes descending from the sky (or out of the rain). The darting, forked tongue of the actual snake further confirmed this view of forked lightning. And just as one striking snake bite produced death, so the similarly striking single bite of lightning also killed trees and people, turning them to stone. The Medusa of legend, then, is the moon, and the snakes about her head are lightning. (Compare here also Heyerdahl's South American sandstone statue, p.229.)

These next comments concerning women and rain, and the moon of course, link directly with the contention of the previous chapter that all religious/magical power once resided in women. First let us just mention the connections we have already seen. Witches and menstruating women are said to be able both to raise storms and to calm them (and these are both old and widespread beliefs). The menstruating woman must not touch water directly. She can spoil well-water, and even prevent the tide from returning. (These negatives are part of the reversed, purging scenario of previously positive qualities.)

Turning to our direct topic, the ancient Mexicans held that the moon was responsible for all flooding 'under the guise of a young and beautiful woman'. The Zuni of South America associate all waters with the moon, and appoint women for all rain-making ceremonies. In Peru and Chile also, rain-making is in the charge of special women priestesses. Throughout all of Asian India likewise magical rites for producing rain were exclusively in female charge. In most of these rites the women danced naked at night around a clay image. (Nor has much changed recently - a *Guardian* report in 1979 states that 'naked women are tilling the fields of drought-stricken Uttar Pradesh State at night in order to try to placate the rain god'.)

Throughout most of Africa also women, once again, are the prime movers in all rain-making ritual. The custom of the Bantu is particularly interesting and informative – very similar ceremonies, too, being found in Nyasaland and the Transvaal.

> *The women remove their clothing and array themselves in head-dresses and girdles made from a particular creeping plant. They set out in procession uttering special cries and singing songs of a revolting obscenity in which all must join. They first proceed to the house of a woman who has borne twins and sprinkle her with water. The procession, still singing obscene songs and performing lascivious dances,*

then proceeds to the wells, which are ceremonially cleaned out. They then go to the grove where the tribal ancestors are buried and pour water over their graves. During the proceedings no man must be found in the path of the women: should any male intruder be met, he is soundly thrashed and otherwise maltreated, and thrust out of the way.[18]

At the end here we have a quite remarkable echo of Bacchic and Dionysian and Mystery rites in the classical world. It will be recalled that Orpheus himself was torn to pieces by such a posse of delirious women.

Both the Zulus in Africa and the Cheyenne in far-away North America, incidentally, believe that if the wife of the male rain-maker becomes pregnant, he loses his rain-making powers – one more interesting, very specific parallel for our collection.

There is much evidence on this occasion also from early and present-day Europe. In recent times in Germany a pre-pubertal girl was stripped and led to some remote spot, where she must dig up henbane with her toes, and perform other ritual acts. Then water was poured over her. In Worms, in former times, during severe drought young women stripped one of the younger girls and took her to the nearest stream to bathe. Meanwhile the others beat the surface of the water with wands. The girl was then led back to the village, walking backwards.

In Rumania, girls clad in green, scanty attire go from house to house singing, while people throw water over them. In Serbia girls dance in a circle round another girl wearing only a skirt of leaves. In Russia, a passing stranger is seized and given a ritual ducking. Such ceremonies, always involving women, and never men, existed or still exist throughout the length and breadth of Europe and the Near East.

The Moon and Mistletoe

Mistletoe is the most sacred plant of all in relation to the moon. Graves notes, almost mocking, that whereas holly and other pagan plants are now allowed into churches, mistletoe is still forbidden.

Mistletoe is revered for its magical properties on at least four continents. It is not simply a plant worshipped and made famous by the Druids. Rather, the widespread reverence and the particular Druidic reverence both stem from a much older tradition. So the Ainu of Japan, whom we have already encountered, consider that mistletoe is a cure for almost every disease. The Walso tribe of Senegambia in Africa not only revere mistletoe, but say if carried on one's person, is a protection against wounds in battle. The Gallos of East Africa also worship mistletoe and keep it in their homes for good luck. The Romans, quite independently of the Druids, again valued mistletoe highly as a medicine, but like the Druids believed it effective only if harvested at certain times of the moon. Modern Italians believe that carrying a piece of the plant will help a woman conceive (so here is a clear fertility aspect). The same belief is held by the natives of Mabuiag in the Torres Straits – yet one more challenging parallel. In ancient Rome, and elsewhere in more modern Europe, there was a belief that mistletoe would extinguish and prevent fires, so that many dwellings and inns kept sprays of it. It was also said to open all locks (a 'Freudian' hint?). In the north of England, in order to ensure the fertility of a herd, the first cow that calves after New Year's Day should be given a bunch of mistletoe (so fertility once again).

The Druidic belief, as we see later, is that if the plant is to be efficacious, it must after harvesting not be allowed to touch the ground. In Cambodia a similar belief exists in respect of orchids, which are likewise parasitic plants and likewise used medicinally. And as we saw in the previous chapter, the important ceremonial pole of the Australian Arunda must similarly not be allowed to touch the ground in the course of its cutting and preparation, and a Polynesian King must also not touch common ground. Certainly we are looking at echoes of the old mistletoe tradition in these four cases. (Nor, of course, must we at all forget the special case of the menstruating woman – see Chapter 9.)

The Celts and their Druid priests were moon worshippers to the core – whatever their professed views on the sun. They observed the 13-month lunar year of 'a year and a day'. Their alphabet consisted of 13 consonants and 5 vowels (and the number 13 as a magical number occurs constantly in their legends and tales[78]). Each letter of the alphabet is named after the tree or shrub of whose name it is the initial letter; and tree worship, as Briffault tells us, is a feature world-wide of worship of the moon.

(There is much that is germane here, although we have not the place to linger – for example, the word for 'willow', the tree which most loves the water, is from the same root as 'witch' and 'wicked'. Of this tree it is said 'the moon owns it'. The word Druid means 'he who knows the oak'). The Celts also practised a major cult of the bear. They traced their descent through the female line. The priests wore white, and so on. We need not continue this list but, clearly, anything the Druids tell us about mistletoe is likely to derive centrally from the old, Neanderthal moon traditions.

In Latin and Greek mistletoe means 'strength'. In Scots Gaelic it means 'all-healer'. As an all-healer, and as an aphrodisiac, it was prized among many peoples, as we have seen. However, while in very many cases ancient herbs and remedies have proved to have genuine medicinal and medical effects, mistletoe has so far not been shown to have any. (But of course, almost anything *can* act as a cure, or a sexual stimulant, if you really believe in it.) So the mighty reputation of mistletoe is *purely magical*. In support of that view, it had to be cut at certain times of the moon's cycle, with a sickle made of gold, and had to be caught in a white cloth so that it should not touch the ground. I am personally sure that the sickle must represent the crescent moon – and if it was made of gold rather than silver, that is perhaps because silver tarnishes so readily.

Common mistletoe is an evergreen. Evergreens as a whole were clearly favoured by the Goddess, since they continue to grow among the other 'dead' plants of winter, when the sun is also absent. The round, white berries of the mistletoe themselves well symbolise the full moon. The plant has a remarkable further property. If a spray of it is kept for several months, the whole turns a golden colour. J.G. Frazer is convinced that here is the mystical 'Golden Bough' of classical legend – and who can doubt him?

Common mistletoe grows only rarely on the oak tree. But it was the oak mistletoe which was most prized. And it was the oak tree which was the most revered tree of all – not just by the Druids, 'they who knew the oak', but throughout the whole of Europe. Why should the oak be special? *Because it is the tree which is most frequently struck by lightning.*[59]

(The circle, then, is complete, is it not?)

I have been unable to find any botanical evidence for the next point – but is it perhaps the case that mistletoe and other parasitic plants grow best on trees which have been damaged by lightning? Does this give the plant a good initial foothold?

I believe we can consider the moon's most frequent striking of the forest's proudest tree by her lightning as a short-hand symbol or allegory of the moon's major activity of striking down the sun, at the height of his powers, on Midsummer's Day itself. Mortally wounded at this point (in Balder's case with an arrow of mistletoe) the vigorous, the apparently invincible, and the golden one, now begins slowly to die. He actually dies (or, like Arthur, goes south to recover from his wounds) at the winter solstice, Midwinter's day. But the moon, in her graciousness (the Lady of the Lake), always resurrects him.

Moon as Serpent, Moon as Dragon

We have had already many references in this book to the moon-serpent-woman connection, and we will not recapitulate all those here. In brief, we have seen principally how serpents are often said to control the waters of the earth and sky, and how it is they who often make women pregnant.

Eliade states that 'there is a worldwide connection between the symbolism of the snake and the moon'.[50] Briffault tells us that moon gods and goddesses are often represented as serpents. Also that in 'all primitive thought' the snake is the emblem of immortality. J.G. Frazer remarks that the moon represents immortality, and that 'renewal of life, and the hope of everlasting life, are indissolubly connected in the five parts of the world [i.e. everywhere] with the moon and the serpent'. Briffault, Eliade and others consider that the link between the moon and the snake in this case is the fact that the snake sheds its skin periodically, and emerges renewed, rather in the way the moon sheds her old self, or changes, and emerges anew. (Certainly I would agree that here is one reason for linking the snake and the moon, but there is, I consider, a much more important and central one – see Chapter 16.) Frazer remarks on the legends of the slaughter or overcoming of the serpent/dragon (regarding dragon specifically, see below) that is said to have begun modern civilisation, and which we find throughout Europe, the Near East, India and beyond – and of course in the Biblical Genesis story. Briffault draws attention to the fact that world-wide all magical powers are said to derive from the moon/serpent.

All these and other points are well covered by a very informative article by S.A. Cook in the old *Britannica* (eleventh edition, 1910, pre-dating both Frazer and Briffault) under the title 'Serpent-Worship'.

Cook begins by confirming that there is 'from all parts of the world a very considerable body of evidence for the prominence of the serpent in religion, mythology and folklore'. He notes, with puzzlement, that there are everywhere stories of the serpent as the guardian of treasure or wealth, particularly of precious jewels. (This idea we can well understand as deriving from the original notion of the serpent as the controller of underground water and ores, and the moon herself as owning all crystals, gem-stones, pearls, mother-of-pearl, shells, and so on.) A snake skin is often kept and touched for luck. Serpents are often associated with water, including specifically sea-serpents. Many kings and rulers in Europe, Arabia, India and China are said to have had a serpent origin. In one or two cases the serpent is specifically named as the mother (n.b.) of all humankind. A conspicuous feature of serpent cults is the prominence of women. Serpents are often offered milk, and are centrally concerned in rites of growth and fertility. Serpents can cause storms (a good link with witches and menstruating women). Some aboriginal tribes will not kill or eat snakes. Many goddesses have serpent qualities.

I would add myself that one further small connection between snakes and water is that rivers are serpentine and 'snake along'. I am sure this imagery was not lost on Neanderthal, and formed one more link in a satisfying associative chain.

We should adduce here also a further *Britannica* article, likewise from the eleventh edition, by W.A. Phillips, under the entry 'Dragon'. Importantly, Phillips begins by stating that in Greece the word *drakon* 'was originally used of any large serpent, and the dragon of mythology, whatever shape it may have assumed, remains essentially a snake'. These are heartening words, for in Chapter 16 we shall be proposing a strong reason why the dragon cannot be derived from the apparently similar lizard or salamander.

The dragon, Phillips tells us, is always symbolic of the principle of evil. Apophis, in ancient Egypt, was the great serpent of the world of darkness vanquished by Ra; and in Chaldea the goddess Tiamat, the female principle of primaeval Chaos, also took the form of a dragon. Dragons keep good things from men – treasure, or whatever – and the slaying of the dragon was often the crowning achievement of heroes (Siegmund, Beowulf, Tristram, Arthur and so on). The dragon ensign carried before an army in battle was almost universal among nations, from Britain (Uther Pendragon, Richard I, and so forth) through to China (where it is the symbol of the land itself, and was the badge of the royal family). The banner of Moses, again, Graves tells us, was that of 'Nehushtan', the Brazen Serpent. The last lurking place of 'real' dragons in recent times was the high mountains – precisely, as it happens, where the last remnants of Neanderthal man gathered (see Chapter 15).

Importantly, the reason why dragons are reputed to breathe fire is, of course, because fire is an attribute of the moon.

Phillips comments that the similarity of European and Oriental snake/dragon myths seems to point to a common origin 'in an antiquity too remote to be explored'. That comment, at least, is very honest. Cook, too, is honestly puzzled to explain the similarities in snake myths and rituals around the world. He can only propose that some common psychological component in the psychology of evolving man must be involved . . . but one can see that he is far from happy with that explanation; and quite right too.

These comments will suffice for our purposes in the present connection. Here, and earlier, we have been dealing mainly with the serpent-moon-woman-water equation. The spider-moon-cross-woman connection is a slightly different one – although of course the unity of all remains – involving earth magnetism. We deal with that subject elsewhere.

Sabbath Moon

The Christian sabbath, no less than the witch's sabbat, is derived from the original once-monthly festival of the moon goddess Ishtar's menstruation (Akkadian *shabbatu* or *shappatu*).[168] This was held at full moon (because, as I have suggested earlier, this is when the moon turns red during an eclipse). Other communities celebrated their goddess's menstruation at new moon, which is when women themselves naturally menstruate. The word sabbath in origin may mean simply 'goddess' – and it is most relevant here that the Jews speak of the ceremony at the start of the sabbath as the welcoming of the 'sabbath bride'.

That none of the above is the product of over-heated imaginations we know from present-day India, where the Mother Goddess is considered to menstruate regularly. Statues of her are hidden away, and then bloodstained cloths are displayed as evidence that she has had her period. The cloths are highly prized for their alleged medicinal properties in the treatment of many illnesses. In ancient Greece, too, the festival of Athene originally involved the washing of her menstrual linen.[168]

All over Africa, Briffault tells us, the day of the new moon is a day of general abstention from work. One tribe calls it 'the Woman's Day'. The two great festivals of the Hindu religion are at new moon and full moon, when there is a strong prohibition on the performance of work. The women of the Aleutian Islands perform rites and dances under the light of the full moon. In the north of England, in living memory, women worshipped the moon, kneeling on a natural ('earth-fast') stone. In Cornwall, in the west of England, it is still said that a particular rock will turn a woman into a witch if she circles it like the moon and then worships the moon on it. (It is perhaps going a little too far to suggest that this rite necessarily displays an *ancient* knowledge that the moon goes round the earth – but that is a possibility.) In Ireland, also, in recent times women prayed to the moon.

Further comment on the moon-sabbath-witch-woman-menstruation link is made, appropriately enough, in Chapter 13. Here we will only remark how strange it is that Margaret Murray, who was so emphatic that the witch-cult was an ancient Diana-cult, nevertheless wholly side-steps the witch-moon link (as well as so much else). Diana, 'the Bright One', the Moon, is goddess of 'the teeming life of nature'. In her sacred grove at Nemi she was especially worshipped as a goddess of childbirth, who granted children to men and women.

Diana is consistently identified with Artemis, likewise a goddess of the moon, of nature in general and fertility in particular. Artemis derives her name from *artos*, meaning bear, a very useful connection for us. Little girls, wearing saffron dresses – which are considered to represent bear pelts – danced in a circle for her. (Margaret Murray this time, as we shall see, was never in any doubt about the importance of such dance.) Here, once again, we have a specific mention of children, and it is becoming clear that children have some special place in the Old Religion. We will take up that point also in due course.

In conclusion, however, we mention the so-termed 'religion of the people' in China. This (at least until the Communist revolution) ran alongside or below the offical religion – although there was nothing actually forbidden about it. In the people's religion the moon received more attention than the sun. One of this religion's three great yearly festivals was the Festival of the Moon. 'It was especially a festival for women and children.... Men never took part in this ceremony.'[81]

So the moon belongs to women – and children.

Stone Venuses and Black Virgins

Throughout Europe from around 30,000 BP onwards are found stone figurines and rock carvings, which are usually referred to as 'stone Venuses'. They show females with grotesquely exaggerated attributes – enormous breasts, buttocks and thighs, hugely swollen stomachs, and so on. Clearly these are fertility symbols, glorifying also the general sexuality of woman. They are considered by orthodoxy to be representations of the Earth Mother.

One paleolithic relief carving from France, however, shows the 'Venus' sitting with a horn in her upraised palm (see *Figure 9a*). On this horn which, clearly, we accept as a symbol of the horned or crescent moon, are carved thirteen notches. It has been suggested – and to whomever first suggested it goes the coveted award of the wooden spoon for academic obtuseness – that these notches represent the number of animals killed in a particular hunt. The notches, of course, in reality, represent the thirteen months of the lunar year.

This Venus alone suggests that all these stone images are symbols not of Mother Earth, but Mother Moon. Strong further support for this view comes from the much later terra-cotta figurines at Cnossos, with their similarly exuberant thighs and breasts (see Chapter 5). Since we know that the Court of King Minos is *nothing but* the Court of the Moon, we are well justified

Figure 9
(a) The Laussel Venus, holding a horn with thirteen notches (paleolithic rock carving from France).

in this case in assuming those figurines to be hers. By extension, all figurines probably are.

On the point that Earth is in fact the Moon's daughter, incidentally, of which I am myself wholly convinced, Shuttle and Redgrove are equally emphatic, stating that just as Mary made God/Jesus, so Isis, Ishtar, Demeter and Artemis have made the world.[168]

Figure 9b shows a drawing of a present-day altar from Otok in Jugoslavia of the Virgin Mary with the crescent moon at her feet. Really, nothing has changed. At the very least, the Virgin Mary has attached much of the general psychological energy formerly devoted to the moon. But there are also considerations a good deal more specific. The so-called Black Madonnas or 'Black Virgins' (we understand the colour black perfectly in our terms) are found in medieval Monserrat and Einsiedelu, where they still call Mary 'the Moon of the Church'.

(b) Portion of a present day church altar, Otok, Jugoslavia. Note crescent moon at Mary's feet.

Three items in conclusion.

In 1901, at Tunis in North Africa, was found 'a huge circle of enormous stumps of trees, ranged round an immense square stone showing signs of artistic chisel work'. Nearby was found a bronze trough and a sickle made of gold, along with a sarcophagus and skeleton. Reporting this find, J.G. Frazer unfortunately fails to tell us how many stumps of trees there were. However, not only is there surprise at 'Druidic' influence extending into North Africa – but we see once again here how Neanderthal could have constructed large sacrificial and votive temples that would, nevertheless, not have survived the passage of time. The tree-circle in Tunis is for us another very fortunate one-off find.

Today we still allow promiscuous kisses under the mistletoe at Christmas time, the winter solstice. Here is a last faint echo of once orgiastic rites. Although we have not so far stressed this point, all 'Neanderthal' and moon ceremony *always* points to orgiastic practice. The point is now made emphatically. There is something very special about sexuality for Neanderthal, which differs significantly from our own, at least public, view of sex (see especially Chapter 16).

Last of all, a word on playing cards. Our present-day playing cards are apparently derived in some way (although perhaps not) from the older Tarot cards, and make their appearance around the fifteenth or sixteenth century. Whoever it was who designed them, however, clearly intended them as a coded statement of the nature of moon religion. There are 4 suits of 13 cards each. If all the face values of the full pack are added together, taking Jack, Queen, King as 11, 12 and 13, then the total comes to 364, the number of days in the lunar year. If we add in the standard Joker, the appropriately odd man out, as a further one, we have the complete 'year and a day'. The colours of the cards are red and black on a white background – the three colours of the moon.

The orthodox Church condemns playing cards as an instrument of the Devil – but without, it seems, understanding precisely why.

11 Gone to Spiral Castle

The story of the Sleeping Beauty is as follows. A great king invites twelve good fairies to attend the christening of his daughter. But a thirteenth wicked fairy, who has not been invited, nevertheless appears and curses the child with death if she should ever cut herself. Despite all care, however, the by now young woman pricks herself on a needle while at her spinning. She falls into a deep, permanent sleep and cannot be wakened. Around her the castle and the land also fall into living death. But one day a brave young knight finds his way to the castle, and at his kiss the princess and the land come once again to life.

In Scandinavian mythology the story of the death of Balder, the most loved of the gods ('the god of summer sunlight'), is as follows. A banquet is held in Valhalla to which twelve of the gods have been invited. While the feast is in progress, Loki, the spirit of strife and mischief, nevertheless turns up as the thirteenth guest. He gives blind Hoder ('darkness and winter') an arrow of mistletoe, and gets him to fire it. It kills Balder. The Saxon version of the story runs a little differently. Here Balder and Hoder kill each other in a quarrel for the hand of the Virgin Moon. Subsequently, however, Balder is resurrected and his resurrection begins the golden age of mankind.

Here now the story of the death of King Arthur. Arthur has in his castle a round table at which he sits with his twelve most favoured knights, a company of thirteen in all. All the knights are loyal to Arthur, except one, Mordred. He is rebellious and treacherous, and one account says of him that wherever he went he ate everything in sight and left the land bare. While Arthur is away fighting in Italy (the south), Mordred usurps the kingdom and marries Guinevere, Arthur's wife. When Arthur returns he and Mordred fight, dealing each other mortal wounds. In an older, French version of the story, a travelling groom stops at a castle in Italy (the south again). Here Arthur is being treated for his wounds 'which break out every year afresh'. In other English legends also, Arthur is said not to be dead, but only sleeping in a hillside. One day he will re-awaken and lead his people again.

The story of the death of Christ is this. Christ (the Light of the World) has a last supper with his twelve disciples, again a company of thirteen. He is betrayed by one of them, the weak and treacherous Judas. He meets his death on the cross, but is resurrected. His resurrection signals redemption and the promise of eternal life for all mankind.

Even at half a glance it is absolutely clear, is it not, that these four accounts are in essence the same story. They are all one and the same story.

They do, in fact, meet the criteria we set up in an earlier chapter. (1) The marked similarities between the stories are too great to allow the possibility of coincidence or independent generation. They must have some common point of origin. (2) At the same time, the equally marked differences between them are evidence of a long period of separation from that common origin.

Leaving aside the nevertheless highly important fine detail for the moment, the main similarities between the stories are as follows: the involvement of a company of thirteen, of whom one proves evil; the death, or 'death', of the most loved one; the resurrection or promised resurrection of the most loved one; the bestowal of general blessings as a result of that resurrection. Finally we mention, since the point is of considerable importance in another connection, that three of the scenarios involve a feast.

The main differences between the stories are these: in three the most loved one is a male, in one a female; in one the central figure is a god (though Christ is also a god), in another he is a warrior-king (though Christ is certainly what we would today call a militant, and the term king is also applied to him), in a third a spiritual saviour, and in the fourth the daughter of a great king.

Let us be clear here and now that the true story line of these four accounts, in the remote antiquity from which they stem, is very, very simple. (How can it ever have been lost sight of – again our academic establishment covers itself with glory.) It is that in the thirteenth month (or, to be precise, on the 'and a day' at the end of the thirteenth month) the moon finally kills the sun but then, in her power and mercy, at once resurrects him. The new-born sun (the 'king for a year', or from some points of view and in some cultures more correctly 'king for half a year') now begins the rise to his zenith that will bring again to us the golden days of summer.

With that said, however, we should point out that in the story line just given, the role of the moon is positive and benign, or at any rate is that of benevolent despotism; whereas in the four stories themselves her role (apart in any case from being only hinted at obliquely) is seen as negative and destructive. This is an instance of pejorative turn-around, already discussed in earlier chapters.

A little later we shall defend the use of the phrase 'remote antiquity' in an earlier paragraph. But first, the fine detail of these four stories will bear further examination.

In Sleeping Beauty the presence or role of the moon is indicated (as in all the stories) by the presence and significance of the number thirteen – but also by Beauty as spinstress and by the blood which runs from Beauty's finger. Is it too daring at this stage to say that the pin which pricks her finger is the same as the spear which pierces Christ's side? No it is not (but see also below). The kiss of the knight who wakes Beauty is the last faint echo of orgiastic rites, just as is the kiss beneath the mistletoe (see also Chapter 13). Finally in this story, the land itself also falls into a death-like sleep. It is, of course, winter, and specifically the midwinter of the thirteenth month, which grips the 'dead' land.

In the Balder story the moon, apart from the number thirteen, is represented by her most sacred plant, the mistletoe. And also by the fact that Balder's mother is Frigg, the Moon Goddess. It is she who obtained the agreement of all animals, plants and objects that they would not harm Balder. But she left out mistletoe from the agreement, because it seemed so harmless. Really! As of course we know from the previous chapter, not only is the mistletoe the moon's most sacred plant, it is also the most powerful plant in the world. So what we have here is either an act of deliberate 'sabotage' on the part of the storyteller, or more likely in this case, a deliberate hiding or masking of the true point of the story. (Incidentally, much of what goes on in respect of these changes to legends over time is not at all unlike the processes of the dream – where frequently the most important is presented trivially and harmlessly, or as an off-centre throw-away. Therefore unconscious processes may be involved in the changes to the stories, as well as deliberate subterfuge or censorship.) There is more, however. Frigg is the goddess after whom we name Friday. It is on Friday that Christ is crucified and dies. By this point in the book, I hope we can accept that such 'slight' correspondences are neither far-fetched, nor in any way trivial. In the Balder legend Hoder is specifically mentioned as representing darkness and winter, while it is Balder, the god of summer sunlight, who now dies, when mistletoe reigns supreme.

In the Arthur story, Mordred is fairly specifically described in terms of winter. Guinevere, for whom the two fight, is the moon (Balder and Hoder fight specifically for the hand of the Virgin Moon) as is the thirteen (as ever). Arthur is the sun – which goes south in the winter, and Arthur is away in the south in Italy (has gone to Spiral Castle) when Mordred usurps the kingdom. In the first part of the year, the spring and summer, the moon is the lover, friend and consort of the sun, raising him to glory at her side. But in the autumn and winter she betrays him (or at least disciplines him) as Guinevere betrayed Arthur, as Frigg betrayed her son. Discipline, not betrayal, is of course the correct word in the true moon religion itself. It is a question of showing who is really in charge, always tempered then with mercy and resurrection.

(In this particular context, we should note Briffault's point that many midsummer festivals are in fact moon festivals. The Celtic midsummer rite in France, for example, was called 'la lunade' and began not at sunrise, but at moonrise. In many cultures the hero, the sun king, is put to death on midsummer's day, not midwinter's day, often by burning. The ancient Celts would have placed him for this purpose, probably along with others, into a great willow/wicker/witch/wicked basket, the moon's basket.

Fire in any case, as we saw in the previous chapter, always represents the moon. The hero sun king, as Graves points out, may well be sacrificed twice a year, at midsummer *and* midwinter. The psychological justification here is that the sun is (a) mortally *wounded* at midsummer, (b) actually *dies* at midwinter.)

The Christ story, apart from the comments we make now, deserves special attention, and we return to it at the end of the chapter. The details we are in the process of identifying are, in this story, even more hidden than in the others – and this time, as I shall be suggesting, for quite deliberate and conscious reasons. The Virgin Mary, however, is certainly the Virgin Moon. Tales of virgin (and at least sometimes moon) goddesses giving birth to (at least, sometimes, sun) gods are in no way uncommon in world mythology. The virgin goddess Rhea gave birth to Zeus, for example. Certainly the mass of the people were never in any doubt that Mary was the Moon. In the previous chapter we already mentioned the Black Madonnas and the practice in their connection of referring to Mary as 'the Moon of the Church'; and showed (*Figure 9b*) one of the very common shrines (and portraits) in churches throughout east and south Europe where Mary is specifically presented in association with the moon. Graves tell us that this connection was savagely – but obviously unsuccessfully! – repressed with 'terrible penalties' by the ecclesiastical authorities throughout medieval Europe. North American Indians converted to Christianity likewise call Mary 'Mother Moon'. But, in any case, we do have our usual thirteen to show the moon's influence in the Christ story.

We have mentioned already that Christ dies on Friday afternoon (Frigg's day, and Frigg also happens to be the goddess of death) and indeed at the start of the Jewish sabbath (originally, as it happens, the festival of the menstruating moon goddess) which commences at dusk on that day. The Bible effectively tells us that dusk appeared as Christ died. In view of significant later discussion, we ought perhaps to mention too (as Graves does) the fact that one of the nails which holds a victim to the cross goes through the ankles (the others going not through palms but the wrists). The spear in Christ's side has already been mentioned in connection with Sleeping Beauty, but both are indicative of something else (see below). The circumstance that Christ was crucified with two others, making a triad, I take to be a nod in the direction of the triune moon goddess (see Chapter 10), as of course is the three of the Holy Trinity (see below). Not all is in our favour however. Christ dies at Easter, which for our purposes is incorrect. But on the other hand he is born correctly at the winter solstice (Christmas).

We spoke earlier of the great antiquity of the material under discussion. Even if these stories were only common Indo-European, we would then have an age for them of some 6000 years. But it is perfectly clear that the many interlinkings and parallels between these stories and others take us into the Middle East and beyond – even if we were to leave aside the fact that the Christ story itself is of Middle Eastern origin. An Indo-European/Middle Eastern connection allows us to think of a plus 10,000 year span (see Chapter 3), but matters do not stop there in any case.

Balder, the sun god, was mortally wounded in the heel, in his case by an arrow of mistletoe. But many other sun gods and heroes also die of a mortal wound in the heel – Ra (bitten on the heel by the snake of Isis), Krishna (a spear in the heel), Talus (Medea's pin), Achilles (Paris's arrow), Mopius (black snake of Libya), Harpocrates (scorpion), and so on. Let us leave aside the strangeness of this wound for a while, and look in detail at one story, that of Ra, the Egyptian God of the Sun.

Amun-Ra and the Snake of Isis

Some historical background is needed here. Amun, not originally anything to do with Ra, first comes to notice as one of the eight gods of Hermopolis in Middle Egypt, where he is the God of Mystery. (Later detail in the footnote to this account will suggest that the eight of this pantheon is the eight legs of the spider.) For 'reasons unknown' (Larousse[81]) the Princes of the Eleventh Dynasty adopted Amun as god of their royal residence in Thebes. Here he became identified with Min, a fertility god. Later again, and again not explainably, he rises to become king of all the gods. He has also by now acquired a family, which happens to be a triad, consisting of himself, the goddess Mut (which means mother) and a son Khonos, who often appears as a moon god. Finally, Amun becomes strongly associated with Ra, so much so that he is now known as Amun-Ra – and 'was even accorded *a divine college of thirteen members*' (Larousse,[81] but my italics). As Amun-Ra this deity is supreme head of the thirteen-pantheon, having undisputed primacy. (The Greeks, in fact, equated him with Zeus – who also ruled over a thirteen-pantheon, as we know from various sources including a Mycenean Linear B tablet[30] – and therefore called Thebes by the name Diospolis, the city of Zeus).

Now we turn to a story concerning the Ra element of the equation. Ra is the all-powerful but ageing (n.b.) master of the universe. Isis, the Moon Goddess, wants his power – but she can only acquire this if she finds out his name, which she does not know. Accordingly, she fashions a snake from his saliva and places it in his path. This bites him, leaving him mortally wounded and in agony. Isis appears, and tells Ra she will cure him (resurrect him) but he must first tell her his name. Reluctantly, but in death agony, he does so.

Let us recast the elements involved here. The ageing sun king (i.e., the sun towards the end of the year) is mortally struck down by the moon (specifically named, but also represented by the thirteen of the Amun-Ra pantheon) in his heel (just like Balder) by one of the moon's most important symbols, the snake (in Balder's case it was mistletoe). Then, having asserted her authority, the moon resurrects him.

Is the re-jigging of the story elements here so unreasonable, especially in view of our earlier stories? As pointed out in Chapter 1 and elsewhere, we must expect our information sometimes to survive only in the form of broken and distorted fragments. In this respect the work of the archaeology of ideas does not differ from that of physical archaeology, or geology.

As with so much of the material we examine however, the ramifications continue.*

* One other anecdote concerning Ra is as follows. Ra grew tired of humanity, and held a council of the gods to discuss his problem. The God of the Ocean, Nun, advised him to sit on the back of Nut, the Sky Goddess, represented as a cow. She ascended with him on her back to become the sky. Ra was delighted to be up there, but Nut was terrified. So Ra ordered eight demons to support her, two at each of her feet. So at this point we have a sky goddess who is, effectively, an eight-legged cow.[81] Does this not remind us a little of the central figure in the zodiac at Beth Alpha?

Symbolism

Is it not a very odd thing, and in so many different countries too, that the all-powerful sun god or hero is killed by a simple wound in the ankle – admittedly sometimes a poisoned wound, but by no means always.

What might this situation signify? Perhaps we could say that the sun is killed, or dies, in the heel of the year, the last or rather unimportant part. This is not a totally unacceptable use of language. However, we can do better than that.

In his *Dictionary of Symbols and Imagery*, Ad de Vries suggests that 'the heel' may be a genital reference. In this respect he says only 'may be' – but in terms of the foot as a whole he is quite emphatic that the symbolism is phallic-genital (with the shoe, also, as vagina). He gives several citations from old texts which have no real meaning unless one understands 'foot' to be genitalia.[195]

De Vries does not suggest this next, but if the foot is the penis, might not the heel be the testicles? This view, if accepted, wholly transforms the interpretation of the death of the sun king. He is castrated before being killed – or is killed by being castrated. The act of castration here is entirely literal (remember, in any case, that all the legendary material we are studying is not imaginative fantasy, but actual *history*) as precisely described by Graves (see Chapter 7). But it is symbolic also – for the moon castrates the sun at the height of his powers on midsummer's day. From that point on his vigour ebbs, and he grows old.

The correctness of this view is supported by the next evidence, which takes us also into the wider arenas of the African and Asian continents. As J.G. Frazer documents, in all parts of the world so far mentioned in this chapter (but, apparently, excluding North and South America, the Pacific and Australia) kings – who were usually thought to be at least semi-divine – commonly (a) either reigned for a fixed term, in the earliest times for six months or a year; but in later times for what appear to be terms related to moon numbers, i.e., 3 years, 7 years, 9 years, (b) or reigned until the first sign of ageing (grey hair, for example), ill-health or later lack of physical or mental prowess. In both cases (a) and (b) the king was then put to death.

We can well understand this practice (though it would appear that Frazer himself did not) in terms of, or in connection with, the small but significant loss of power, the instant beginning-to-age, of the sun immediately following midsummer's day – though again it would seem that the peoples involved had themselves altogether lost this understanding. As so often, they were maintaining an ancient tradition without appreciating why.

Interestingly, Margaret Murray, who tended to be completely blind to matters tangentially though, nevertheless, importantly related to witchcraft, eagerly fastened on and supported the notion that after a fixed term of reign the king must die (though she, too, showed no awareness of the connection with the sun's behaviour). She believed that witches executed, or brought about the execution, of several highly placed individuals in historical time, including King Edmund (AD 946), Edmund Ironside (AD 1016), William Rufus, Thomas à Becket and Joan of Arc/Gilles de Rais.[134] I am myself inclined to accept Murray's evidence – even though she missed the most obvious case of all, as we shall argue, that of Christ.

The Holy Grail

As with many legends, there are several versions of the story of the Holy Grail. Again as with other legends, the manifold versions do not weaken the content or message of the material in any way. On the contrary, the multiplicity and spread tells us both that the story-line has been in existence for some time and is of considerable importance. The story has, in fairly recent historical times, become Christianised, although its origin pre-dates Christianity. For most people today the Grail is the cup from which Christ drank at the Last Supper, and which was also subsequently used by Joseph of Arimathea to catch the blood which flowed from Christ's side while on the cross, when he was pierced by the Roman soldier's spear. There is, incidentally, some evidence that the real Joseph of Arimathea really did bring something, perhaps the cup/Grail to Glastonbury in England, after the death of Christ. However, as stated, these events, if they occurred, do not mark the beginning of the Grail story – they are at most a continuation and adaptation of it. Aside from the Christian connection, the Grail story is also heavily associated with King Arthur and his knights, whose mission it became to find the lost Holy Grail.

The composite story of the Grail is this. A knight arrives at a castle by the sea. He is received into the castle, and within, after a banquet, he observes a procession of maidens and knights, or perhaps priests, who collectively bear a lance or sword which drips blood. The blood is caught in a silver chalice by one of the maidens. The legend tells us that the knight is supposed to ask about the meaning of the events he witnesses, in particular the question: 'This cup which bleeds, what is it for?' But out of politeness he remains silent. Continuing the details of the story however, at the centre of the mystery is a wounded king. He has had a spear thrust through both thighs. On account of his illness, the land has become barren. It is the Wasteland. As we learn from some versions of the story, if the correct question, in some cases three questions, are asked, the king is cured and the Wasteland restored to fertility. The full possible list of questions is: (1) Whom does this Grail serve? (2) What is the Grail? (3) Where is the Grail Castle that is surrounded by water, that is everywhere at once and that is invisible?

For me, what we are dealing with in the Grail story is but one more version of the four stories with which we began this chapter. For we are told that the wounds of the Fisher King of Grail Castle have been caused by a spear through both thighs. A very odd-sounding wound, is it not? What we are really speaking of here is certainly the knife through both testicles – and we also understand that the spear in Christ's side is another disguised reference to castration. Shuttle, Redgrove and others have proposed that the Grail and Grail Castle are really the menstruating vagina/vulva. Certainly I accept this concept and symbolism as an underpinning idea. But the Grail legend – like the deaths of Balder, Arthur and Christ – is nevertheless concerned specifically with the (yearly) castration and execution of the sun king. This act does, certainly, un-man the king, removing his sexual gender and turning him into a menstruating woman. In the real ceremony the blood which flowed from the king's genital wounds would have been caught in a vessel, passed around and drunk. Probably the High Priestess herself ate the testicles. Subsequently the rest of the sacrifice's blood would also have been consumed, and the body eaten.

What the Grail legend is trying to tell us is that unless these (ancient) mysteries are understood for what they are, and unless the rites are duly performed (the king's wounds *must* break out every year afresh), life on earth will not be renewed. The Wasteland will remain permanently – as it did when the ice-sheets marched down from the north, and stayed. (We must well understand that for Neanderthal *winter really meant winter*. Can we really grasp the awfulness of the winter in Europe during an ice age? Classic Neanderthal did.) Just like the Australian Aborigines and the American Indians, Neanderthal believed absolutely that the world continued only because of mankind's observance of the correct religious rites. Or rather, he did not believe this. He knew it.

How much of this detail Celtic priests, for example, understood is hard to say. Certainly, however, Druidic knowledge was closer to the truth than the highly elaborated but basically empty conceits of the kabbalists, alchemists, Gnostics, Rosicrucians and others, who were nevertheless drawing on the same ancient traditions (see below).

The Grail legend, in any case, is in no way simply some parochial French-German-British story-cycle. J.L. Myres tells us that the earliest versions of the Grail story have 'a marked affinity' with Adonis/Tammuz worship. In both the Grail and the Tammuz accounts, he says, we have a castle at the sea shore; a dead body on a bier; the identity of this is not revealed, and it is mourned over with solemn rites, especially by women; a wasted country whose desolation is mysteriously connected with the dead man, and which is restored to fruitfulness when the questor asks the meaning of the mysteries he beholds; and the talisman of a ritual feast, involving a sustenance-providing, or blessing-providing, sacred vessel.[136]

'A marked affinity' is absolutely correct. We also see now that the Biblical 'Last Supper', specifically, is nothing other than a fragmentary part of the Tammuz rituals. It is interesting how often the name Tammuz (the consort of Ishtar) has cropped up in these pages. He is, incidentally, the yule log which we burn at Christmas time. The 'castle by the sea' is a further item of interest – and of course nothing in these tales and legends is there by chance. We saw already that in Scandinavia the stone mazes were often situated on islands or close to the sea (Chapter 5). Whenever we find a reference to the sea, we are speaking of the queendom of the Moon Goddess. 'Another spot famous for the worship of [the Japanese moon goddess] Benten is Chikubushima in Lake Biwa. The island rises steeply from the water.... There stands a shrine dedicated to Benten, whose music is heard in the waves and ripples that beat against rocky cliffs....'[120]

So the monarch of the sea-girt Grail Castle is the Fisher King, wounded in both thighs. Bran, the hero, was similarly wounded through both thighs when he invaded Ireland, and Bran had once been a sea god. Christ also, wounded in ankles and side, was a Fisher of Men, who walked upon the water.

Alchemists, Gnostics, Kabbalists, Rosicrucians and Others

All the many secret, semi-secret or heretical movements found during medieval times throughout Europe and the Middle East, and often also in Asia, can be well understood to be groups nursing fragments of the Old Religion and the Ancient Knowledge, this dating essentially from the age of Neanderthal. These groups cannot be, and have not so far been, well understood, or even understood at all, in any other terms. Here we have a set, and a very extended set, of otherwise impenetrable mysteries of obscure origin which the explanatory power of our present model is able to make good sense of; although the word 'sense' should perhaps be written in inverted commas.

When one says that these groups were nursing fragments of the old traditions, three extending comments should be made.

(1) Those concerned had no real idea or understanding of what it was they were guarding and transmitting down the generations. They did understand, however, that it was very ancient. Thus the kabbalists said that their wisdom came direct from Abraham (who, as we saw in Chapter 10, happens to come from Ur, the moon city of the moon people). The Hermetic writings are traced back to the Egyptian god Thoth, the thrice great, and god of wisdom, fully identified with the Greek Hermes, the thrice great, i.e. Hermes Trismegistos, from whom the movement takes its name. (But as it happens, Thoth is a moon god; and Hermes, who carries a staff around which two serpents are twined, comes originally from the Arcadians, the people of the bear, who also worshipped Artemis and Pan.)

(2) These various 'wisdoms' as we find them 'going public', at least in a limited sense, roughly from the time of Christ onward, do all have a heavy overlay of 'thought' produced during our own historical times. The greater part of this later material has no discernible value at all – although the alchemists, for example, like the numerologists, did occasionally stumble across genuine scientific truths. We do not, I think, do this overlay material any great injustice if we describe it as mysticism for the sake of mystery, wrapped in endless philosophical and metaphysical meanderings. A few examples follow below.

(3) Many and perhaps all the movements involved have crosslinks, one with another. Thus alchemy links with kabbala, kabbala with Gnosticism, Tarot with alchemy; Rosicrucians link with Alchemists, Templars with Gnostics. This particular observation is in no sense a discovery of mine. It is a position which all commentators well recognise, and which was also clear to the initiates of the movements themselves, hence of course their regard for, and traffic with, each other. So Richard Cavendish remarks that 'alchemy grew up in the same area and at the same time as the kabbala', and tells us, for instance, that the steps of making or finding the alchemical Philosopher's Stone were often diagrammed in the form of the kabbalistic Tree of Life. Also that 'many of the basic ideas of the kabbala are also found in Gnosticism'. I do, however, myself take these many interconnections as supportive of my own particular position – that all these movements and philosophies are fragments of one whole. There are, I would add further, also quite specific *continuities* involved, the deliberate handing-on of traditions and secrets – or if not that, then nevertheless the conscious taking-over of traditions – done with full awareness. In these terms I consider that the Knights Templar were a conscious continuation of aspects of Druidism and the Arthurian tradition (and in the German version of the Grail story, *Parzival*, the Templars are specifically made the guardians of the Grail – see also below); further, then, that both the Garter Knights and the Freemasons were a conscious continuation of Templar traditions.

Let us start by looking at some precise detail. In this there will be no requirement for any careful sifting or judging, nor shall we need to labour our points. The precise kinds of symbols and connections we have been examining throughout the book are on immediate, and continuous, view.

A very common symbol of the alchemist's work is a snake or dragon forming a circle by swallowing its own tail. This emblem bears the motto in Greek *en to pan*, all is one. (It would be nice to think that the individual who assigned that motto understood that all forms of esoteric thought arise from one single source and are all aspects of the self-same tradition. Incidentally, this motto contains three words and seven letters. The 'one' can be achieved, numerologically, by adding $3 + 7 = 10$, and further $1 + 0 = 1$.) The cyclic nature of the symbol is, I would suggest, nothing other than a representation of the natural yearly earth and sky cycle, where all returns in due time to its starting point. For as we see later, much else in alchemy echoes the literal letter of the old moon religion.

The major task of the alchemist's work was the search for the Philosophers' Stone. This was said to be a stone or substance that would, variously, turn base metals into gold; cure the sick and crippled; restore youth, virility, innocence; resurrect the dead; and confer immortality. Initially, there were said to be four recognisable stages in the work that would tell the adept he was on the right track (the 'four' probably being designed to accommodate the notion of the four elements – earth, air, fire and water – but both arising, I suggest, rather from the function of four as a moon number). The instruction was that when one heated, treated and modified some initial common substance – which was never named or specified beyond that – the mixture in the retort would pass from black to white to yellow to red. This is already excellent news, for three of these colours are those of the moon. But the news gets better. By medieval times the number of stages, and colours, had been reduced to three, – black, white and red! This situation is of course perfect from our point of view – for now we have not only the three moon colours, but one of the most central moon numbers, three.

The colour of the finished Philosophers' Stone (although there were differing minority views) was almost always said to be red. This red substance would turn 'leaden' metals to gold; and in respect of people confer youth, virility and resurrection. Have we, then, met anywhere in this book a red substance which (or rather, the Mistress of which) could cause the dead or 'leaden' land to become gold once more, which conferred eternal renewal (in all senses of the term) and could resurrect the dead – notably the dead sun king, but also, through reincarnation, the dead generally?

As already said, we do not need to labour these connections. Is it not totally clear that the alchemists were working with a much distorted memory of red ochre, and of the powers of the (menstrual) moon which it once symbolised and represented?

We need not linger further with alchemy, except to say that its purposes and explanations were always almost as much spiritual as chemical, and to mention Chinese alchemy. The leading alchemists in China had decided that the Philosophers' Stone was red cinnabar (mercuric sulfide). One said that this, combined with honey, and taken for a year, would restore youth, and enable the individual to fly. Taken for longer than a year, it would confer immortality. Tche'fou 'purified' the cinnabar with saltpetre. After taking the result for thirty years, he became like an adolescent and 'his hair (including his body hair) had all become red'. A strange thing indeed to happen to a Chinaman, and we consider red-haired men further in Chapters 13 and 15. Red cinnabar recommended itself to Chinese alchemists also because at relatively low furnace temperatures it turned into silver mercury – so that they no doubt presumed it had originally passed from white to red, the last stage of the Great Work. Neanderthal man would certainly himself have observed red cinnabar, which is a crystal, occurring in the neighbourhood of volcanic activity, both good reasons, apart from the red colour, that would highly recommend cinnabar as an important moon substance. (Neanderthal himself would probably not have been able to produce the temperatures necessary to smelt red cinnabar. But he just *might* have observed the transformation in the area of volcanic activity.) At any rate, a concluding point to make here is that the ideas of alchemy were in no way confined 'merely' to Europe, the Middle East and India.

We need not be so detailed in looking at other esoteric disciplines and beliefs – sample comment alone will suffice. So we read for example that the adept of the kabbala must follow the spiral convolutions of the Serpent of Wisdom 'rising in green coils from Malkuth to Kether'. We are also told that the serpent of Wisdom is female. Hermes/Thoth, when beginning to write the numerous Hermetic texts (some of which do indeed date back to pharaonoic times) saw a vision of the Great Dragon of the Universe, which symbolised the Mind of the Universe and Universal Life. Perhaps this is why Hermes's staff bears two entwined serpents (although that, I consider, is certainly also a stylised umbilical cord, two veins wrapped round a central artery). Seligman tells us that some Gnostic sects also worshipped the serpent; Cavendish that the Waldensians, an off-shoot of the Cathars, worshipped the Dragon of Revelation. Already also we have met the serpent as the guardian of (mundane) treasure world-wide. But Jill Purce suggests, and I would agree with her, that the snake is as well protecting the sacred pearls of wisdom and divine knowledge. Purce speaks also of the Indian tradition, where the demons and gods respectively (and so dualism – see below) haul on Sesha, the cosmic serpent who is wrapped around the world's axis, thereby turning the central pole. (We should note here also that aboriginal peoples often conceive of the sea as a great snake coiled around the earth.) 'Within the body of man, this is [held to be] the circulation of the subtle energies, visualised in the Hermetic, Kabbalistic and Tantric traditions.'

In the *Sepher Zohar*, one of the basic kabbalistic texts, we find such statements as these (gently described by Richard Cavendish as 'mystifyingly obscure'): 'And the dignity of dignity hangeth from the seven conformations of the cranium. This is the head of the venerable and Ancient One, which is divided into thirteen portions'; 'When the thirteen fountains of the rivers of oil descend, all these are mercies'; 'Seven, which are called the eyes of Tetragrammaton . . . and it is written . . . upon one stone seven eyes,' and so on. There are three (n.b.) basic books of kabbalism. In the *Sepher Yetzirah* we can further read of 'the three Mother Letters' and the 'seven double letters'. The references to three, seven and thirteen are all that we require from this 'information' here. As already noted elsewhere, however, the important major arcana Tarot card of Death and Resurrection is numbered thirteen. (But the most important card of the major arcana is that of the Holy Fool, which is 'only' the Joker of our habitual pack. This card and its significance will concern us again in Chapter 13.)

Gnostics, like alchemists, held that a spark of Divine Life had fallen from heaven and was now imprisoned (a) in all matter, (b) specifically in man himself. Gnosticism, like Hermetism, believed in a knowledge of divine mysteries directly or intuitively perceived, and reserved ultimately for an élite. That which was written down, in the esoteric texts, was the least of this knowledge – much was transmitted by word of mouth only to the true initiates. In all the teachings we are considering, dualism is a central idea – and not just simply the dualism of the divine and the mundane. The Cathars or Albigensians specifically held that Lucifer or the Devil was not just a fallen angel, but another separate power in the universe, opposed to God.

One view of alchemists was that alchemy had originally been taught to 'the daughters of men' by the 'fallen angels'. (I would myself prefer to say, as already suggested, taught to the fallen angels by the daughters of men.) Then, one of the two main strands of Gnosticism (the other involved complete asceticism) taught by Simon Magus and Menander, spoke of 'the existence of a subordinate female creative principle, superior to world-creating angels', and encouraged the use of magic. (Is this not – to put it very simply – the repressed moon religion versus the now dominant sun religion? After all, the Gnostic Jews did set out to build a thirteen-zodiac with a central eight-legged moon goddess.) This branch of Gnosticism was later accused by the Church of compulsive promiscuity and the use of sex as a religious rite – in other words, orgiastic behaviour. So here we are, then, in more senses than one, squarely in the domain of witchcraft and Satanism. Those (orgiastic) devotees also held, like the Cathars, that the Devil was a separate power in the universe, equal to God (in our terms, not Devil and God, but Moon and Sun).

The Cathars or Albigensians – the people of Albi – took their second name from the town of Albi, one of their main centres, which just happens to mean white – so the town of the White Goddess, perhaps. At any rate, Cathars/Albigensians subscribed to the doctrine of reincarnation and to a recognition of the female principle in religion. The 'Perfects' of Catharism, the true initiates, were of both sexes; and the Cathars had colleges openly devoted to the study of the kabbala. We noted already in an earlier chapter the close relations also between the Cathars/Albigensians and the Templars – that both wore a secret, sacred cord, for example – and the strong links between the trappings and structure of the latter with Garter Knights and witchcraft. So we could go on here almost indefinitely pointing out specific links and parallels among all these various movements and creeds.

It is preferable, however, to now show that these parallels and connections are indeed not accidental, but that they argue strongly for a *continuity* of aims, purpose and understanding, usually fully deliberate and conscious. It is quite true what the alchemists said – they are all one.

The Templars and the Priory of Sion

There appears to be no general recognition by commentators that the Knights Templar represent a continuation of Druidic tradition – or perhaps, as ever, we should rather say that both are a continuation of something far older. (In that respect let us be clear, for instance, that though the Druids made much use of the stone circles of the British Isles, they did not build them.[20])

First, the Templars shared with the Druids the practice of wearing a white tunic. This is no trivial or accidental item. One of the Rules of the Order stated: 'It is granted to none to wear white habits, or have white mantles excepting the . . . Knights of Christ.'

The Templars also shared with the Druids/Celts the practice of wearing a torque or cord. However, whereas the Celts wore them openly, the Templars wore theirs only secretly. Here is a mark both of the great significance of the cord and of the fact that it was too much of a give-away, too obvious an indicator, to be acknowledged openly. Incidentally, the torque was also worn by Teutonic tribes, who were not Celts. They wore it as a sign of allegiance to their fertility goddess, whose image also bore it (see Chapter 13).

A very important further link between Templars and Druids/Celts is the cult of the severed head. Only one text seems to have picked up on this significant matter, *The Holy Blood and the Holy Grail*, which we shall be looking at in some detail. However, the authors of that book have not noticed that the spot where Christ was crucified is Golgotha, the place of the skull. (Such a detail, as ever, is neither trivial nor accidental – any more than it is accidental or trivial that the place where the seven-and-thirteen Neanderthal bear altar was discovered is called Drachenloch, the lair of the dragon.)

The cult of the severed head, then, was an important Celtic practice. It signifies literally what it implies. The Celts removed the heads from their sacrificial victims and placed them in specially prepared niches at shrines and altar sites. (Interesting, of course, that Neanderthal man had done precisely the same with the heads of bears: the Celts themselves being also noted bear worshippers.) As for the Templars, they were said (both before and at their trials) to worship a bearded head, called Baphomet. One possible meaning of this name is 'source of wisdom'.[5] As it happens, the escutcheon of the Founder of the Templar Order was three black heads on a gold field. A thirteenth-century Templar portrait of a head was found at Templecombe in Somerset, England, which has a reddish beard. (On the subject of red-headed men see Chapters 13 and 15.) Then, in connection with the Templar trials of 1307, a Templar reliquary was found in Paris in the shape of a woman's head, 'a great head of gilded silver, most beautiful, constituting the image of a woman'. Inside this reliquary were two skull-bones (Golgotha: the place of the skull) wrapped in a cloth of white linen, in turn wrapped in a red cloth.[5] (So we have now seen the colours black, red and white in association with the severed head – how most coincidental.) A serial number in the reliquary incorporated what is certainly – in view of later evidence – the astrological sign for Virgo (♍), LVIIIm. So this, in any case, is head number fifty-eight in a series; and probably represents the head of the Virgin Mary, the Virgin Moon. (*Is* it a coincidence that the words Mary and moon, and also mother, all happen to begin with m, and that the sign for Virgo is the same letter? In many lands around the world the word for mother begins with m because, it has been suggested, this is the first consonantal noise which a baby makes.) Lastly, the sign of the skull and crossbones is ascribed to the Templars in several legends, a story certainly accepted by the Freemasons, who therefore adopted the skull and crossbones as one of their own important symbols.

Golgotha, the place of the skull. This is the right moment to point out also that, at the end of the rites, the head of Tammuz is flung into the sea (and the head of Orpheus into the Milky Way).

Let us look at some of the specific charges levelled at the Templars at their trials:

Item, that in each province they had idols, namely heads . . .
Item, that they adored these idols . . .
Item, that they said the head could save them . . .

Item, that it could make riches...
Item, that it made the trees flower...
Item, that it made the land germinate...
Item, that they surrounded or touched each head of the aforesaid idols with small cords, which they wore around themselves next to the shirt or flesh....[5]

Here we are squarely back with a central theme of our book – rites of fertility and renewal. Incidentally, the authors of *The Holy Blood and the Holy Grail* also suggest that the skull and crossbone legends may be references to such beliefs. There is more to this particular theme. In the special Templar Mass, Psalm 67 figured centrally. It is a very short psalm of only seven – seven? – verses: (1) God be merciful unto us, and bless us; and cause his face to shine upon us: Selah, (6) Then shall the earth yield her increase....

Might the first verse be a reference to the sun? Certainly in verse six we have the hint of fertility.

We have to remember that the Templars, if they were indeed, as must seem certain, practising ancient fertility rites, necessarily had to be very circumspect about it. They may have chosen Psalm 67 – and there had to be *some* reason for choosing it above all others – because they could use it publicly, but meanwhile knowing secretly what it meant for them; perhaps in something of the way that Scottish clansmen, taking the loyal toast, would pass their glasses over the finger-bowl, to signify that their allegiance was to the king 'over the water'.

There is, also, the matter of the strange word 'Selah', repeated twice in the psalm. The Templars used to shout this word, as well as another without any apparent meaning – 'Yallah'. We can only guess what this word without meaning is doing in the psalm in the first place. But, at any rate, many other mystical groups shouted meaningless words in their ceremonies, including Gnostics, witches and Satanists. (Are these, perhaps, where they are not manifestly distorted Latin, Greek or Hebrew, fragments then of Neanderthal tongues?)

Some years ago, Michael Baigent, Richard Leigh and Henry Lincoln published their formidable, cautious and very well-researched book *The Holy Blood and the Holy Grail*. Its central conclusion is that we best interpret certain significant events of the last 2000 years in Europe as acts of conspiracy, covering up the fact that Christ did not die on the cross, but lived to produce a family. His descendants, the authors maintain, are alive to this day. This is not a theory which I find to have any merit. Is it likely, for instance, that one of what must cumulatively be several hundred descendants would not have spoken up publicly? However, much of the admirable research carried out by these authors is – if they will forgive me – strongly supportive of suggestions made in the present book. (After all, their canvas is a mere 2000 years long, and only Europe wide!) Of the fairness of my view of the evidence here, the reader can be his or her own judge.

The story told by Baigent and his colleagues begins in a sense with the mystery of Rennes-le-Chateau. In the parish church of this small village the local curate certainly did discover, in 1891, documents dating from 1244 and 1644 respectively. He probably also found a buried (Templar) treasure. In connection with the mystery of Rennes-le-Chateau there has been appearing in France, since 1965, a series of equally mysterious documents and books. One of these, titled *Le Serpent Rouge* (*The Red Snake*), was published or at any rate appeared publicly for the first time in 1967. The main bulk of this text consists of thirteen short, well-written prose poems of one paragraph each, 'reminiscent of the work of Rimbaud'. Each poem/paragraph corresponds to one of the signs of a thirteen-zodiac. The thirteenth is Ophiucus the Serpent Holder, which is placed between Scorpio and Sagittarius. We note that this extra sign, as in the case of the extra sign in the thirteen-zodiacs of Beth Alpha and the Mound Builders, is inserted on the left side of the usual twelve-zodiac.

The document speaks of a red snake 'cited in the parchments' uncoiling across the centuries. This comment the authors consider to be a reference to a bloodline. However, this symbol and its colour is already familiar to us from many other contexts which have nothing to do with bloodlines. The entry for the sign of Leo contains these words: 'From she whom I desire to liberate. . . . Formerly, some named her ISIS, queen of all sources benevolent. . . . To others she is MAGDALENE, of the celebrated vase filled with healing balm. The initiated know her true name: NOTRE DAME DES CROSS.'[5]

The reference to Isis here of course takes us back a very long way before the time of Christ.

Baigent and his colleagues demonstrate that the Knights Templar were backed, financially and otherwise, by an older organisation known as the Order of the Priory of Sion, of whom the Templars were the military arm. The Priory of Sion seems traceable back to the abbey of Notre Dame de Sion near Jerusalem, dating from the fourth century AD. The founding of the Templars dates from 1118. However, already in 1188, only seventy years after, a formal split occurred between the Priory of Sion and the Knights Templar, as a result of an incident referred to as 'the cutting of the elm'.

Briefly, a group of knights led by Philippe II of France had a serious fight, resulting in many casualties, with a group of knights led by the elder son of Henry II of England, Richard Lionheart (later to be Richard I, who tied cords around the legs of his knights in battle, as we saw in Chapter 6). The serious skirmish, which took place at Gisors in France, was about whether a certain old elm should be cut down or not. The French won the argument and the elm was cut.

For whatever precise and actually unknown reasons, the Templars and the Priory of Sion then parted company, each now having their own Grand Master instead of a common one. The first separate Grand Master of the Priory of Sion was Jean de Gisors. As a kind of subtitle, the Priory also now adopted the name Ormus. The device for Ormus consisted of the zodiac sign for Virgo, ♍ with the other letters, o, u, r, s, entwined within it. *Ours* is the French word for bear. What is Ormus?

The French for elm is *orme*, a corruption, however, of early French *olme*, which derives from the Latin word for elm, *ulmus*, as does our own English word elm. It looks very much then as if *ormus* is a back-formation to a non-existent Latin form of the bastard French *orme*. The sole purpose of creating this artificial Latin word would seem to be to have the symbol for Virgo (alias the Virgin Moon, alias Virgin Mary) plus the letters of the French word for bear, *ours*. So the device and motto would seem to be telling the initiate, or gnostic one, the Virgin Moon leads the cult or the people of the bear. (We recall how the word min-o-taur employed a very similar device in Chapter 10.)

The view gains further credence from the fact that the name Ursus (the Latin for bear) frequently occurs in Priory documents.

Further again from the fact that the Rennes-le-Chateau mystery had involved Poussin's painting, *The Arcadian Shepherds*, which incorporates the Latin phrase *et in Arcadia ego*, 'and I am in Arcadia' (verb 'to be' understood). Also again, from the circumstance that one of the later Grand Masters of the Priory of Sion, René d'Anjou, an important Renaissance figure, showed a great interest in Arcadia. The central river of actual Arcadia in Greece flows underground. The phrase 'underground stream' comes then to refer to all esoteric and occult thought. What, however, Baigent and his co-authors do not show that they know is that the Arcadians, literally the people of the bear, worshipped Artemis, the moon-bear goddess, and Pan and Hermes-Trismegistos-Thoth, likewise associated with the moon, but also with the Hermetic writings. Once again, this frame of reference takes us back two to three thousand years before the time of Christ, which is not especially useful for the authors concerned. These appear, also, to appreciate not at all that the bear cult itself, along with the number thirteen, has a history of over 75,000 years.

In this particular connection, however, one of the repudiations of the Christian faith made by the Templars at their trials was that it was 'too young'. (Baigent and his colleagues do not face up to this definite rejection of what they consider the mystery is all about, namely the offspring or descendants of Christ.) The Freemasons and other writers on the subject themselves maintain that the Templars were 'custodians of an arcane wisdom that transcends Christianity itself'; and symbolic carvings on Templar premises strongly suggest that they were well acquainted with alchemy, numerology, astrology and other such matters. It is said that the Templars may have financed the building of the Gothic cathedrals – in which case they would have approved the labyrinths prominently inlaid in their floors (see Chapter 5). The Freemasons, by the way, claim that Ormus was an actual Egyptian sage and Gnostic adept, who lived in the early years of the first century AD. This Ormus allegedly converted to Christianity, and gave his followers a new symbol – a red or rosy cross. This story and notion is probably the forerunner of the Rosicrucian movement and its rose cross. But let us not forget that the Templars also wore a red cross, the splayed eight-point variety. The Priory of Sion *also* described itself as 'the Order of the true Red Cross'. Both the colour red and the cross itself are, of course, clear grist for our own mill. Lastly here, the word Ormus also occurs in Zoroastrian thought, where it means light or enlightenment.

The list of Grand Masters of the Priory of Sion includes Nicolas Flamel (a prominent alchemist), Leonardo da Vinci, Robert Fludd (an exponent of Hermetic doctrine), Johann Valentin Andrea (one of the founders of the Rosicrucian movement), Isaac Newton, Victor Hugo, Claude Debussy and Jean Cocteau.

The hero of J.V. Andrea's fictional story, *The Chemical Wedding*, is Christian Rosenkreuz (Redcross), who wears a white tunic with a red cross on the shoulder – very much like a Templar therefore. Around 1618, however, Andrea also set up a network of more or less secret societies known as the Christian Union. Each society or branch was headed by an anonymous prince assisted by twelve other persons – a coven of thirteen, therefore – divided into four groups of three. Baigent and his co-authors have no comment to make on these covens of thirteen, just as they had none on the thirteen-zodiac of *The Red Snake*. The founding of these secret groups of thirteen of the Christian Union was an extremely daring and dangerous undertaking, in view of the witch trials which had been in progress in Europe for almost 200 years. The avowed purpose of the groups was 'to preserve threatened knowledge', and they literally aided the escape of many philosophers and esotericists from the turmoil in Europe to the relative safety of England. These refugees, and the Christian Union itself, may have been the starting point of the Masonic Lodges.

The Grand Masters of the Priory were officially called 'Nautonniers' or navigators. Perhaps like real navigators they steered by the Great Bear. The fourth Grand Master of the Templars was a Cathar, as was perhaps the first. When hundreds of thousands of Cathars were massacred by the Church during the so-called Albigensian Crusade, many sought refuge with and were helped by the Templars. The last of the Cathars, though offered a full pardon, instead chose martyrdom. (Just before the end, something was daringly smuggled out of the beleaguered Cathar garrison – was it the Grail?) Similarly, when later the mass arrests of the Templars themselves took place, the knights – who were the very last people to submit readily in battle – offered no resistance at all and surrendered themselves passively. We could say that both these groups went willingly to their fate.

This brief review of Baigent, Leigh and Lincoln's material will suffice for present purposes. Aside from their central claim that the matters they have researched concern the existence of blood-relatives of Christ, I find their observations both perceptive and accurate (although not necessarily adequate). Like Murray, Frazer, Briffault and Graves before them, they have had the courage to argue for continuity where the academic establishment perceives none; and reasoned action where that establishment sees only nonsense.

The Christ Story

Non-religious commentators (and even some religious ones) fully agree that the collective material we know as the story of Christ contains elements borrowed or accreted from earlier pre-Christian beliefs and legendary accounts. The view is entirely commonplace among scholars. The present Church itself of course never publicises such matters. It will not tell us, for example, that one of the first miracles attributed to the orgiastic god Dionysus was turning water into wine.

The reasonable (or half-hearted) position of the scholars will not do for me. In now over twenty years of researching and considering the material of the present book, I myself find no way of avoiding one of two conclusions.

(1) That among those who gave the Christian faith its present form – and we are speaking not just of those active during Christ's life, but of those who contributed in the several generations thereafter and who edited the sacred texts – there were powerful men who were, secretly, wholly devoted to the Old Religion and its ways. They were what we today would call double agents. While outwardly helping to formulate a new religion which would break decisively with the past, they secretly ensured that the most potent symbols, rituals and concepts of the old tradition were firmly enshrined at the very heart of the new order.

(2) That those – all of them this time – who founded the Christian faith were not double agents at all. They were single agents, collectively devoted to the Virgin Moon (to the female principle), to the Goddess of Wisdom and all her causes. But they saw that times were changing, had indeed already changed. The

new moods, variously, of sun worship, the male principle, rationalism, scientific enquiry even, had gained considerable ground on all sides. The Old Ways were under considerable threat as never before. But those we are speaking of were determined to hand on the core of the old tradition (of the magical path) to future generations, in a form in which those who looked hard enough, who were knowing or gnostic enough, would always still recognise for what it was. Accordingly, the founders of Christianity re-fashioned the Old Faith in a new format, shone upon it something of the more modern light. In this attempt they were very like marketing managers today – they looked for a new image, a new package, that would sell a product fast going out of fashion. The product itself was not basically changed – only the packaging, the inessentials.

My stronger inclination is to the second view presented above.

What cannot be denied, in any case, is that the Christian religion does incorporate, in easily recognisable form, and at its heart, all the major elements of the old moon beliefs and rituals.

Thus Christ – as in many similar stories involving a sun king or hero who is sacrificed, but then immediately resurrected, in order to bring new life and hope – is a member of a group of thirteen, signifying the thirteen months of the lunar year. As sun king Christ is frequently identified with Light, and is portrayed with the shining nimbus about his head, so that we cannot fail to recognise this aspect. (Judas of course is Loki, Mordred.) Like some other ancient sun kings/gods also he is born of the Virgin Moon (the Virgin Mary). He is born at the winter solstice, which is correct, but dies at Easter, which is not. However, spring is one of the four main festivals of the lunar year, and some sun heroes had their principal festivals then, for example Krishna. The Christian Easter remains, in any case, a moon festival, which is why it varies its date from year to year. The date is determined by the appropriate new moon.

Christ dies on the cross, the ancient, world-wide, pre-Christian symbol of the moon, and in case we miss that point, speaks seven times from it.

As with all sun kings, Christ is castrated before he dies – the 'spear in the side'. (And, of course, he went willingly to his death.) The blood is caught, as it should be, in a vessel. Why, the doubter should ask himself, was Joseph of Arimathea, or whoever, waiting ready with a vessel (or at any rate was said to be waiting in later popular accounts)? There is not a great deal you can do with a cup of blood on a warm afternoon in the Middle East two thousand years ago – unless you intend some ritual purpose with it.

The consumption of Christ's blood, and the devouring of his body, is in any case absolutely literally performed in the Catholic Mass. The congregants are assured by the priest that the Host and the wine are *literally* the body and blood of Christ. There is no play-acting here. (But no one asks, why are we doing what they did in the wildwood five thousand, ten thousand, fifty thousand years ago?)

The three of the moon is present in the Christ plus two thieves who are crucified, but much more importantly in the Holy Trinity. The real Trinity, naturally, is the Virgin Mary, Father-alias-Holy-Ghost, and Christ. Historically, as we have seen, nobody has been fooled by the deliberate shunting of Mary to the sidelines. Moreover, Christ receives gifts from three wise men, is tempted three times in the wilderness, is denied three times by Peter, appears risen three times to the disciples, and so on.

Much else is preserved in the further detail of the religion. White is retained as the colour of virginity and purity, the colour of the girl before menstruation and intercourse. The well-known pronouncement, though your sins be as scarlet, I will wash them white as snow, is quite certainly a reference to the washing of the goddess's menstrual linen. Black is still worn by the living as the colour of death. The Pope, the leader of the Catholic Church, is buried in a red shroud, the traditional red ochre of Neanderthal man, the goddess's menstrual blood. So there we have our white, red and black. The symbolic immersion of the individual in *water* at christening, and the literal immersion at baptism, also the practice of sprinkling holy water – why, the congregant dips the hand in water and makes the sign of the moon cross with it on entering the church – all these are sheer moon ritual. Let us not forget the pre-Christian ritual immersion of menstruating women in water world-wide. The fish as the symbol of the early Christians and the eating of fish on Fridays among both Catholics and Jews, are again ancient moon signals. And of course the sabbath itself is, in origin, the festival of the menstruating moon goddess.

It is not a case, at all, of what has been included. It is a case of what hasn't.

In fact I would go further, and propose that Christ's death was specifically engineered by the moon worshippers – echoing here the spirit of Margaret Murray, although with a particular view that she did not actually express.

However, this last major attempt to perpetuate the Old Religion failed, as was perhaps inevitable. It is the top-dressing, the essentially undesired elements of the new package which prevail – the patriarchal, sex-denying, woman-denying elements. The followers of the Old Religion (many of them highly placed as we have seen, and will see further) and of the philosophies and beliefs which developed from it, feel they have to retreat into their own private acts of worship – from the Templars at one end, through Cathars, Waldensians, Gnostics, to witches at the other – and their own private debate. Only the Virgin Mary herself offers some hope of sustenance in the scholastic sterility and sexual repression of Catholicism, and the then yet more barren, life-denying wastelands of the Protestant ethic. Finally, in time, even the Catholic/Protestant accommodation fails, falling itself victim to the ravening male principle and its flagship science. For all its many horrors, moon worship was nevertheless life-affirming. The computer, however, is not even alive.

12 Left Out

On one clear count we can indict both orthodox and unorthodox writers equally. For in neither camp has it occurred even to a single individual that each of the despised, persecuted, denied, repressed, hated and lost elements of human cultures world-wide (menstruation, the labyrinth, the moon, thirteen, the spider, the feminine, witchcraft, matriarchy, the occult, and so on) might somehow all belong together.

Certainly many of the outstanding writers whose work we have (gratefully) drawn upon did perceive some of the inter-connections. Thus Graves is in no way blind to the importance of the number thirteen in his pursuit of the White Goddess. Briffault understood the significance both of the spider-moon and the woman-magic connections in his argument for a once matri-archal style of society. Frazer, in his successful bid to demonstrate the central importance of the King Who Must Die rituals, also gathered vital information on much else of outstanding importance – menstruation, mistletoe (another of Graves's contributions of course), the worship of the Pleiades – but bequeathed these only as unintegrated fragments; clearly he appreciated the great import of these matters – but was unable to say what that was.

All these and other writers can be fairly said, nevertheless, to have *majored* on one, or at most two, elements of the lost, arguing then fiercely that this or these are the overriding, paramount, dictating factors. Thus Frazer and Briffault have nothing to say on the number thirteen or the labyrinth. Briffault has nothing to say on menstruation taboos. Margaret Murray saw only witchcraft and the number thirteen – and not even the totality of those – but not the moon, not menstruation. Graves discusses nothing outside the European/Middle East arena, has one mention only of menstruation, fails altogether to see the spider. So we could go on.

Yet there is one item which all with one technical exception (Margaret Murray) have overlooked, and how they managed to do so is very, very hard for us to understand. For even if one glances, just casually, and as a complete novice, through the ancient sources and materials, how can one possibly miss it? The item is the very central question of left-handedness.

Where shall we begin? Anywhere will do. Black magic and the occult, then, are often referred to as the left-hand path. Witches danced anti-clockwise, as did originally the Whirling Dervishes (though today these whirl clockwise). In medieval portraits the raised devil steps from the pentagram with his left hand outstretched. Again, at least fifty per cent, and probably more, of the spiral labyrinths (and certainly all the major ones, such as the Cretan labyrinth) have a left-hand entrance.

In all Indo-European and many other languages of the world the word for left also means something extremely derogatory. '*Lyft*' in Old English means 'weak, worthless, womanish'. *Gauche* in French also means awkward. Latin *sinister* has the same connotations as our own use of that word. Italian *mancino* means dubious, dishonest. In Japanese *hiddarimaki* also means mad. Among the Nyoro in Africa left means hated, while for the Kaguru of that continent it means unclean and weak, and for the Gogo stupid. Among the Rotinese of Indonesia left means foolish and ignorant. We will amplify further on these attitudes shortly. But there are other purely linguistic aspects.

In all Indo-European languages, for example, the root for the word right spawns a great number of other, always favourable words – for instance, in English: correct, direct, rectitude, erect, erection, rector, regal, royal, regime, rights, forthright, upright and so on. The root of the word for left, however, produces no other words whatsoever. But what left or left-handed does produce is a great many basically uncomplimentary epithets, thus English: cack-handed (which means 'shit-handed'), squiffy, wacky, bollock-handed, molly-handed (which means 'soft-handed'), coochy, southpaw, cowpaw and so on. I have not, so far, seen any comment by linguists or philologists on the significance of this rather remarkable situation.

Some non-linguists, at least, imagine that our attitudes towards right and left are heavily influenced by the Old and New Testaments of the Bible. However, the linguistic material cited above long pre-dates the existence not only of the Bible, but also of Christianity. Nevertheless, the material of the Old and New Testaments is itself of great relevance and interest.

The left hand in the Bible is actually condemned more by implication than by direct statement – that is, more by lavish praise of the right hand. (It is Islam which is much more openly condemning of the left. That credo instructs specifically that the right hand must be used for all honourable purposes, the left for all unclean bodily functions – cf. here our own cack-handed. The Koran tells us that on Resurrection or Judgement Day God will give each person a book of his deeds, into his right hand if the verdict is salvation, into the left if eternal damnation. And Tabori writes: 'Allah has nothing left-handed about him, since both his hands are right hands.') By way of praise of the right hand in the Bible, then, Psalm 110, verse 1, tells us that the resurrected Christ reigns in honour and power at the right hand of God: 'The Lord said unto my Lord, sit thou at my right hand': a view subsequently echoed throughout the New Testament. So Acts 5:31, 'Him hath God exalted with his right hand to be a Prince and a Saviour'; Ephesians 1:20, 'Which he wrought in Christ, when he raised him from the dead and set him at his own right hand'; Romans 8:1, 'We have such an high priest, who is set on the right hand of the throne of the Majesty in the heavens.' And so on. However, this is not simply New Testament usage, nor applied solely to Jesus, thus I Kings 2:*19*, 'And the king rose up to meet her, and bowed himself unto her, and sat down on his throne, and caused a seat to be set for the king's mother; and she sat on his right hand'; or Psalm 45:*9*, 'Kings' daughters were among thy honourable women: upon thy right hand did stand the queen in gold of Ophir'. So 'it is not by chance that in pictures of the Last

Judgement it is the Lord's raised right hand that indicates to the elect their sublime abode, while his lowered left hand shows the damned the gaping jaws of hell ready to swallow them'.

But compare here, just in passing, the following extract from Margaret Murray's *Witch Cult in Western Europe*. She tells us – rather engagingly imagining we shall have no problems with medieval French – that in the Basse-Pyrénées in 1609 one could '*en chasque village trouuer vne Royne du Sabbat, que Sathan tenoit en delices comẽ vne espouse privilegiée*': 'one could in every village find a Sabbat Queen, whom Satan kept in delights like a favourite wife'. The account continues '*...luy baisent la main gauche, tremblans avec mille angoisses, & luy offrent du pain, des oeufs, & de l'argent: & la Royne du Sabbat les reçoit, laquelle est assise à son costé gauche, & en sa main gauche elle tient vne paix ou platine, dans laquelle est grauée l'éffigie de Lucifer, laquelle on ne baise qu'apres l'auoir premièrement baisée à elle*'. ... kissing Satan's hand, trembling with a thousand anxieties, offering him bread, eggs and money; these the Sabbat Queen accepted, who was seated at his left side, and in her left hand she held a loaf (*pain*?) or a metal disc, on which was carved a likeness of Lucifer, which one only kissed after having kissed the Queen'.

Here, then, we see the left hand and side playing precisely the role which the right hand and side play in the Bible. (Orthodoxy claims in this respect that witches, satanists and black magicians were merely reversing the order they perceived in Holy Writ. But, as usual, the case is the opposite of that which orthodoxy maintains – it was the Church that reversed the practices of the Old Religion, as we shall further see. And whichever view is correct, the Knights and Ladies of the Garter favoured the left. Surely in this they were declaring their true allegiance?)

References to the left in the Bible are by no means as derogatory as they are often claimed to be. (So that a theologian's view that 'Christian saints in the cradle were so pious as to refuse the left breast of their mothers'[138] would seem to be drawing on some broader frame of reference.) In fact references are basically not unfavourable, and were perhaps once even less so. Instances of the alleged deceitfulness of the left hand, for example, arise from Ehud's assassination of King Eglon using the left hand (Judges 3:*21*) and Joab's similar assassination of Amasa (II Samuel 20:*9–10*). Granted both men did use pretended friendship to approach their victims, at least Ehud's use of his left to strike the blow cannot be faulted, since we are told he was left-handed! (So, perhaps, was Joab – the text can be so read.) Moreover, Ehud's action was certainly, in principle, sanctioned by the Lord, for not only was King Eglon holding the Israelites in slavery, 'but when the children of Israel cried unto the Lord, the Lord raised them up a deliverer, Ehud, the son of Gera, a Benjamite, a man left-handed' (Judges 3:*15*).

It is worth our lingering for a further moment over Old Testament left-handedness, for it has some distinctly odd aspects. There has, I would suggest, been tampering with and editing of the text, such as we already suspected with regard to the number thirteen (see Chapter 9). Ehud is a left-hander, even though he is of the tribe of Benjamin – which just happens to mean the tribe of the son of the right hand (*ben yamin*). Moreover, among the Benjamite warriors 'were seven hundred chosen men left-handed; every one could sling stones at an hair breadth and not miss'. (Nothing derogatory about this reference, in any case; and the use of 'seven' is perhaps noteworthy.) Then I Chronicles 11 gives a long list of individuals, who were David's 'mighty men', who gathered round him in Hebron following the death of Saul. There is no suggestion that these were some kind of sample of Israelites – indeed, it seems clear that these were all the fighting men that Israel could muster at that time, drawn from all tribes and subtribes. Chronicles continues: 'Now these are they that came to David . . . the mighty men, helpers of the war. They were armed with bows and could use both the right hand and the left in hurling stones and shooting arrows out of a bow, even of Saul's brethren of Benjamin' (which presumably means 'just like the Benjamites').

But isn't there something wrong here? Shouldn't that read 'who could use both the left hand and the right' not 'both the right hand and the left'? For in 'both . . . and' sentences we habitually put first that which is the more unusual. Consider these hypothetical examples. 'Lord Young possesses a Rolls Royce and a bicycle. But he uses both the bicycle and the Rolls when he goes to see the Queen.' 'Mr Smith, who lives in central London, owns a car and a horse. But he uses both the horse and the car for going to work.' See how the meaning is lost here if we say 'but he uses both the car and the horse for going to work'.

So what we have in these Old Testament references, in summary, is this. There are many good – very, very good – fighters in the Israelite ranks who are either left-handed or ambidextrous: and the ambidextrous ones, it seems, are remarkable because they *also* use the *right* hand. Not only are these remarks not at all derogatory, but, point two, we also seem to have a strong hint that left-handedness is the norm. The text further appears to say 'and as is well known the tribe of the son of the right hand is noted for this sort of left-handed chap'. All very odd. And one last comment. The tribe of Benjamin is the youngest tribe. Does that mean that the older tribes (i.e., Israel in the past) were the sons of the left hand?

In case we seem to be getting too cosily European and Middle Eastern, let us look further at the picture world-wide. The material we have here, incidentally, is largely thanks to Rodney Needham and his contributors in his volume *Right and Left*.[138] But two points by way of opening: there is a universal and uniform attitude to left-handedness; and it is deeply unfavourable. 'The power of the left hand is always occult and illegitimate, it inspires terror and revulsion.... Beings which are believed to possess dreadful magical powers are represented as left-handed.' Once again also, and we cannot make this point too often, we have here a world-wide phenomenon transcending all national and cultural boundaries. Further, in these attitudes to, and treatment of, the left hand we find a picture which very closely resembles what we found in our considerations of menstruation (Chapter 8). Is that resemblance a coincidence? Hardly – for world-wide we find that the left hand is associated with the *feminine*, even though in all ethnic and social groups so far tested *there are fewer left-handed women than men.* A remarkable situation. (We have again been very, very lucky here – for had there been more left-handed women than men there would have been no point to capitalise on. It is because normal expectation is *reversed* that we have another significant lever for our central argument.)

As usual, we can begin our review almost anywhere; so overwhelming is the evidence that it requires no subtle or carefully balanced argument.

Among the Maoris, then, the right hand is considered to be male and active, the left to be female and passive. And likewise in the Arab world, on the other side of the globe, the left is female and the right male. In Africa men are habitually buried lying on their right side and women lying on their left side. Similarly again amongst the North American Indians the right represents bravery and virility, the left death and burial. In Asiatic India, too, right and left are clearly identified with the male and the female respectively. 'The clearest statement of this association of sides [with sexual gender] is the frequent iconographic representation of Siva as Ardhanarisvara . . . the right side of the figure has the hip, shoulder and chest of a man, while the left side is fashioned with the thigh, waist and breast of a woman.'[10] In classical Greece also the Pythagorean table of opposites contained the same right-male, left-female dichotomy, and Anaxagoras considered that the left testicle was responsible for female children, the right for male babies.

But let us meanwhile not neglect the wholly derogatory associations. Throughout India the left is considered to be 'polluted and inferior to the right'. In China, as soon as children are capable of picking up food they must be taught to eat with the right hand. We saw already the associated meanings of the word 'left' in some African tribes. But in fact 'dirty' is a common description of the left throughout Africa (how close this attitude is to the Islamic traditions). In some African tribes women are not allowed to use the left hand while cooking, and in others they must never touch the husband's face with the left hand. Again how very closely these prohibitions parallel the rules governing the menstruating woman. But there is likewise physical abuse too – for in the Dutch Indies the left hand of the child is tied to its body, 'for long periods', to teach him or her not to use it, while in parts of Africa metal rings are used for the same purpose. And once again as in the context of menstruation, a number of peoples punish the left arm by actual mutilation. In the classical Greek and Roman world the left is – merely! – universally unlucky.

The left-female connection (against all logic) is remarkably persistent – as is also the connection of the left with death, a further problem for linear thought. For why, on the basis of any normal logic, should the left signify death? So in South America not only is right good and left evil; but again right is life and left is death; and right is the man and left the woman-child. (Some tribes, such as the Mapuch of Chile, say specifically that the left is associated with children.) Among the Nyoro of Africa, after a child is born, the father digs a hole in the floor of the hut to bury the placenta – on the right side of the door if the baby is a boy, and on the left side of the door if it is a girl. Among the Kaguru a left-handed boy is given a nickname which means 'like a wife'. The Atoni of Indonesia, again, associate the left with the female – but the detail of their beliefs is remarkable. They say that the outer section of a house, and the attic, belong to the male; but the inner or back section of the house, particularly the left side of the inner section, belongs to the female. (Here, I consider, they are speaking not just of conscious versus unconscious, but of actual functions of the brain – see Chapter 17.)

The Taradja of Indonesia demonstrate very strong connections between right and life, and left and death. They say quite specifically that the left represents the dead, who are in the underworld, and who come to life at night. They further say that the dead do everything precisely the other way round from the living. 'The living do everything with the right hand... the dead do everything with the left.' Also the face, the feet and the chest of the dead are turned backwards. (There are many connections we could develop here. Our own vampire comes to life at night, the Chinese vampire has his head turned back to front, and Lilith, the night-hag, has her feet turned round the wrong way.) But the Taradja do not go in for half measures. The dead actually walk upside down. And not only do the meanings of language reverse – so yes means no, right means left, and so on – but the words are actually spoken backwards. Finally, they say that the dead are pitch black in colour.

Indonesia as a whole is special, and very consistent, in its regard of the left. Moreover, as we see, matters concerning the left readily spill over into wider contexts. The Ngaja of southern Borneo also say that the dead reverse all the meanings of words in this life – so right is left, straight is crooked, sweet is sour, and so forth. The Batuk of Sumatra again say that the dead reverse everything – walk backwards, go about by night instead of day, use the left instead of the right.

Without wishing to go into these matters too deeply at this point, it would seem that the Indonesians generally are working with a much more vivid memory of Neanderthal than most. As already indicated, I think that Neanderthal was almost certainly left-handed, probably a buttock-presenter instead of a head-lowerer, and at least semi-nocturnal, particularly in the area of his religious activities. But there is a possible alternative framework operating here too – I would prefer to say an additional framework. Mirrors are a recent invention, but the surface of pools has always been there. When we reach our right hand out to scoop water, our reflection in the water reaches out its left hand to us. Our reflection is left-handed – look in the mirror and see for yourself. Not only that, but our *shadow* is left-handed. Stand so that your shadow is thrown on a wall or rock face. Reach out your right hand towards it, and your shadow wil give you its left hand. Moreover, when you move away from the wall, there is your shadow below you, walking upside down.

In general we have no hard statistics on the incidence of left-handedness in aboriginal peoples, or outside modern Europe and America as a rule. However, Cyril Burt, who is reporting here not his own work, but that of others, writes in 1937:

> *It would appear that in prehistoric races, as in primitive tribes of today, the tendency to right-handedness was somewhat less universal than it is amongst ourselves. . . . An examination of throwing sticks yields proportions of 10 to 15 per cent left-handers, or slightly larger. Wm. McDougall and others who have tested primitive communities . . . report a decidedly smaller preponderance of right-handed persons. The evidence from Paleolithic implements, cave drawings and methods of working flints also suggests a high percentage of left-handers: one observer puts the proportion at least as high as 33 per cent.*

In no way, however, should we imagine that the question of left-handedness is of no concern in today's world, or at any rate not in Europe. As with all the matters this book considers, this matter too shapes our thought and our institutions right to the present day.

In the Japan and nationalist China of the present (little information comes out of mainland China) zero or near-zero rates of left-handedness are reported, for there left-handedness is still 'corrected' (or 'righted') in early life. An ingenious study by E.L. Teng and her colleagues was, however, able to show the true position in Taiwan (nationalist China). On the surface the research team found only 0.7 and 1.5 per cent of the population using the left hand for writing and eating respectively. But 18 per cent of the population reported that they had been 'corrected' in infancy – and this 18 per cent used their left hands for minor tasks, which the genuine right-handers, who reported no correction, did not. (Thus the true incidence of left-handedness among Chinese is roughly double that reported among Europeans.) As to this question of correction here, one might feel – oh, well, that's China and Japan, after all. It will come as a surprise then to learn that present day Italy (the home of those gifted sinistrals Michelangelo and Da Vinci) also reports zero left-handedness. It seems scarcely believable, but Italy still corrects all its left-handers, as H.B. Young and R. Knapp assure us in their 1965 report, *Perceptual and Motor Skills.*[208]

In Britain we have, however, also no cause for smugness. A survey of schoolchildren in 1937 reported 5.8 per cent of boys to be left-handed, and 3.7 per cent of girls. A survey in 1959 found 6.7 per cent of boys left-handed, and 4.4 per cent of girls. Another in 1976 returned 11.3 per cent left-handedness for boys, 8.8 per cent for girls.[69] We have of course no reason at all to suspect that more left-handers have been born in the last fifty years. No, what we are seeing in these rising figures is the effect of the *very recent* liberalisation of attitudes towards left-handedness, a process which is probably not yet completed.

Again in present-day Europe we have just the faintest echo of the ancient, world-wide association of the feminine with the left. Today women still button their coats towards the left, while men button them towards the right.

Buried under or within the universal despisation and persecution of left-handedness are just occasional hints that the left was once honoured and propitious. As already noted, the usual Arabic word for left, *simal*, connotes general ill-omen and uncleanness (and a left-handed person means one who is difficult, arduous and troublesome). But there is another word for left, *yasar*, which also means 'auspicious'. The Indian Tantrists themselves call their worship of Shiva and Shakti the left-hand path, and mean it with approval. When the Nyoro of Africa consult the cowrie divination shells in times of trouble, the diviner casts them with the left hand. At the Nyoro manhood ceremony, the king has his right arm bare and his left arm wrapped – but the three (n.b.) women present who stand on the king's left (n.b.) have their left arms bare but their right arms wrapped. The Kaguru, when practising divination, say that the signs (favourable or unfavourable) must appear both on the left and the right before the prognostication can be regarded as complete. In ancient China, under some conditions, the left is considered honourable (and, it must be admitted, male). Lastly, in our own country, a woman wears her wedding ring on the left hand – and while that is from one point of view only a further acknowledgement of the feminine/left connection, marriage is, after all, a holy and a desirable state.

Margaret Murray gives us very useful material concerning the left hand. We saw already that the Sabbat Queen sits on the left side of the Devil. Murray tells us, further, that those who join a coven receive from the Devil a mark in their physical flesh, which shows they have indeed committed themselves to his service and worship. The Devil will make the mark with his left hand, sometimes using his fingernails, or perhaps a pin of 'false gold'. The mark was habitually, though not invariably, said to be made on the left side of the acolyte's body – the left shoulder, the left hip, the left wrist or hand, the left buttock, the left thigh. Mentioned also is the white of the left eye. The mark could be a cut or deep scratch, or a tattoo. At witch trials body-search was made of those accused to discover this Devil's mark, or witch mark. Of course almost anything at all would serve the court's purpose for this – a wart, a mole, an old injury scar – nor did it matter from the court's point of view on what side or part of the unfortunate accused's body it was found. Finally, Murray emphasises that witches, like fairies and elves – and she is in no doubt of that connection, as we saw in Chapter 10 – danced anti-clockwise.

Though she records these details, Murray makes no attempt to account for the role of the left, nor to use it as one of the links between the various witch traditions in various parts of Europe, a cause to which she was otherwise dedicated. Still less did she use the left (or other material) to link witchcraft with any wider framework (outside Europe, say). In her subsequent book, *The God of the Witches*, published ten years later, she dropped the subject of left-handedness. In short, like everyone else, she completly failed to appreciate its central significance.

Richard Cavendish has one potentially intriguing point. Apart from reminding us that in ancient Babylon omens on the left were unfavourable, those of the right propitious, and that in Homer birds flying left or right were likewise bad or good omens respectively, he goes on to suggest that left-handedness may be more frequent among homosexuals: an interesting idea, for which however no statistical support currently exists.

When explanation would orthodoxy have for the events of this chapter, even if it bothered to consider them? Why should the left and left-handed individuals be universally reviled and persecuted? Why should the left be associated with the feminine – given especially that there are fewer left-handed women than men (also in Teng's study, incidentally)? Why should the left be connected with death and with the dead? Why should it be associated with children? Why also should the left be equated with particularly virulent magic? What, in short, is there in the behaviour, style or appearance of left-handers which would justify any of the epithets, treatment and despite used against them? Quite apart from the 'mighty men' of ancient Israel, consider the following sample of left-handers: Beethoven, Michelangelo, da Vinci, Goethe, Nietzsche, Holbein, Landseer, Cicero, Tiberius, Lewis Carrol, Chaplin, Judy Garland, Paul McCartney, Cole Porter, Danny Kaye; John McEnroe, Jimmy Connors, Pelé, Babe Ruth. Are these people weak, worthless, awkward? Bear in mind, too, that especially in modern times left-handers grow up in a world full of equipment designed for use by the right-handed – telephones, doorknobs, typewriters, hand-writing. They are environmentally disadvantaged from the very start, to say nothing of other people's attitudes. Yet they often become not simply proficient, but the very highest word in excellence in their particular fields.

Orthodoxy can offer no explanations. But we can. We can say that once, long ago, there was a highly intelligent, mysterious and 'magically' adept variety of very strange-looking human beings, who lived by night, and were left-handed. And (hard to believe) they were ruled over and led by women. These people are all dead now, long ago, we killed them. But in their dying they gave us one last miracle. For when our own main ancestor, right-handed man, interbred with those magicians, a new type of human being came into existence (ourselves, that is) whose innate abilities and capabilities outshone those of each of the parent groups.

We can describe that biological miracle either in the very words of the ancient texts: '... when the sons of God came into the daughters of men and they bore children to them ... *these* ... were the mighty men of old, the men of renown' (Genesis 6:4, italics added). (Interesting, of course, that this passage occurs in Genesis, the Book of Origin.) Or we can couch it in the language of science: when two distantly related varieties of animal or plant are cross-bred, the offspring frequently show what is termed 'hybrid vigour', that is, dramatic new qualities which are present in neither parent.

There is only one potential problem. Sometimes these hybrids are unstable. They then seek, continually, to devolve back into the two parent strains.

A Note on Nocturnalism

For the nocturnal creature, be that bird, rodent or man, the 'day' begins at nightfall. As it just so happens, the Druids did, and the Jews do, consider that the new day begins at dusk, a very odd idea indeed for a *daylight* creature to generate. So the Jewish sabbath runs from dusk on Friday evening to dusk on Saturday evening, and the commencement is announced by, of course, three blasts on the ram's horn (again a horn) at the appearance of the first star. Jewish and Islamic months and festivals also begin at the rising of a particular moon. Such against-daylight-logic ideas must, surely, derive from a nocturnal (Neanderthal) moon-worshipping culture.

13 Lindow Man

In Humberside in the north of England, on a small island in a great tract of marshes, is the village of Haxey. Here is enacted annually the Haxey Hood Game, on the twelfth day of Christmas. There is no doubt at all that this game was once something much more serious, and took place, I suggest, not on the twelfth, but on the thirteenth day following the winter solstice.

The story which is told of the origin of the Haxey Hood Game is as follows. In medieval times Lady de Mowbray was riding to church one Christmas Day when a fierce wind blew the scarlet hood from her head. Twelve men ran forward and picked it up for her. So pleased was Lady de Mowbray with this gallantry that she left a parcel of land, called the Hoodland, from which the income would pay for a hood and costumes for an annual contest between twelve villagers wearing scarlet jerkins and caps. One of these, known as the Lord or King, carries a wand made of thirteen strands of willow, bound around thirteen times.[177]

With what pleasure we can greet these by now old friends – the story as such, of course, is just a fabrication – a woman who wears a scarlet hood, heading a coven of thirteen, all of its members dressed in red. And here is the willow, the wicked-witch-willow, the tree the moon owns, that make the witch's broom, and is sacred, too, to poets. For Orpheus received his gift of mystic eloquence by touching it in a grove sacred to Persephone.

Another member of the Haxey coven is the Fool, with blackened face. Towards the end of the proceedings, at the Old Cross (of course old, of course cross), a fire is lit at his feet and parts of his clothing set alight. In an older version of the Game, the Fool sat during the 'Smoking' in a loop of rope suspended from a tree.

Still earlier 'Fools' did not escape so lightly.

Lindow Man sleeps quietly now in a glass container in the British Museum. The visitors who gossip and push around the container do not wake him. Two thousand years ago, after a meal which included mistletoe pollen, he had been stunned by two, or possibly three, heavy blows to the head as he knelt. Then he had been strangled with a stick twisted in a cord tied about his neck, until the neck broke. Lastly his throat was cut, at the jugular vein, to produce the ritual blood. To this death, however, as in many other cases, it seems he went willingly.[177] There is in fact no doubt at all that Lindow Man's death was a ritual sacrifice (as also the mistletoe indicates). The 'three-fold death' which he died is actually a commonplace of Irish and Welsh legend. Sometimes the victim is strangled, stabbed and drowned; sometimes strangled, stabbed, and burnt.

In some communities, then, the sacrificial victim was burned and his ashes scattered. But often, especially it seems in north-west Europe (though it may be that only there are conditions favourable to preservation) the body of the victim was consigned to a surface of water – the sea, a lake, a bog. Under this last condition the bodies are sometimes almost miraculously preserved.

We have not moved away from the Haxey Hood Men. For they are called Boggans or Boggins. This name is one variant of a set of names applied to a class of fairies or elves – bogies, bogey-men, boggarts, bugbears, bog bears and so on, associated with bogs and marshy places. From the same verbal lineage comes also Puck (alias Robin Goodfellow). Margaret Murray proposes that all these variant names derive from Gaelic *bouca* or Slavic *bog*, both meaning god.

Many hundreds of preserved bog bodies have been found throughout Europe, as far south-east as Greece. It is likely that the sacrificial rite we are discussing extended further, but that the conditions for preservation elsewhere were absent. The finds 'show a strong bias to the prehistoric period' – that is, the further back we go, the more bodies are found. The oldest reach back some 10,000 years.[177] Interestingly, we are speaking then of the end of the last ice age. Did the formation of bogs only begin at that point? Certainly we cannot say with any sureness that such sacrifices did not occur before 10,000 BP.

Sufficient bodies have been found, even though only lately have proper recording procedures been followed, for generalisations about them to be possible. A few, of course, represent cases of accidental death, or are the outcome of murder or private quarrel. The greater bulk, however, are clearly sacrificial victims. P.V. Glob reports that analysis of the stomach contents of a number of victims (Grauballe, Tollund, Barre Fen) shows no trace of summer or autumn fruits, nor any trace of greenstuffs. The implication, and certainly Glob concludes this, is that the sacrifices were made at mid-winter or at latest early spring, and were clearly designed to invoke the return of summer.

Many victims were obviously individuals of standing. Such can be inferred both from the value of articles placed with them, and from the fact that their hands show no traces of toil. 'For a community with few resources, the most valuable object which they had to sacrifice could have been a man or woman of status and they may have gone willingly to their deaths.' Not infrequently the victims were naked, except for ritual items. Thus Lindow Man had the noose about his neck, and a fox-fur band on his left arm. Tollund Man, in Denmark, wore only a belt and a pointed skin cap. It has been suggested that the Arthurian story of Gawain and the Green Knight, as well as other similar legends, commemorates and enshrines the elements involved here – including the next fact, namely, that many of the bog victims had been beheaded. Sometimes only the head is found. In the Arthurian story Gawain beheads the Green Knight – but is himself protected from beheading by a silken green riband tied about his waist.

Clearly two matters we have already investigated are concerned here, the first being the cult of the severed head, found not only among the Celts and the Templars, but in the Middle East, for example as part of the Tammuz myth (see Chapter 11). The second matter is that of the cord or garter, also worn by prehistoric shamans, witches, Incas and Templars (see Chapter 6).

The bog bodies have two even more exciting aspects. The pointed skin cap of Tollund Man has already been mentioned. Not a few of the bodies are in fact capped, hooded or caped, though often otherwise naked. Does this circumstance not remind us powerfully of the capped, hooded and caped menstruating women and pubertal girls of Chapter 10? Lady de Mowbray, too, wore a hood – and further examples follow below.

The second item concerns the hair, which is often very abundant, but more especially the hair colour of the victims. The following notes are taken from two books, *Lindow Man*,[177] dealing with Britain, and P.V. Glob's *The Bog People*,[61] which is concerned with Denmark. 'The skull, with its long plait of auburn hair.' 'The hair was on the legs and generally over the body, and had been of a dark red colour.' 'The skull of a female with a plait of thick reddish hair adhering to it.' 'The remains of a human skull, with a great abundance of hair, of a most beautiful auburn.' 'The hair was long and of a reddish colour.' 'Hair well preserved and dark-red in colour.' 'A considerable amount of hair survived, reddish brown in colour.' 'Reddish beard.' 'Curly red hair.' 'Hair had been perhaps golden red.' 'Reddish stubble on chin.' 'Red-brown hair.' 'Reddish coloured hair.' 'Red brown hair.'*

The suspicion that red-haired individuals were sacrificed more often than others is strikingly borne out by quite other evidence, which we look at in a moment, but also by other aspects of the bog burials themselves. 'A portion of a garment made of skin covered with reddish hair.' 'Fragments of red deer bone.' 'A skin cape of reddish brown leather.' Legend itself also sometimes records the red hair: 'At the top of a mound which overlooks a lake called the Lake of the Cauldron I saw a huge man with yellow-red hair emerging from the lake...'[177]

J.G. Frazer tells us that red-haired men and red oxen – who were said to represnt Typhon, the enemy of Osiris, the (nominal) sun god – were sacrificed to Osiris in ancient Egypt to ensure the fertility of crops. (It is of course an interesting question whence they might have obtained red-haired individuals in that part of the

* Sometimes the staining action of the bog water prevents judgement of the victim's original hair colour. The main staining effect, where present, produces yellowing or browning of the hair (as well as of skin, nails, etc.).[177]

world.) In ancient Rome also, at springtime, red puppies were sacrificed, again to ensure fertility. Still in Rome, generals parading in triumph and magistrates presiding at the Games had their faces reddened with vermilion. At festivals the face of the eagle who represented Jove was likewise dyed red. 'So important was it deemed to keep the divine features properly rouged that one of the first duties of the censors was to contract for having this done.' In Greece, during rites, the face and sometimes the whole body of Dionysus, the wine god, was painted red.

The Jewish Talmud has a lengthy section (in the *Seder Tohoroth II*) on the use of sacrificial red heifers for the purpose of purifying the Temple ('the residue of the ashes of seven red cows' and so forth) and absolving personal sin – as also described in the Bible, Numbers 19:

> *And the Lord spake unto Moses and Aaron saying... speak unto the children of Israel that they bring thee a red heifer without spot... and Eleazer shall take of her blood with his finger and sprinkle her blood directly before the tabernacle seven times... And a man that is clean shall gather up the ashes of the heifer... it is a purification for sin.*

So both the red cows as well as some of the bog victims are burned. Placing them in fire, of course, delivers them to the moon, for fire is one of her most important symbols – the other being water – where many other victims are also placed.

Finally, Richard Cavendish mentions a number of superstitions concerning red-haired individuals – for example, that in Scotland and Ireland a fisherman who met a red-headed woman on the way to his boat would turn back. In medieval France it was claimed that poison could be made more virulent by being strained through people with red hair(!).

There is a mixture of respect and hate in these various practices and observations. But at any rate, the sacrifice of red-haired men and red oxen in Egypt, and red puppies in Rome, in both cases specifically to increase the fertility of crops, fairly certainly confirms that red-haired individuals were more likely to become sacrificial bog victims than others. Why, however, should this custom have arisen? Is it simply because red-haired people and animals suggest an association with red ochre? No, I think the reason is other than this. For there is very strong evidence to suggest that Neanderthal man was red-haired. This material we shall be considering in Chapter 15, but already in Chapter 7 we saw that red hair is not uncommon, for example, among Australian Aborigines.

Two last points on the bog sacrifices. The victims were usually strangled with a cord, sometimes a plaited cord rather like a torque. In any case, however, the fertility goddess of those north European tribes is depicted wearing a torque or cord about her neck – so that we must assume that the cord and the sacrifice were on her account. Also, a plaque on the noted Gundestrup silver cauldron (which, however, did not originate at Gundestrup) shows a sacrificial victim being bled into another cauldron, from which springs a Tree of Life. Meanwhile warriors pass by in procession. We are reminded here of the events observed in Grail Castle.

At Cogul in north-east Spain is a paleolithic drawing of a round dance. There are nine dancers, all of them women, and all wearing peaked hoods. They are circling about a small figure, which may or may not be a child, and may or may not be a sacrificial victim. Many thousands of years later a medieval painting shows twelve dancers, all wearing peaked hoods, who form a moving circle round Robin Goodfellow.[134] The ring dance, Murray tells us, usually moved anti-clockwise. A further late medieval drawing appears in a book titled *Robin Goodfellow, his mad prankes and merry jests*, published in 1628. Here we see twelve dancers in pointed hats and cloaks circling the superimposed figure of Robin Goodfellow. This is evidently an older portrait from another source – for there is nothing merry or prankish about this Puck. He wears a hat with two horns, has a cruel expression, and holds a broom in his left hand and a club in his right. This is a coven master, the devil himself. Fairies and elves, again, also danced in circles – and so perhaps boggarts too.

The Morris Dance of medieval England consisted of two opposing groups of six dancers, sometimes with blackened faces, and with a fool running among them – and so once again a coven of thirteen. This dance was an aspect of the Maypole festivities. Similar dances are found throughout Europe, the Middle East, India, and parts of Central and South America. In origin, the current *Britannica* article on dance suggests that these dances may be celebrating the resurrection of a god, i.e., the fool. However, as a model I would be rather more inclined to take the two lines of dancers of the South American fertility dance described in Chapter 7, with the scarlet 'fool' (in this case explicitly the moon) prancing between them. But both explanations are suitable, and both assign the origins of this dance to antiquity. Given the obviously once much higher status of the fool, we need not hesitate to link this figure with the same major symbol of the Tarot deck.

Robin Hood and his 12- strong merry band, living as they did in the greenwood, can hardly be missed as a coven. Neither 'Robin' nor 'Hood' would appear to be accidental names (many witches' familiars were named Robin). A recent suggestion is that this legendary band had its origin in a form of Morris Dance – and that is of course a perfectly acceptable idea.

The many interconnections of the events we are describing are clear without laboured argument. By way of two further precise connections between the bog sacrifices and witchcraft we can cite Murray's comment that 'the importance of the lace or string among witches was very great' and that all descriptions of the devil's costume always included mention of a string or garter. Secondly, de Lancre's comment, reported by Murray, that the sabbat should be held near a lake, stream or water of some kind. (However, a crossroads is also a spot favoured by witches for rites – this a last dim memory, I suggest, of the fact that the cross represents the moon.)

The bog sacrifice directly involved the leaders of the community, and the continuance of the Old Religion in recent times has likewise involved the highest to the lowest – the whole community in fact. On no other basis of course could a Celtic altar, complete with the names and portraits of Celtic gods, have got itself built into the choir of the Notre Dame cathedral in Paris, or a large stone penis have been carved inside the altar of a London church.[67] In a church in Braunton, Devon, the initials of some of the owners of the pews are carved upside down. Here is a clear public admission of allegiance to, and membership of, the Old Religion – reversal always signifying that. Some pews have only one initial upside down, also strongly suggesting therefore various ranks within an alternative organisation.

14 Uncommon Ground

This chapter begins with a statement of what it is not about. The opening here sets out specifically to set aside books and theories which, in principle, appear to cover the same ground – so which, again in principle, might be supportive of – the present book. Instead, the purpose of this chapter is very different, namely, to use for my own ends statements and evidence from authors who very much do not support the kinds of attempt this book makes.

First, then, the act of demolition.

By no means a small number of authors have attempted in the past, and still attempt today, to use parallels which they observe or think they observe between different human cultures widely separated in both space and time, as the basis for some general statement about the origins of man. The more sensible of such statements involve theories of 'diffusionism'. The argument here is that civilisation began at one particular point on our planet, and then spread subsequently through migration to all other parts. (The present book is, of course, exactly such a diffusionist view.) Diifusionists divide roughly into two groups, the old ones and the new.

The early diffusionists at the beginning of this century and before were often extremely learned individuals, those such as Gerald Massey, Elliot Grafton Smith and W.J. Perry. Wading through the erudition of these books is – with no disrespect – like wading continuously through chest-deep water. All these books nevertheless fail, in my opinion – and not because they do not contain good insights or because they are difficult to read. It is because the time span the authors are forced to work in – that they force *themselves* to work in – is far too short. For what these books say is that around 5000 years ago the bearers of civilisation set out from some central point, usually either Egypt or Africa, and carried the seeds to all other parts. The setting-out point of these alleged voyagers cannot go back more than 5000 years because earlier than this, in the view of these authors that is, there would have been no civilisation for them to carry. These voyagers, however, would also have had to be very intrepid, since they managed to reach, and influence, every part of the world – Europe, Asia, North America, South America, the Pacific, Australia. Yet if such recent vigorous migration had indeed occurred, and shaped civilisation world-wide, then it would necessarily have left some deep mark in legends around the world. We find however no such marks, anywhere. Then again, just to touch on detail for a moment, it is no good Massey showing some interesting parallels between the actual vocabulary of, say, Maoris and Egyptians, and then suggesting on this basis that the Maoris had an Egyptian origin. For after only a mere 5000 years we would expect still to see very substantial parallels not just in occasional words (Massey's examples are in any case debatable) but in syntax, grammar and so on. But it *is* very remarkable, for example, that both the ancient Egyptians and the Maoris had the same name for their sun god, Ra. It would, I think, be salutary for our present-day philologists and other academics, despite the above disclaimers, to go back and read the books of these early diffusionists for themselves. These should not simply be written off.

There are substantial diffusionists alive today, such as Giorgio de Santillana (see Chapter 4, and below) and Thor Heyerdahl (though he is really only a partial diffusionist). But most modern diffusionists, such as James Churchward, are considerably more lightweight than their scholarly forerunners, although that on the other hand is not to say that they are altogether uninformed or unqualified. (I am, for instance, especially grateful to James Churchward for drawing my attention to the Mound Builders' thirteen-zodiac.) Where most present-day diffusionists break down irretrievably, in my own view, is in their belief that civilisation arose from some lost continent, that is, from some variation or other of Atlantis. Here one is not as such against the idea in principle of some natural cataclysm (flood, earthquake or whatever) destroying a reasonably advanced culture – precisely that did actually happen in the case of Minoan Crete. But we *do* have to insist on at least one or two genuinely identifiable artefacts from the alleged civilisation. (We cannot, also, be especially happy over the site of alleged Atlantis not having yet been located, but let us leave that one.) Fairly substantial groups of escapees of the Atlantean disaster apparently brought their knowledge out with them. Did they not manage to bring *any* (reliably identifiable) trinkets or other artefacts – a few coins, perhaps? And then, why did they not, after the escape, write – or if they had no writing, orally construct – a detailed account of their own history and a report on the disaster itself? Our experience in this present book is that important oral items of this kind do not get lost. (Why, the Australian Aborigines even still have a legend explaining how the white swan became black; though there never have been any white swans in Australia.)

There is one other variety of author – the best of whom is someone like Andrew Tomas – who believes that all civilisation on this planet was seeded initially by visitors from outer space. Most of these books are worth no serious consideration, mixing fact with fiction, juggling the dates of history to suit their convenience, using logic which an intelligent ten-year-old could fault. Some are a complete disgrace. Jacquetta Hawkes pointed out, in the *Sunday Times*, that the photographs in Erich von Däniken's books include 'more than forty well-known forgeries'.[86] Were that statement not true, of course, Däniken and his publishers would have sued the *Sunday Times* and Hawkes for a very large amount. (For those who would like to read an account of the demolition of the foolishness and outright lies which characterise most visitors-from-space books, L.D. Kusche's *The Bermuda Triangle Mystery Solved* is recommended.) However, the ultimate failure of the space-visitor theory of civilisation is not in the quality of the writers, but in the failure of anybody to produce one single, solitary physical or manufactured item of extra-terrestrial origin.

No author likes to be taken for a crank. For those in academic employment there are also dangers other than bruised feelings. I know myself of academics who have been advised to drop certain lines of enquiry, if they are seriously interested in promotion. With that said, and bearing in mind also Robert Bolt's advice that no one should deliberately seek martyrdom (*A Man for All Seasons*), there does nevertheless come a point, if integrity is to be preserved, where uncomfortable evidence should force one to take up an, if necessary, uncomfortable position. The authors whose work we now discuss are, in my own opinion, too much in love with comfort. We cannot, of course, see into their respective private thoughts, so we do not know quite why they walk away from the evidence – or rather, from the consequences of the evidence. For they do report the evidence in question, otherwise we should not have it. Clearly, then, they realise at some level that the point or points in question are important, for they 'confess' them. In more extreme instances however, having confessed, they then seek specifically to deny, as in the case of the first author we now consider.

But before we actually come to him, let us look back to W.H. Matthews's comment in Chapter 4. We recall Matthews had been considering the matter of the labyrinth drawn in the sand for the Spaniard by the Pina Indian in 1761. Matthews said that if that labyrinth could be shown to predate the Spanish invasion of America, it and the Cretan labyrinth would have a common origin of astonishing antiquity. In other words, he was fully prepared to face the implications of what he was saying, in effect – 'look, if this is true – *if* it is true – then, by heavens, the whole damned structure we're working with at present is no good; take out just *this* one, and the whole house of cards of our current understanding of the evolution of human civilisation collapses.'

Apparent and certainly striking similarities in ancient astronomical/ astrological traditions around the world (some of which we considered in Chapter 4) are often commented upon. In his book *The Origin of the Zodiac* Rupert Gleadow examines some further of these similarities, with a view, however, to explaining them away. He takes, for instance, the twelve signs of the ancient Greek (from Babylon) and the ancient Chinese zodiac, and considers the often noted similarities between them. He has two 'explanations' for these similarities: (a) there is no great similarity after all, (b) such genuine similarities as exist are to be accounted for by the ancient Chinese and Babylonians exchanging ideas in these matters.

Let us look at his first explanation. Here, first, are the two zodiacs in question. *Greek:* Aries, Taurus, Gemini, Cancer, Leo, Virgo, Libra, Scorpio, Sagittarius, Capricorn, Aquarius, Pisces. *Chinese:* Rat, Ox, Tiger, Hare, Dragon, Serpent, Horse, Sheep, Monkey, Cock, Dog, Boar. Leaving aside the question of position for a moment, the similar signs in these two zodiacs are said to be, respectively: *Greek:* Taurus, Leo, Scorpio, Sagittarius, Capricorn, Aquarius; *Chinese:* Ox, Tiger, Serpent, Horse, Sheep, Monkey. Gleadow himself agrees that it is not altogether unreasonable to equate a lion with a tiger; a scorpion with a serpent; a half-man/half-horse with a horse; a ram with a sheep; and a man with a monkey. But, he insists, only one pairing is in the correct (second) position, Taurus and the Ox. The rest are out of position. Nevertheless, Gleadow has overlooked two very important further statistical features of this material. (Possibly he fails to consider them out of something of the same frame of mind that orthodox scientists have in respect of the footprints of Bigfoot. As we see in the next chapter, science fails to observe what these footprints actually tell us, because of their prior assumption that these prints must be fakes.)

The first point which Gleadow (and all the others) fail to appreciate is that the apparently similar items in the two zodiacs *are in exactly the same order or sequence*: that is, (a) follows (b) follows (c) follows (d), etc., in both cases. So what are the statistical odds of these six items occurring in the same sequence in the two different lists by chance? The odds (these and other calculations kindly performed by William G. Duffy) are 719:1. In other words, only once out of a total of 720 occasions could we expect to find two identical sequences of six in two such lists. (It is, incidentally, of no consequence at all how many other items there be in the lists concerned, or at what intervals in the lists these other non-relevant items fall.)

However, the odds just given are in fact a dramatic understatement of the true odds involved. The question we have to ask is, out of what available *parent* population of animals or beings have the 12/6 symbols of the two lists been drawn? Except in the case of Taurus (see Chapter 4) there is nothing in the actual constellations themselves which forces the choice of any animal or person. (Unless there once was, many tens of thousands of years ago – but that, of course, would suit our general argument equally well – again see Chapter 4.) So how many possible animals/beings, real and hypothetical, were available to the Chinese, and to the Greeks for choice purposes, and from which population did they make the selections which we see before us? Was it twenty animals, thirty animals, fifty animals? How many? Once we have decided on the number possible available for choice – and that would be no easy task – we then have a different statistical problem, namely: what are the odds against a particular six animals in a sample of twelve animals, drawn randomly from a total population of X animals, occurring in the same sequence as those same six animals in another sample of twelve animals drawn randomly from a total population of Y animals? In the circumstances we can give no precise answer, but we are speaking of odds of at least tens of thousands to one.

Gleadow tells us, further that, 'Kio, which was called the Root of Heaven and the Chief of the Asterisms, was the star Spica; and it is curious that Spica was also the sidereal marking star of the [western] zodiac, as we shall see later. This may be only chance, but the Chinese could equally well have chosen several other equatorial stars, particularly Makab, Altair, Antares, Alphard, Procyon, Betelgeuze or Hyades.' Gleadow goes on to note also that the Chinese had the same names as the Babylonians for the constellations of the Great and Little Bear, Draco, Corona Berenices, Orion and Andromeda. Further, that 'Mars in Fang (which is part of Scorpio) in ancient China has the same effect as Mars in Scorpio in Babylon'. He gives then another seven examples of the same kind of parallel – one being that, in China, Mars was called by the name of the constellation Boötes, just as it was in Babylon.

Fully aware that despite his judgement of the unimportance of the similarities between the Greek/Babylon and the Chinese zodiacs (the Chinese zodiac 'does not bear much resemblance to our western zodiac') and constellations, there clearly remains something to explain, Gleadow proposes that the two communities must have directly influenced each other. I find it rather hard to imagine under what precise conditions Chinese and Babylonian astrologers could have met, overcome a formidable language barrier, and persuaded each other of the rightness of particular names and attributes which have no observable necessity. Clearly, in any case, in other instances the two peoples have not taken on each other's ideas in a direct sense at all – there are only echoes or tangential relationships (a scorpion is not a serpent, a man is not a monkey, and so on) and occasional parallels within very different overall structures. For example, the Chinese do not even use their zodiac for the same purposes as the Babylonians (and ourselves). What we seem to have here, once more, are (a) similarities too great to be argued as the result of chance or independent generation, (b) differences too great to be anything but the result of prolonged separation from some common inspirational source.

But in any case, even if one were to insist that, no matter what the linguistic or geographical barriers, there *must* have been some perfectly normal traffic in, and exchange of, ideas between Babylonian and Chinese astrologers, there remains the small matter of Mexico.

The parallels between Mexican and Chinese/western astrology and astronomy have aroused comment throughout modern times. When the explorer and scientist Alexander von Humboldt returned from Mexico in 1816, he announced in a book (*Vues des Cordillères*) that he had discovered striking similarities between zodiacs there and in Tibet. Similarly, Bernadino de Sahagun, writing in Spanish a little later (*Historia de las cosas de la Nueva España*, Mexico, 1829) considered he had identified a series of signs closely equivalent to that of the Old World zodiac. We come to one or two of those correspondences later.

Let us now, however, look closely at a table reproduced by Gleadow. This is taken from Fritz Roeck *(Kalender der Tolteken*, Vienna, 1922). Of it Gleadow writes: 'Roeck has the following comparative table which he believes to indicate some continuity of cultural contact, rather than just the expression of similar archetypal ideas in different places.' (Again that infuriating use of the word archetypal as a catch-all 'explanation'. I have not yet seen one writer, who uses the expression, make any attempt to define it, much less therefore to assign limits to its operation. Is a Yorkshire pudding archetypal? Is a publisher's contract archetypal?)

The table produced here (*Table 1*) is a simplified version of

Gleadow's, in which I have deliberately included only the stronger elements. There is nothing illicit in this step, for Gleadow does not consider there to be genuine correspondences anywhere within it. Nor, however, are the other correspondences unimportant, or contrary to what is shown here – but they would necessarily involve us in a much longer debate. The table is concerned with the names or attributes of the four main directions of the compass. (Why human beings should say that there are four principal directions to the compass, as opposed to eight, or ten, or twenty-four is a situation itself by no means self-justifying – but we shall leave that matter for Chapter 16.)

Table 1 Representations of the powers of the four directions of the compass in four countries.

	Egypt	*Tibet*	*China*	*Mexico*
	The 4 sons of Horus	Portents of the 4 seasons	4 Cosmic Beings	Ritual masks of the 4 Regents
South	Hawk	Garuda-vulture	Red Bird	Vulture
West	Jackal	Black Dog	Spotted Dog	Dog
North	Dog-headed Baboon	Horse and Rider	Black Warrior on Tortoise	Death's Head
East	Man	Man-Dragon	Green Dragon	Crocodile

We can see at once why Roeck was so impressed with his finds, but equally fail to see why Gleadow is not. The weakest line here is North. A dog-headed baboon is hardly a horse and rider (though in both we have one creature on another). Then we have the death's head. We cannot fairly say that a death's head resembles a horse and rider – unless perhaps the rider had a death-aspect of some kind. Unfortunately the illustrations themselves are not shown. The East line, on the other hand, is not weak – for though a man does not resemble a crocodile, the man-dragon gives us a bridge (just as, in other circumstances, the Greek mythological Centaur, half-horse, half-man, could give us a bridge between man and horse). The West and South lines are very strong.

If all the figures in all four lines were accepted as (originally at least) one and the same, what would be the statistical odds of finding them all in the same order in all four columns by chance? The odds would be 24 to the power of 3, that is, 13,823:1. Only once in 13,824 occasions would we expect to find the situation we actually have occurring by chance. Even if we disallow one or two items, the odds against chance remain formidable.

Ah, but we have overlooked one thing. From what possible *parent* population of available symbols were the four items in each column in any case drawn? It is very hard to set any kind of limit on those parent populations, especially since we must allow the possibility of mythical and composite figures. We flounder in an almost limitless range of possibilities. But certainly overall we are talking of real odds of millions to one against chance.

Gleadow however writes: 'It would be guesswork to try to establish any definite theory of Toltec astronomy being copied from that of China or derived from Babylon, *although some influence may have percolated*' (italics added). But what does this mean – 'may have percolated'? When percolated? Under what precise conditions percolated? One simply cannot make statements of this kind, and then change the subject. For if there *is* influence then, as we know, the history books have to be re-written.

C.A. Burland gives us further information on the matters that so impressed Humboldt and others.

> *An indication of the extreme antiquity of the zodiacal constellations can be seen in ancient Mexican stellar linkages with the stars of the four quarters of the sky in which* [*western*] *Scorpio was also* [*for the Mexicans*] *a Scorpion, Aquarius and Pegasus were taken together as the sign of the Rain God Tlaloc, Taurus with the red star Aldeberan was taken as the Fire Sticks of the Fire God who was Lord of the Year, and the space between Aldeberan and Alcyone was taken as the commencing point of the year as in so many other calendars. The Sickle in Leo was the Crook held by Quetzal-coatl, Lord of the Breath of Life.*[21]

This is not all that Burland has to contribute to our theme. In another book he writes: 'The singular parallels between modern witchcraft and the ancient Mexican worship of the goddess Tlazolteotl are not likely to indicate a common material origin, but rather a psychological need.'[23] Burland does not use the word archetype itself, but nevertheless takes the same timid road. What are these 'singular parallels'? Why does Burland not tell us about them, and allow us to make up our own minds? I have looked through Burland's other books, but the details in question do not seem to be anywhere given – there is only one hint, in *The Magical Arts*. Here Burland tells us that in ancient Mexico broomsticks were associated with witchcraft. So *this* is a common psychological need, or archetype? Really, what on earth are these people talking about?

A wooden medal is also deserved by A.A. Abbie. Again there are two points, the first positive.

> *... the Old Testament. There we discover that a man might not marry his mother, sister, sister-in-law, daughter, daughter-in-law or aunt. Jewish polygamy and concubinage made it necessary to extend some of these classes, so that the mother category included step-mother, secondary wife and any concubine of the father and any aunt; that is, every woman who stood in the relationship of 'possible' mother. Similarly, the 'possible' sister group included legitimate sister, half-sister, step-sister, illegitimate sister and sister-in-law. The whole system has obvious similarities to the Aboriginal kinship system.... Even the secondary obligations have similarities: if a Jew died childless his brother was expected to lie with the widow until she had a child; if an Aborigine dies his brother takes over the widow(s).*[1]

Thus far so good, a contribution without hedging or equivocation. (In respect of the last custom above, incidentally, which is known as the Levirate, Briffault tells us that it is 'well-nigh universal' among aboriginal peoples.) But now to the wooden medal. Abbie comments: 'Indeed, many Aboriginal myths have an echo in classical mythology' – and then changes the subject! *What* are the echoes of which Abbie speaks? Well, luckily we know of one – it is the story of the maidens of the Pleiades which we considered in Chapter 4. But *why* does Abbie not go into details – clearly at some level he considers the link important, otherwise he would not mention it at all. This is the 'confessional' aspect described earlier: 'I've observed it, I've confessed it, I've put it on record, now I can drop it.'

Peter Lancaster Brown, already mentioned in these pages, gives us perhaps the reason why these various authors do not follow through. In the notes to one of his books he comments on the similarities between the Pleiades legends in Aboriginal Australia, ancient Greece and among the North American Indians.

> *It has always surprised me that the hyperdiffusionists of the Elliot Smith school apparently overlook this most remarkable coincidence in astronomical mythology as ammunition to support their crank theories. Another remarkable astromythological coincidence is the independent adoption of the Bear Legends for Ursa Major by the Greeks and the North American Indians.*[111]

What Lancaster Brown seems to be saying here is – 'hey, don't get me wrong, I'm not one of those diffusionist cranks – that's not me at all'. Well, if Lancaster Brown does not think that this 'most remarkable coincidence' (parallel might have been a braver word) is due to diffusionism, then *what does* he think it is due to? On the one hand his words make it quite clear that he appreciates the basic importance and singularity of his two observations (Pleiades and Great Bear). But on the other hand he is not prepared to discuss them further. I do happen to know that Lancaster Brown has collected a great deal of information world-wide on the Pleiades. Why does he not get this together, publish, and face the possible implications? 'Look, chaps, this Pleiades business – I don't want to rock the boat too much – but there is something definitely strange about it, which ought to be looked into and which might – er – which *might* produce a few changes in our view of how civilisation first came about.' Is it too much for us to ask that of him, and the others also of course?

Mircea Eliade is obviously very clear about the parallels in myth and cultural practice to be found world-wide – one could quote him almost endlessly, but five brief further examples will suffice, all taken from his book *Patterns in Comparative Religion*: (1) we are driven to connect *all* the various initiation ceremonies with the lunar myth (italics added), (2) there is a world-wide connection between the symbolism of the snake and the moon, (3) there is a world-wide connection between the gods and goddesses of fertility and the moon, in all races and religions, (4) the cosmos pictured as an immense tree has its counterpart in innumerable other traditions, (5) the most striking parallel to the Australian reenactment of the 'Creation' is to be found in post-Vedic India.

So there are no doubts regarding either Eliade's awareness or his commitment. But where is his explanation for the world-wide parallels he observes? As far as my own reading of his books yields, he seems to offer none.

However, in this latest respect he is in distinguished company – for neither J.G. Frazer nor Robert Briffault had any central explanation for the spread of the detailed similarities they perceived world-wide, and so devotedly recorded. (At one point Frazer cites a missionary, Father A.G. Morice, who wrote a paper in 1888 on the similarities between the customs of the Chippeway Indians and those of the Hebrews in respect of menstruating women. Father Morice gets a *real* medal.) Frazer and Briffault are certainly not classifiable as diffusionists. Reading both these authors one seems to detect their sense of underlying helplessness, regarding explanations, in the face of their own evidence. To use a modern metaphor, although they box wonderfully, they simply do not have the knock-out punch. This is why, I think, their books are not infrequently referred to as flawed masterpieces.

Giorgio de Santillana has gathered important evidence of planet-wide parallelisms, some of which were cited in Chapter 4. Why, he asks, as a further example, did the Mexican god Tezcatlipoca first drill fire in the year two-reed (two-acatl) and Prometheus steal fire from the gods concealed in a hollow reed; while in Sumeria the word for reed, *gi*, also means to burn, and the god of fire is Gibil? Santillana is a dedicated diffusionist in belief, though he avoids a commitment to any particular area as a starting point. He speaks of the 'tantalising fragments of a lost whole' and 'the clues to a gigantic puzzle which is waiting to be reassembled'.[162]

My own feeling, too, is that any reasonable person who takes the trouble to examine the evidence – and most do not – will find him or herself led to these same metaphors.

15 Wild Men

The generic term 'wild man' occurs in cultures throughout Europe, Africa and Asia in historical times. This term overlaps with another reference that we are familiar with: the Yeti or 'Abominable Snowman'. This second generic term is, this time, found world-wide, including therefore among American Indians and Australian Aborigines. Interestingly enough, the Australian Aborigines refer to their creature as the Yowie.[70]

Our concern in this chapter is with the wild men, not with the Yeti, although we cannot in fact always be sure to which of these two phenomena the sketchier sightings relate. The Yeti is almost certainly a non-human primate – which may exist as at least two distinct varieties, large and small – adapted to living in remote, high-lying mountain areas. Incidentally, I would think it far more likely that the Australian Yowie is an idea which the Aborigines brought with them (from India) rather than any such actual creature in their present environs.

There is no ground whatsoever for scepticism on the subject of wild men, despite the fact that western science wholly excludes them (along with so much else) from its consciousness. The most solid report of all, nevertheless, one among many such, comes from the Caucasus. Here, in the later half of the last century, a wild woman was captured and, eventually, lived freely among the villagers of Tkhina on the Moki river. This woman, whom the villagers called Zana, was covered with reddish hair, had a muzzle-like prognathous jaw, large eyebrows and big white teeth. Ultimately she produced four children by human fathers. In 1964 Professor Boris Porshnev, Director of the Modern History Department of Moscow Academy, interviewed two of Zana's grandchildren. They are described as of somewhat negroid appearance, with very pronounced jaw muscles and jaws. Their father is reported as having had curly hair and prominent lips, and being small in stature. Their aunt had been a very strong woman, with dark, hairy skin.[167] (Extensive body-hair in women is a feature entirely absent in all present human populations, with the marginal exception of the Hairy Ainu in Japan. Here of course is further evidence of the very long genetic separation of the Neanderthal and Cro-Magnon types – see Chapters 1 and 17.)

Zana was what is usually referred to as an 'almas'. There are many other local names for these people (and people is what they are) who are reported from various locations in an area stretching from the north of Afghanistan through to central China in the east. As far as possible from here on we will use the term almas in respect of wild men living at the present time (meaning today, now, on this very planet) and during the past hundred years; and wild man for the older historical reports of this phenomenon, including such from Europe. For we cannot be sure that there was not more than one distinct variety of wild man in older times.

Almas and wild men have interest for the present book for two reasons. First, there is the point that Neanderthal man (and there can be no reasonable doubt, as we shall further see, that the almas and wild men are surviving or relict Neanderthals) lives on in appreciable numbers beyond the date of his alleged disappearance 25,000 years ago. Such survival allows us to be confident of an extended period (a) during which Cro-Magnon and Neanderthal continued to interbreed and (b) during which Neanderthal customs, rituals and beliefs could be studied, copied and absorbed by our own direct (and by now genetically mixed) ancestors. We can then also see in this context that all stories of trolls and monstrous dwarfs living in mountain fastnesses, and of elves and hobgoblins abroad at night, likewise of bogies, boggarts, boggins, bogbears, bug bears inhabiting the centres of trackless marshes (and, incidentally, John Napier[137] tells us that these were indeed associated with phantom bears in the popular mind, so yet another link with bear-worshipping Neanderthal) are *all* not fairy-stories or fantasies, but actual historical accounts of surviving groups of Neanderthals.

We are also interested in reports of almas and wild men for a second very important reason – that is, because they confirm conclusions we have reached already through entirely other lines of approach.

Thus, for example, we learn that Zana had fine teeth – 'big white teeth'. In Chapter 7 we noted that Australian Aborigines (who happen to be, by general agreement, the most physically 'Neanderthal' population alive today) and Eskimos have the finest teeth of any existing human population. We shall also have further important comment to make on teeth a little later.

Zana was covered with reddish hair. How very interesting. So let us now, additionally, glance through some of the reports of sightings of almas, drawn from a variety of sources: 'hair predominantly reddish-brown'; 'reddish-gray hair all over'; brown to reddish hair'; 'reddish-black hair'; 'reddish-brown hair'; 'thick greyish-red hair'; 'covered with reddish hair'; 'thick reddish hair on its body'. Certainly other colours are also mentioned, namely black, brown and yellow (and sometimes hair colour is not stated at all). But the red element is clearly the most frequently mentioned.

A critic might comment, oh well, once these stories get started, however that may be, any elements mentioned in the first ones will tend to be included in later proliferations of the original hysteria. There may be some truth in such a view. But what of the circumstance, purely coincidental perhaps, that in ancient Egypt red-haired men were sacrificed to ensure the fertility of crops? These men were said to represent the 'enemy' of Osiris – and despite the latter's clear moon antecedents (see Chapter 13) he is certainly outwardly and nominally the sun hero. Then, after all, Zana, an absolutely authentic case, was quite definitely red-haired. And then of course there is the matter of the apparent predominance of red-haired individuals in the Bog Sacrifices (again Chapter 13). One more coincidence, perhaps?

It is a common saying in Poland that all red-headed Poles are Jews. Then, the German-Jewish radical, Daniel Cohn-Bendit, is not called Danny the Red simply because of his left-wing views, but as much because of his distinctive carroty hair. In a German-Jewish family of my own acquaintance, both the father and mother had a slight touch of auburn. (Though what I first noticed about the man was his glass eye and a good deal of gold bridgework in his mouth. These were a legacy of being struck across the face by a Nazi with a bicycle chain, that being the kind of thing Cro-Magnon does to Neanderthal.) One of their children had likewise a touch of auburn, but two had flaming red hair. In due course the daughter herself married, and had six children, all with the same dramatic red hair. Yet red hair is hardly the first characteristic one expects to find in an ethnic group originally from the Middle East. As I have argued in earlier books, however, I do myself consider Jews to have an unusually high concentration of Neanderthal genes.[65,67]

Let us here briefly look at some of Thor Heyerdahl's very relevant evidence in these connections.[88-9]

The mysterious statues of Easter Island in the Pacific are said unequivocally, by the Easter Islanders themselves, to be images of their ancestors. Each of these statues, prior to later decay, had placed upon its head a large red stone, which was not a hat but a 'top-knot' of hair. So the statement is quite specific – our (distant) ancestors had red hair. 'Formerly,' Heyerdahl says, 'the Easter Islanders always walked about bare-headed; their hair, regularly cut above the ears, was artificially rouged. . . .'

Nor is this by any means all. Heyerdahl comments: 'We have seen how the black-haired Polynesians in many of the islands imitated the natural hair colour of the *uru-kehu* [the red-haired ones] by plastering or painting their own hair red.' He writes further (quoting now J.S. Polack in 1838): 'The red ochreous earth called *kokowai* is in great request among the [Maori] beaux and belles of New Zealand. . . . This material of embellishment is rubbed over the body from the head, including often the hair. . . .'

Heyerdahl is trying to show that the Polynesians are really American Indians. So he draws attention here to a comment by G. Dixon (in 1789) on North American Indians: 'The long black hair of the . . . Indians would have been an ornament to them were it not for the large quantities of grease and red oker constantly rubbed into it.' (We can absolutely agree with Heyerdahl that the North American Indians and the Polynesians do have this identical cultural practice in common, not however because they are racially descended one from the other, but because in the very distant past they shared a common cultural background.)

Two more of the authorities cited by Heyerdahl are, first, E. Best writing in 1924: 'Among the black-haired natives of New Zealand . . . reddish hair of a wavy type is extremely persistent.' Of the same Maoris in 1922 P.H. Buck said: 'The general hair colour is black, but brown and reddish hair occur. Certain tribes have been stated to have had more than their share of red hair, and in these tribes it is said to occur in certain families.'

Another observation of Heyerdahl's own is that among the 2000-year-old mummies of Peru there are 'a great number with reddish-brown hair . . . sometimes even clearly wavy in texture'. Heyerdahl also discusses a Tiahuanaco statue – Tiahuanaco having been the most vigorous and widespread culture of the area prior to the rise of the Inca culture. The statue in question is large and carved entirely in red sandstone. Two rays of lightning meet at the forehead and continue down the sides of the face. On each side of the body is a serpent figure. Heyerdahl believes that the lightning is suggesting 'flame-coloured hair', which may well be so. However, we are very familiar with red (the whole statue), lightning zig-zags, and serpents. We could not ask for better evidence of the involvement of the moon in all this.

I would suggest here that from 30,000 years ago forwards – the time of the initial meeting of Neanderthal and Cro-Magnon – the priestesses and priests of the moon religion had often been red-haired, and that both this characteristic and the priestly privileges had been the preserve of certain families (just, perhaps, as the priests in ancient Israel were always Cohens). By 5000 BP this concept of the red-haired priests had been lost – but it was still at that time considered, in Egypt and Europe, that the sacrifice of red-haired individuals was the most 'valuable' sacrifice: and generals and magistrates still artificially reddened their faces at important occasions. The 'red-haired priest-king' idea seems to have survived intact for rather longer in North/South America and Polynesia.

Interestingly enough, in his novel about Neanderthal man, *The Inheritors*, William Golding gives his Neanderthals red, curly hair. Curly hair, in any case, is another item on my own list of Neanderthal qualities.

But back to the wild men of Europe and Asia.

Descriptions of captured wild men, alive or dead, lend very strong, I would say conclusive, support to the view that these are indeed surviving Neanderthals. An anthropologist, Michael Wagner, had this to say of a captured wild youth in Germany in 1784.

> *His forehead was strongly bent inwards.... He had heavy brown eyebrows which projected far out over his eyes.... His mouth stood out somewhat... the back and the chest were very hairy; the muscles on his legs were stronger and more visible than in ordinary people.... He walked erect but a little heavily. It seemed as if he would throw himself from one foot to the other. He carried his head and his chest forward.*[7]

This is a strikingly accurate description of known features of Neanderthal. The walk is precisely what the physical structure of classic Neanderthal leads us to expect – the massive body and wide pelvis, the slightly bowed legs, the broad feet. But Michael Wagner himself had never heard of Neanderthal man. The first fossil of Neanderthal was discovered in 1856.

Here now is an extract from a report by Major-General Topilski of the Russian army, concerning a wild man shot by bandits in the Pamirs, filed in 1925, but published first in 1964 in *Moscow News.*

> *At first glance I thought the body was that of an ape. It was covered with hair all over.... The eyes were dark and the teeth were large and even and shaped like human teeth. The forehead was slanting and the eyebrows were very powerful. The protruding jaw bones made the face resemble the Mongol type of face. The nose was flat with a deeply sunk bridge. The ears... looked a little more pointed than a human being's.... The lower jaw was very massive... powerful chest and well-developed muscles... the feet much wider and shorter than man's.*[209]

Items to emphasise particularly here are the 'large and even' teeth, the deeply sunk bridge of the nose (known as the nasal notch and, as it just so happens, the Australian Aborigines have the deepest nasal notch of any currently living human beings) and the wide, short feet. It is a thousand pities that Major Topilski did not notice whether the big toe was shorter than the other toes. For we know that Neanderthal man had a distinctive short big toe, whereas Cro-Magnon had a long big toe, as do most people living today. *Figure 10* shows a footprint of actual prehistoric Neanderthal man preserved in clay, along with an almas print found in fresh mud recently in Asia, and an again prehistoric preserved footprint of Cro-Magnon. Note the short big toe of Neanderthal and the current almas 'Bigfoot'. Were western scientists less preoccupied with dismissing all evidence concerning almas as nonsense, they might have observed this striking feature of the almas's foot.

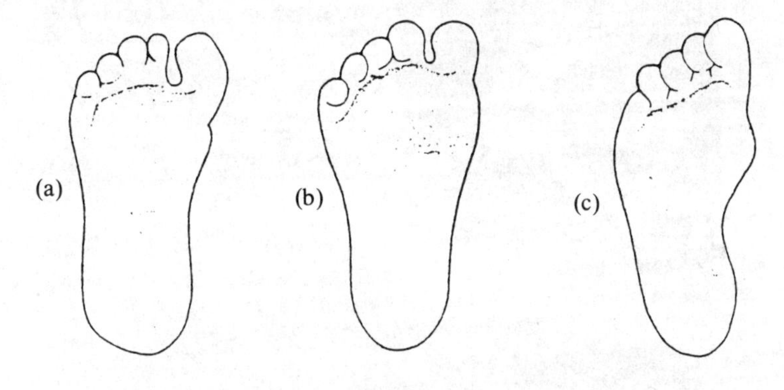

Figure 10
(a) Prehistoric Neanderthal footprint preserved in clay. (b) Footprint of an almas (Bigfoot) found recently in fresh mud in Asia. (c) Prehistoric Cro-Magnon footprint preserved in clay.

There are many portraits of wild men preserved throughout European and Asian history in stone, wood, paintings and drawings. Karin Cross, researching a book on unusual items in churches, turned up references to twenty-nine carvings (of which she kindly sent me details) on her first library visit. There are probably hundreds in all. A most superbly naturalistic stone portrait exists on a thirteenth-century French church. Here, with his captor, is the image of a living Neanderthal (*Figure 11a*). Many of the representations in the various art media are stylised. Sometimes these wild men lie at the feet of knights on carved tomb slabs, alongside the hunting dogs. These men were probably indeed hunted for sport in early medieval times. Mock wild men also took part in carnivals of the time. However, the stylised portrait shown in *Figure 11b*, from a church in Devon, is truly remarkable for us. The artist clearly intends to draw attention to the white, even teeth. There is nothing rotten about them (a fact which alone may have impressed people of the time), but the upper front incisor is missing.

Neanderthal skulls are found in Israel, Gibraltar and elsewhere, in which one or both of the front incisors have been deliberately removed during life.[166] Aboriginal Australian boys also have one or both upper incisors removed during the

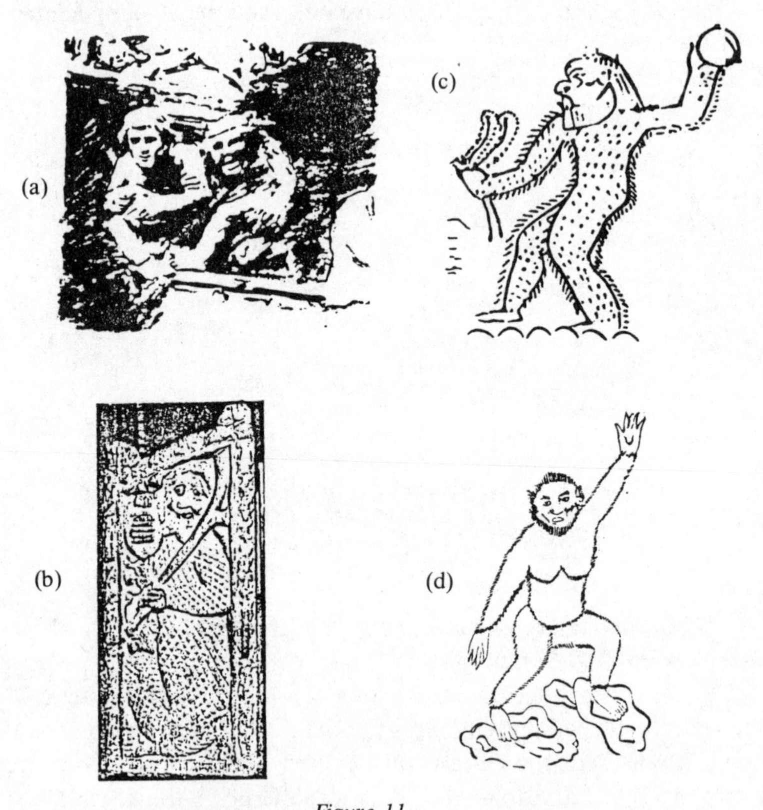

Figure 11

(a) Peasant and captured wild man from thirteenth century French church (Provence). (b) Stylised wild man from Devon, England, church, indicating possible ritual removal of upper front incisor tooth. (c) Wild man using left hand to throw a rock (?), Carthaginian bowl design (seventh century B.C.). (d) Mongolian wild man with left hand raised (eighteenth century Tibetan manuscript).

ceremony of initiation into manhood. In the circumstances, then, we seem to have a Neanderthal ritual custom stretching unbroken from actual Neanderthal times through medieval Europe and into present day Aboriginal Australia.

If the medieval Devon portrait is accepted as evidence of ritual removal of incisor teeth, then we here also have evidence that at that point in time Neanderthals were still numerous enough, and still organised enough, to conduct religious ritual.

The satyr, faun and silenus of classical times, often pictorially represented, are clearly stylised wild men. In some cases they are shown with all-over curly body-hair, though in others the hair is straight. Whether or not fauns and satyrs are accepted in evidence, bands of *actual* wild men on occasion attacked outlying towns in ancient Greece. One such event is recorded pictorially on a Carthaginian bowl (around 2600 BP). Here we see a wild man throwing what is probably a rock with his left hand, *Figure 11c. Figure 11d* shows a drawing of a wild man from an eighteenth-century Tibetan manuscript. This one is standing on rocks and appears to be waving, using his left hand.

Is it not remarkable that the only pictures we have that show wild men actually doing something show them using the left hand?

We note further that the man in *Figure 11c* has pointed ears, a feature also noted by Major Topilski. By pure coincidence perhaps, elves, goblins and fairies are also traditionally drawn with pointed ears. Note, further, the deep nasal notch.

There is a further behavioural item. Fauns and satyrs in classical literature are altogether renowned for their sexuality, and stylised drawings often show the males in a state of full erection (see Shackley's *Wild Men*). Albert Magnus, in the twelfth century, describes the male of a pair of wild people captured in Saxony (the woman soon died of dog bites). The man's 'lack of reason', according to Magnus, was evidenced 'by his ever trying to accost women and exhibit lustfulness'. Michael Wagner's wild boy, likewise, behaved thus: 'As soon as he saw a woman he broke out into violent cries of joy, and tried to express his awakened desires also through gestures.' These, we must stress, are actual wild men, not Greek tales concerning them. We have noted repeatedly the orgiastic nature of the echoes of Neanderthal ritual which come down to us in historical times. Was the exceptional lust of

Neanderthal male for female Neanderthal one potent reason for his acceptance of her social supremacy?

Many accounts mention the strong eyebrows of the almas. Zana had 'large eyebrows'. In Topilski's specimen 'the eyebrows were very powerful'. Wagner's boy had 'heavy brown eyebrows which projected out far over his eyes'. This external feature augments the heavy, projecting bone brow ridges which underlie the eyebrows – and provide us with one more vital clue to our understanding of Neanderthal. This matter is reserved for Chapter 17.

To conclude here, what we undoubtedly see in the almas is the fossil skeleton of Neanderthal given flesh, life and movement. The distinguished Mongolian scientist, Professor Y. Rinchen, collected many eyewitness reports of sightings of almas from shepherds and tribesmen during a period of fifty years. Again and again they are described as having sloping foreheads, prominent eyebrows and large jaws. Descriptions of the now tragically dwindling almas groups (yet we could *still* save them) continue to come in. An account from the early 1970s, published in the magazine *Mongolie* in 1980, is as follows.

> *... half men and half beasts with reddish-black hair. ... The back of the head has a conical shape as it were* [on this feature see Chapter 17], *the forehead is flattened, prominent brow ridges and a protruding jaw. The size of a medium height man, an almas walks with his knees bent, stoops, as is in-toed. Almas are easily frightened, suspicious ... and lead a nocturnal life.*[167]

How very clever of these Mongolian peasants to know all the anatomical characteristics of fossil Neanderthal. The almas 'lead a nocturnal life'. How also remarkably coincidental that their comment is in favour of the views of the present book.

16 The High Civilisation of Dreams

Empire

In 1936 a Frenchman, Xavier Guichard, published a 558-page book, printed at his own expense and titled *Eleus Alesia*. Most of the 500 copies were then destroyed in an accident. The book survives today only in one or two European museums. It has never been translated into English. One of the few sources of information of the book's contents is Francis Hitching's *World Atlas of Mysteries*, on which the present summary is based.

Gathering the subject matter of *Eleus Alesia* occupied most of Guichard's life. His findings are remarkable. He showed that the basic place name Alesia (derived from what he considers to be an Indo-European root *alès, alis* or *alles*; and signifying a meeting point to which people travelled) had been given to many hundreds of sites in Europe and beyond. All the sites involved are of prehistoric origin. The name has never been given to a town or village founded in historical times.

Most instances of the name occur in France, where there are over 400 sites. But the names extend as far as Kalisz in Poland, Eleusis on the Nile Delta, Eleusis in Greece, Allessano in the heel of Italy, La Aliseda in southern Spain, Calais on the north French coast, and Elisenfeld on the north German coast. There are no names at all in Britain, a fact which may be significant.

Guichard spent much of his life visiting the many sites in question, and established that they always had one of two characterising features: (a) they were on hills overlooking rivers, (b) they were built around a man-made well of salt or mineral water.

Guichard came to other conclusions. He considered that all the sites lay on lines radiating like the spokes of a wheel from the town of Alaise in southern France. He believed (1) that twenty-four extended, equi-spaced radiating lines, together with (2) a further four based on sunrise/sunset at the two equinoxes and the summer and winter solstice, touched every site.

Here we begin to run into problems of assessment. Maps as we find them in atlases are flat, but the real surface they represent is part of the curve of a sphere. To arrive at a flat model a notional projection has to be used, and there are different systems of projection which yield slightly different results. For reasons which are not stated, Hitching has reproduced not Guichard's original maps, but maps of his own, using a different projection technique. Even so, the degree of fit between lines and sites remains absolutely remarkable. A further possible query for me hangs over the total number of lines involved. On the basis of the information provided by Hitching it would seem that two of the equinox lines might be redundant. Were that the case, then we would have, instead of a total of 28 lines, a total of 26, which obviously from my own point of view would be far more satisfactory – for 26 is 13 × 2. My wish to 'force' the data into meaningful moon numbers is not entirely the result of megalomania. For when we look at another set of radiating lines, far distant in time and space, at the Inca capital Cuzco, we find moon numbers to be very much operant.

However, let us leave such speculation in respect of Guichard's lines, and summarise what he has established beyond doubt.

It is beyond doubt that many hundreds of inhabited towns and villages over a vast area bear a place name derived from one root name, Alesia. It is beyond doubt that all of these sites were so named prior to historic recorded time. It is beyond doubt that the names cluster most thickly around the town of Alaise in southern France, and become sparser as we move away from that centre. It is beyond doubt that a regular system of straight lines drawn as radiating spokes from Alaise as centre or hub touch (or in a minority of cases only, very nearly touch) all the sites in question. It is beyond doubt that all the sites overlook a river, or enclose a man-made well, not of ordinary water but of mineral or salt water.

In view of the evidence presented throughout this book, this last reference must alert us strongly to a probable moon influence. A significant further question also arises – how did prehistoric man decide where to dig in order to find underground mineral water? Is there some rational, conscious way of deciding? Or are we talking here again about the extra-sensory capacity of dowsing?

There is another important connection with our general subject matter. The Greek town of Eleusis, one of Guichard's towns, and whose origins are lost in the mists of pre-Homeric times, was the centre of 'the most famous and secret religious rites of ancient Greece', known to be in existence already in 5000 BP. Little is known about the rites themselves, even though they persisted as the major, twice-yearly Athenian festival throughout the lifetime of the Greek empire. In general terms, however, they were fertility ceremonies, connected with the corn-moon goddess Demeter and her daughter Persephone. Certainly originally these were orgiastic – involving, as Frazer puts it, 'indecencies, licentiousness, obscenities'. More than just orgiastic in fact, for human sacrifice would certainly have been involved. The cult of Dionysus was a further aspect of these Mysteries, run solely by priestesses. Any man who intruded on these rites was torn to pieces, as no doubt were the sacrificial victims themselves. We have seen echoes of that particular situation persisting in late historical Europe and Africa. (It is an interesting reflection that in former times it was men who were put to death for violating female religious rites; whereas among the Australian Aborigines and the North American Indians, it is women who are put to death for violating male religious rites.)

Is it pure coincidence that this same Greek Eleusis just happens to be one of Guichard's sites?

My own view, very much, is that Guichard's research has succeeded in locating the outlines, the physical remains, of the Neanderthal empire. Whether or not we accept *alès/alis/alles* as an Indo-European root is immaterial. I suspect that we are dealing with an Indo-Europeanisation of a Neanderthal word – but perhaps the sites were renamed at some point.

A number of other items impress me. First, that most of the sites are in France – that is, in western Europe, where classic Neanderthal evolved. Classic Neanderthal was the extreme variety, squat, barrel-bodied, powerfully muscled and no doubt extremely hairy – very much the typical troll in fact – as adaptational response to the extreme cold. We noted that there are no Alesia sites in Britain, or in Europe north of Calais (with the one exception of Elisenfeld). During the ice age the glaciers had advanced permanently as far as London, and roughly along the same parallel throughout Europe.

Now, if the descendants of Cro-Magnon named the sites from 10,000 BP onward, which was when the ice age came to an end, why are there none in Britain and Scandinavia, which then became free of ice? One would have expected at least a few. The same arguments, and another, apply to the warm interstadial around 30,000 BP which first tempted Cro-Magnon into Europe. This other argument is that at *that* point Europe was still occupied by Neanderthal, whom Cro-Magnon was in the process of replacing. These were hardly conditions in which one would easily be able to set about establishing a grid of named sites.

The grid we are discussing is really an item that could only be set up during a very long, settled spell of occupation by one unified people. Again, such conditions hardly existed after 10,000 BP (when the re-emergent ice-sheets once more retreated) for almost at once the various nations and peoples we know today began to come into existence. It is really highly unlikely that in such times of ferment the agreement and co-operation required for the establishment of some overriding network could have been achieved. On the other hand, however, Neanderthal had occupied the whole of the area we are discussing, continuously and unchallenged, for something like 100,000 years and more. These are the right conditions for large-scale consolidation and for putting down these kind of roots.

We have already discussed aspects of the Nasca lines of Peru (Chapter 5). There appear to be three kinds of phenomena here. One is the animal and maze drawings. Another comprises long, straight, isolated lines which can run on for miles, and are apparently aimed at particular events on the horizon, such as sunrise or moonrise on given dates, or star risings. Re-alignments sometimes occur in these lines either in response to, or in order to test, the occurrence of precession (see Chapter 4). The third phenomenon, which we are concerned with here, are points or centres where lines radiate or converge. Here the lines are like 'the spokes of a cartwheel'. The word line itself, or *ceque*, Tony Morrison further tells us,[132] has a definite religious significance. Dotted along these radiating lines at intervals are small shrines. We shall return to these shortly. But does not this picture of lines radiating (sometimes for appreciable distances) from a centre, and dotted with shrines, remind us very much of the lines, and the towns, radiating from Alaise in France?

Further evidence comes from the Inca Temple of the Sun at Cuzco, several hundred miles away from the Nasca lines, Cuzco being the ancient Inca capital. Writing in 1653 a priest, Father Cobo, kept records of structures and customs that were very quickly destroyed by the Spaniards. Father Cobo reports that from the Cuzco Temple of the Sun as a centre, lines radiated in all directions. Four main lines divided the city into four main quarters – and these lines extended right through the Inca Empire. In each of three of the quarters were three groups of three lines. (As we shall see, three is the Incas' most important sacred number – so the moon influence here is quite clear.) The fourth quarter contained either fourteen or fifteen lines – Father Cobo is not sure which. Fifteen would be better, for our purposes, since it is a multiple of three. The total number of lines, forty-two, is alas not a multiple of thirteen. The radiating lines, in Inca times, extended well into the open countryside beyond Cuzco. Along each of the lines were many shrines, as at Nasca, between four and fifteen per line. Some shrines were or are springs, some hills, others just open places.

The following comments on shrines are important. At Nasca, which in general is a smaller-scale phenomenon, they consist often of heaps of stones or boulders. The commonest number of boulders in a shrine is three. At the shrines sacrifices were made – small animals and trinket offerings at small ones, large-scale human sacrifice at others. Those sacrificed were often children.

Human sacrifice was the most valuable offering that could be made and such sacrifices were generally performed in times

> *of great need: famine, epidemics or disaster in war. Also Inca ceremonial occasions often involved ritual sacrifices and at one 'coronation' 200 children were slaughtered: they were selected for their perfection, like the animals used in lesser sacrifices. The children had to walk round the shrine three times. The older ones were made drunk on chicha, a maize beer, and then,* after being strangled with a cord, *their hearts were cut out to be offered, still beating, to the blood-spattered shrine.*[132] *(emphasis added)*

There is much here to remind us of material we have already studied. Highly significant, certainly, is the strangling with a cord – exactly the method used in the Bog Sacrifices of Europe.

Three appears to be the most sacred number of Inca life – there were also three kinship groups in Inca society, for example. Perhaps we should stress here, having not so far done so, the great importance of the number three throughout *Asia* – from where of course the distant ancestors of the Incas once came. (Europe and the Middle East we have already considered in some detail on three – though we did not discuss its central role in fairy-tales.) The translators of the significantly named book *Three Lives* (which is about 3500 years old) tell us that a flick through any Chinese dictionary will produce a flood of items concerning three: the Three Principles (essence, breath and spirit), the Three Primordial Powers (heaven, earth and water), the Three-Inch Golden Lilies (the bound feet of women), the Three Principles of the People, the Three States of Existence, the Three Religions (Buddhism, Taoism and Confucianism), and the Three Holy Ones of the Three Religions. The translators cite one dictionary with almost three hundred entries including three. They conclude that three has a 'very highly charged significance' within the boundaries of each of the specific faiths of Buddhism, Taoism and Confucianism, and equally across the spiritual and geographical boundaries of all three.[146]

Next to the importance of the Inca three, however, seven is also very much to the fore. On the *quipus*, bundles of knotted string extensively used to record information – which, unfortunately, we are completely unable to decipher – the most common numbers found are, by far, seven and multiples of seven. 'Seven had obviously been an important number... Erlund Nordenskiöld noticed the recurring seven, and so developed the idea that it was a sacred number.'[132] Here is a further seven, then, which Geoffrey Ashe seems to have missed (see Chapter 11).

One last point before returning to the significance of the Alaise, Cuzco and Nasca lines – for it is nevertheless important that we establish links also in our standard material between Inca Peru and Europe. The more and clearer such links we find, the stronger the case then for speculative links also. So Tony Morrison writes again:

> *The most famous of the ancient Cuzco races was held at the boys' puberty festival: after sacrifices of llamas had first been made at Huanacauri and then in the Great Plaza, the boys raced recklessly down another steep hill, Anahuarque. At the 'finishing post' young maidens are said to have 'waited upon them with vases of maize beer'.*[132]

Are we not powerfully reminded of the maze race in Finland 'where a girl stood at the centre, while the boys raced for her along the winding paths'?

The lines radiating from the Temple of the Sun in Cuzco – might they not well represent the sun's rays, given very much the fact that we are speaking of sun worship here? I would accept that these are indeed the sun's rays, not just at Cuzco and Nasca, but at Alaise also. Nevertheless, we shall see in the next section that this interpretation does not in fact conflict with an overriding moon interpretation.

However – with that said – are not the radiating lines at Alaise, Cuzco and Nasca *really* the radial lines of a spider's web? And are not the shrines along them the joins of the connecting spiral thread? And is it not probably further the case that the worshippers went not up and down the straight lines (which would be in any case a little boring) but instead followed the spiral spider path from shrine to shrine *across* the lines – starting at the outer edge probably, and working towards the great central shrine? Here could be a good reason also why the Alesia towns become sparser as we move away from Alaise – because the spirals of the web become wider. The spider's web is dense towards the centre, spaced out towards the edge.

The image here is clear, I think. One may of course reject this as a mere coincidence, or consider its choice an undue forcing of the evidence. But the image as such is, clearly, potentially there. We have the centre of the web – the central shrine. We have the radial lines from it, which are clearly drawn. And we have the idea of the approaching, spiralling worshippers, marking in the non-visible spirals of the web with their footsteps. The additional and undisputable fact that five of the twenty-six Nasca drawings contain spirals, and that another is actually a giant spider, must further support this last interpretation.

Did therefore the Neanderthal peoples of Europe undertake vast pilgrimages, lasting sometimes years, through the great spider web of Europe around Alaise? Yes, I think they did. Why not? In our own historical times people have made trips to Jerusalem, and to Mecca, that also lasted years.

Now, I think, we catch a glimpse of the glory of the spiritual empire of Neanderthal, the mass of people wheeling slowly, night by night, about the central shrine of Alaise ('a meeting place to which people travelled'), as the great stars wheeled also above them.

Cosmos

We come in the next section to further detail on Neanderthal religion. Here we first look briefly at actual and possible Neanderthal cosmology.

I think myself, though there seems no way of proving it apart from the suggestions in Chapter 10, that Neanderthal understood that the sun was a fixed point, and that the earth and the five other visible planets revolved about it – but in his philosophy or metaphysics this schema took a particular form. For Neanderthal, the sun was the centre of a web. The sun's straight rays (observable in any forest where the sun penetrates) were the radial lines of the web, and the planets described the spirals. The moon herself was the spider. People and animals were the spider's children (spiders do produce teeming myriads of tiny offspring). In terms of objective logic the picture is, of course, faulty – but it is perfectly acceptable within the boundaries of religious logic.

Rays and magnetism were somehow connected. On earth, the splinters of lodestone (see Chapter 2) pointed always north and thus gave the north-south axis. The motions of the moon and sun east-west and west-east gave the other axis of the four-point compass.

The magnetite needle pointed always north, and in the north sky was the still centre of the heavens, about which all the other stars and constellations turned. Perhaps for Neanderthal the stars and their Pole Star centre were the Great Web, the moon, sun and planets the Lesser Web. The north in any case was obviously the home of the moon for another reason: as you approached north everything became white, the moon's own special colour, including all the animals. Guarding the way finally were the massive white polar bears, larger even than the huge brown bears. In the sky the seven Polar Bears of Ursa Major guarded the eight stars of the constellation we call the Little Bear (but did Neanderthal call it that?), or the Little Dipper, that contains the Polar Star itself.

Let us dwell on this last point. The constellation at the very centre of the sky contains eight stars. Could Neanderthal possibly have viewed that situation as a coincidence – of course not. The central constellation of the sky has eight stars, just as the spider has eight limbs.

Perhaps for Neanderthal it was to her home in the constellation of the Pole Star that the Moon, and in her incarnation as the Ice Queen, went during the three days when absent from our skies.

Religion

Neanderthal religion was satisfying and sustaining to its people to an extent that is very hard for us to grasp – for do not forget also that they were inventing the world for the very first time. We see a little of that sustaining power among Jews, joyfully welcoming the Sabbath Bride each Friday evening during all their centuries of exile and persecution, and again in the current, unfortunately mainly negative, fanaticism of Moslems. For orthodox Jews and Moslems alike, prayer and observance is not just the major activity but the very purpose of each day. Jews pray a minimum of three times a day ('would that man would pray all day' – Rabbi Yohanan). Moslems are enjoined to pray five times, but tradition has it that this was once fifty times.[92]

For Neanderthal, sex itself was a religious rite, and in fact the most important religious rite of all – as it was also for witches,

Satanists, and in the early Mystery cults of the Near and Middle East, and again among some aboriginal peoples of the present day. An echo of this situation survives in the Jewish religion, where husband and wife are told to make love on Friday nights, for then the chances of a 'high soul' reincarnating in their child are greater.

Like all adequate religions, Neanderthal religion had a place and an explanation for everything. For example, sap rose in trees in spring, just like the spring tides, because all liquid was under the direct control of the moon. Therefore trees were sacred to the moon, since they were full of liquid – but then, so was every living thing. Liquid *is* life. But in trees they actually observed the sap rising, at the moon's call.

Ritual practice and prayer would have taken up the greater physical, as well as the metaphysical, part of every day that could be spared from life's necessities, as was till recently the case with Australian Aborigines and American Indians. Perhaps once during his or her lifetime the individual Neanderthal made all or part of the great spiral pilgrimage to Alaise. (This is no outrageous idea, for aside from the pilgrimages to Mecca and Jerusalem already mentioned, we have also in our own times the walkabout of the Aboriginal initiate, the *wanderjahre* of the apprentice, and the Grand Tour of the wealthy youngster.)

We have already discussed many other features of Neanderthal religion throughout the book – circumcision, the role of salt, blood, human sacrifice and so on – and will not take space here to discuss these further (see Index). But perhaps we should put stress, in case the point has been missed, on the fact that Neanderthal was a thorough cannibal – that is, in a religious context. Children especially were sacrificed and eaten – but precisely because these were most valued and most loved. (This circumstance of child sacrifice is why also witches, Jews and others were accused, quite wrongly, of eating children. It was said specifically that Jews slaughtered Christian children and used the blood for their Passover bread. These are actually dim memories of Neanderthal times, in this particular case of the spring rites.) The sacrifice and eating of an individual, adult or child, conferred nothing but blessings on him or her in the after-life, and ensured speedy and fortunate reincarnation. Frazer tells us that the American Indians of recent times had no fear whatsoever of death. The same was so of the Celts. For Neanderthal the position was quite simply that there was no such thing as death – only change and rebirth.

We have still not answered the central question, why should the spider and the snake have been chosen as the major symbols of Neanderthal moon religion? For, as already pointed out, there seem no obvious links at all between, particularly, the spider and the moon.

It is true that the snake sloughs its old skin periodically and is 'reborn' new, somewhat in the way that the moon is born anew after her cycle. And it is true that snakes wind along, something like rivers, and quite often enter water. Yet these are not specially compelling reasons – for other creatures also shed their skins, and swim. It is true again, in a sense, that the moon can be thought of as drawing up the tides by invisible magnetic threads. But once again, here is hardly at all a compelling reason to use the spider as a major symbol.

The central reason for the choice of spider and snake is disarmingly simple. Whereas in the vast majority of species of animals readily on view the male animal is larger than the female, in both spiders and snakes *the female is larger than the male.* A society led by women would naturally find these two exceptions to the standard rule both at once important and satisfying. Put it another way. Would men be likely to make such a choice?

There is more. The male spider has to be very careful with the female, especially when mating. Otherwise she kills him. He must approach her slowly and humbly, playing little 'tunes' on the strings of her web, until such time as she signals back that he may draw near. Sometimes she kills him after the mating anyway! In the male spider, the sexually dominated and manipulated Neanderthal male, victim of his own insatiable lust, also saw himself mirrored. Out of precisely this situation the legendary stories of Circe and the Cave of the Lady Venus arise, where men are sexually enslaved to women. Once again we understand that these legends are not fantasies or fairy-tales (in the usual sense) at all, but statements of historical fact.

A further point to note here is that *in the lizard the male, in accordance with the usual rule, is larger than the female.* Here is another important reason why we must see the dragon always as a stylised snake, never as a stylised lizard (see Chapter 10), and these circumstances again very much underline the specificity of the snake as a symbol choice.

Magic

For Neanderthal, magic and religion would have been indivisible commodities; or for that matter, life, religion and magic. So we speak now of magic rather as perceived by Cro-Magnon and by our own culture.

There are today men in eastern countries, although some westerners can also duplicate the effects, who can drive skewers and knives through their flesh, without feeling pain, and without the removed implements producing bleeding, or leaving anything other than the faintest marks in the flesh. Others can cause bleeding from an open wound to stop, or start again, simply by taking thought. Others can similarly stop their hearts beating, without ill effects.[70] These results have all been achieved under test conditions in laboratories – which is not to say, however, that one finds them discussed in standard text books.

Theresa Neumann, a twentieth-century German stigmatic, who died only in 1962, could produce the wounds of Christ on her body at will, and also weep tears of blood. Such individuals are actually not at all uncommon in devout Catholic communities. In 1933 the psychiatrist Alfred Lechler published his report on one of his patients, Elizabeth K. She could produce the wounds of Christ on experimental command, cause them to bleed or stop bleeding, and weep tears of blood. In the medical journal *The Lancet* in 1946 and 1948 Dr R.L. Moody published independently witnessed reports and photographs of patients who could reproduce wounds suffered in childhood on their bodies, simply by talking about them.[114,130]

We need not continue this catalogue. Suffice it to say that most, if not all, Neanderthal individuals could almost certainly and readily produce even stronger effects than any of those noted here. For that part of the brain that governs these and other autonomic responses is principally the cerebellum, and Neanderthal had a much larger cerebellum than either Cro-Magnon or ourselves (see Chapter 17).

By the very same token, Neanderthals were probably excellent subjects for hypnosis. Under conditions of hypnosis and/or hysteria these people could probably produce feats of strength and endurance that Cro-Magnon found quite staggering and even appalling. From such circumstances arise then perhaps stories of 'monsters' and 'supernatural beings' who cannot be killed except by, say, being pierced through the heart (as with Dracula and others) or by being beheaded. Is this perhaps also where the cult of the skull begins?

We need hardly mention, except in passing, the phenomenon of trance and 'spirit possession'. These would have been much to the fore in Neanderthal ecstatic religious ceremony.

Neanderthal's undoubted knowledge of the curative properties of herbs has already been discussed (Chapter 8). The precise extent of his medical expertise remains a matter for speculation. However, in legends we sometimes find what appear to be (and certainly could be) garbled accounts of quite remarkable medical knowledge. For example, in Greek legend, Prometheus was punished for stealing the secret of fire from the gods. The punishment given was for his liver to be pecked out and eaten by an eagle. Why the liver – an odd choice – why not the heart, or eyes or whatever? After being eaten, Prometheus's liver always grew again, so that the punishment was eternal. It just so happens that we know today that the liver is the only major internal human organ that is capable of regeneration. Then again, in both Europe and China, tradition has it that one of the ways of driving off a vampire is by the use of fresh garlic. As recent research shows, however, eating fresh garlic rapidly, within days, significantly reduces the level of blood cholesterol, a major cause of heart attacks. Did Neanderthal understand that garlic is good against 'that which harms the blood'?

Neanderthal may or may not have known of alcohol. But we can be quite certain that he had discovered the mind-altering and hallucinogenic qualities of some mushrooms and other plants. Graves tells us that some of these were used in the orgiastic Mystery rites. (It is most interesting, of course, that the fairy-folk are typically associated with mushrooms and toadstools.) When, therefore, we find tales of the lone traveller in distant hills or forests, who meets strange people who give him food or drink, whereafter he is transported to fairy land, it is quite clear that we are discussing the administration of mind-altering drugs. What else could the unwitting recipient think, other than that he had been transported to another world? So yet again we see that fairy stories are statements of historical fact.

The further probability is that Neanderthal also possessed what are usually called extra-sensory or paranormal abilities beyond the level at which we observe them in our own time. Such matters, like so much else in the present book, are totally ignored or scorned by the academic establishment. But as Kathleen Raine remarked, the paranormal does not require the permission of science to exist. Ronald Rose reports that Australian Aborigines sense the death of members of the tribe who are away on hunting trips or other business. Such awareness often takes the form of hallucinating the absent individual's totem animal.[159] Telepathy, then, as well as the ability to perceive aspects of the future paranormally, were fairly certainly in Neanderthal's mental armoury. Once again, these matters appear to be connected with the functioning of the cerebellum.[69]

Legend

The whole of this book is really concerned with different aspects of the legend of Neanderthal. Many of the matters studied have of course hitherto *not* been perceived as cultural and verbal traditions and practices deriving directly from Neanderthal times and actual Neanderthal existence. That position, one hopes, will now change.

Here we can mention a further point of some importance. The skull of Neanderthal man shows that, from his receding forehead, heavily armoured bone projected out over the eyes, as it does also in the case of Australian Aborigines (see *Figure 13* in the Appendix). Sometimes this projection took the form of a continous shelf of bone, but more often it divided at the centre, between the eyes. As we know from actual living almas (see Chapter 15), out of those brow projections also sprouted strongly projecting eyebrows. It is not at all unusual in nature to find bony projections further augmented by hair, fur or feathers – the furred hump of the American buffalo is a good example. We also see such projecting eyebrows in occasional human males today – for instance in the Labour politician, Dennis Healey.

Do we not understand that these bony projections, and the augmenting eyebrows, are horns? I am sure that Neanderthal, proudly, perceived his species as 'the horned people'. To Cro-Magnon also – whose skull had no such bony projections at all, see *Figure 13* – these were horned human beings. Add to the picture, further, the short, powerful body of Neanderthal, and his manner of walking with a slight forward inclination (see Chapter 15) – and we have the bull-man, the creature with the body of a man and the head of a bull.

Here is the deepest and most central meaning of the figure of the Greek Minotaur. The Minotaur is Neanderthal man. That, however, is not at all to say that our earlier interpretations of this figure are either incorrect, or alternative. (It is all one.)

Much follows from this picture. Here is why the Christian devil, along with Pan and other figures, has horns. Here is why two raised fingers connotes rampant sexuality. Here also is why the Vikings and other peoples wore helmets with horns. As with the snake worn at the Pharoah's forehead and the dragon-winged helmet, these are all essentially the same statement: we have conquered the people of the bull/of the snake/of the dragon, and taken their powers to ourselves.

Again we see what a powerful and comprehensive explanatory tool we have in the model proposed by the present book.*

A last word on the topic of the Neanderthal 'empire'. In terms of places where the fossil bones of Neanderthal are found, his geographical range was from Africa in the south to northern Russia in the north, and from the French seaboard to western Russia and the Middle East in the east. His remains are *not* found in central or eastern Asia. (Finds in Mongolia are very late, not earlier than 20,000 BP, and Myra Shackley, for one, considers these to be displaced, refugee and not indigenous Neanderthals.) We need to be quite clear that in the period when Neanderthal flourished, and of which we are speaking, there were no men of any kind in central or eastern Asia, or in North or South America, or in the Pacific, or in Australia. The diffusionists we spoke of in Chapter 14 had great and, indeed, insuperable problems in getting their 'seed' civilisation transported around the world. The present book has much smaller problems in this respect. The cultural ideas it discusses did not spread to Asia, America, the

* Neanderthal is, of course, also the hairy creature that moves about by night, drinks blood, is ruled by the moon – the werewolf, vampire and so on. Again, all legends are history.

Pacific and Australia in any *secondary* sense. The ideas were brought with them on a purely primary basis by the first inhabitants of those areas.

Though widespread by some standards, then, Neanderthal distribution was nevertheless relatively contained, and in any case continuous. Throughout the entire area the ideas and the culture described in this book held sway, with but minor variations here and there.

Are we suggesting that everyone in this none the less broad geographical area spoke the same language? No, not at all. How then was communication achieved? The answer lies, I think, in the situation which prevailed subsequently in North America and Australia. In North America there were at one time as many as 1000 different languages. In Australia there were perhaps 600 languages. But on both these continents a sophisticated sign language had been developed, which enabled every Indian, or Aboriginal, to talk to every other.

Precisely the same situation existed, I suggest, throughout the entire Neanderthal empire. I consider this view confirmed by the fact that ancient magicians casting spells are always said to make mysterious passes with their hands. These for me, must be the remnants of the Neanderthal *lingua franca* of signs. It is very possible that *the basic native language* of Neanderthal was *also* partly composed of signs. This interesting possibility, however, seems never to have occurred to our academic and scientific establishments.

17 Biological Imperative

In 1979 a study of handedness among 1045 students at an American college produced the following results. Those majoring in music showed an incidence of left-handedness of 14.9 per cent. The visual arts majors had a 12.2 per cent incidence in this respect. But the science majors showed only 4.4 per cent left-handedness.[150]

Some would wish no doubt to argue that some kind of environmental pressure must be operating to force lefties into the arts rather than the sciences. I think, rather, that students are naturally drawn into areas where their talents happen to lie and where they feel most comfortable. Perhaps one might also like to reflect what environmental pressures operated in the case of Nadia, a left-handed autistic child. At the age of three and a half Nadia 'suddenly' began producing the most remarkable drawings, and continued to do so for several years. Her studies of people sitting with crossed legs, of horses approaching head-on at full gallop, would not be out of place in Leonardo's sketch books. Nadia's case and many examples of her drawings can be seen in Lorna Selfe's book about her.[164] Among aspects of the case which particularly interest me is, for instance, the fact that when she dressed herself Nadia would often put her clothes on the wrong way round.

There are very many aspects of left-handedness which relate to the issues raised in the present book, but for which we have no space here, and details of which can be found in my earlier books.[64,69,72] All these are part of what I used to call the Dark Continent, a vast tract of unknown territory which has so far never been explored. Nowadays I tend to call it the Dark Planet – a planet which has not only never been investigated by establishment scientists, but whose very existence is denied by them.

What, however, of the findings of Teng's study of a Chinese population, which we looked at in Chapter 12, where an overall incidence of 18 per cent left-handedness was reported? Left-handedness is anathema in China, as we saw, so the physical predisposition *itself* can in no way be environmentally induced – that predisposition has to be biological and genetic. What might be the biological explanation of left-handedness, both in China and elsewhere?

The answer, for myself, is transparent (and has only in a secondary sense to do with hemispheres of the cerebrum). For it just happens to be the case that Asiatics have a far larger cerebellum than western Europeans, 'very incompletely covered by the cerebrum'.[17] It also just happens to be the case that the cerebellum itself is left-handed, in a very precise sense. For whereas in the case of the cerebrum or main brain (however the description 'main brain' is entirely chauvinistic – since the cerebellum is in many respects more highly evolved than the cerebrum[69,72]) the right side of the body is governed by the left cerebral hemisphere, and the left side by the right cerebral hemisphere, in the case of the cerebellum the left hemisphere governs the left side of the body, and the right hemisphere the right side. As a consequence of this very odd arrangement, impulses between the two major brains, the cerebrum and the cerebellum (a very heavy traffic, incidentally), must cross over *en route* in order to reach the appropriate but, in fact opposite, hemisphere.

Let us describe the situation at once more simply and more dramatically. When the cerebrum 'looks at' the cerebellum it has the same experience as we have when we look at ourselves in a mirror. Our mirror image is left-handed. When we reach out our right hand towards it, it reaches out its left hand to us. The cerebrum likewise confronts an image of itself that is opposite-handed.

What then is the relevance of these various speculations and propositions for our subject matter? The relevance is that Neanderthal man had a far larger cerebellum than either Cro-Magnon or ourselves – far larger even than the cerebellum of present-day Asiatics. Moreover, Neanderthal also had a relatively smaller cerebrum than either ourselves or Cro-Magnon, as the backward-sloping forehead already indicates.

To accommodate his larger cerebellum, Nature extended the back or occiput of Neanderthal's head in a large protuberance or bun, sometimes called the 'occipital rose'. The Mongolian and other tribespeople, as we saw, include this skull feature in their descriptions of present-day almas. Obviously they had read up the subject beforehand.

The large cerebellum of Neanderthal is one of my reasons (but only one among many) for suspecting that this variety of man was left-handed. The question of Neanderthal's possible left-handedness need not at all, however, remain a matter for speculation. His handedness could be demonstrated at this very moment by two methods, one direct, one indirect.

Writing in the 1920s, Sir Elliot Grafton Smith, one of the diffusionists we met in Chapter 14, by profession a distinguished anatomist and anthropologist, demonstrated that the right arm of adult right-handers is longer than their left arm simply through use, even though at birth the two arms are the same length. So, likewise, for the left arm of left-handers. Smith and his associates also established that the examination after death of slight markings on the inner skulls of individuals, due to the differing action of the dominant and minor cerebral hemispheres, could establish whether the individual had been left-handed or right-handed during life. I have not seen either of these techniques since refuted – but nor does either seem to have been taken up. Nevertheless, the position is that the examination of the fossil remains of Neanderthal man could at this moment demonstrate his handedness.[172]

One of the several possible indirect approaches to the question is as follows. Neanderthal, particularly classic Neanderthal, was extremely short. The average height for classic Neanderthal males was 5 ft 4 in, for females 4 ft 10 in. (Here are Margaret Murray's 'little people', whom she postulated but could not find: she simply did not look back far enough.) Cro-Magnon was tall – the male's average height was initially thought to be 6 ft, females some four inches shorter, but later finds have somewhat reduced those original estimates. To this information concerning height we add the fact that some living individuals today possess the short big toe of Neanderthal. We then add the, this time, hypothesis that Neanderthal was left-handed. It should be the case, therefore, that, when large samples of present-day human beings are examined, more males and females who are below average adult height for their sex and also possess a short big toe should show a higher incidence of left-handedness. (I have personally located a number of individuals with all three attributes, but have not succeeded so far in obtaining funds for a full-scale enquiry.)

The subject of the present book, however, is not in the first place biological, but psychological, cultural and sociological. We are therefore not concerned centrally with the correlation of physical factors one with another, but in correlating such factors with personality attributes. One would be interested to show, for example, that left-handed individuals, or those with a large cerebellum, were more interested in religion, especially in ecstatic or mystical religion, than those who are right-handed or have a small cerebellum.

After a lecture which I gave at a denominational, that is, Catholic College of Further Education in London, one of the novice nuns, a Chinese girl, herself left-handed, approached me and told me that she was herself interested in the question of handedness. She had formed the impression that there were, among the students and novices of the College, more left-handers than one would expect on a random basis. She promised to do a proper count and send me the results. For whatever reason, I never heard further from her. Perhaps she abandoned the enterprise herself. Possibly the authorities of the College intervened. Hopefully this last comment does not sound too paranoid, but in my experience such intervention is far from rare.

The issue of left-handedness could be very usefully pursued in connections likely to cause maximum discomfort for the orthodox establishment. Is it the case, for example, that left-handed individuals would score higher in tests of telepathy and precognition than right-handers? Oh, but surely that possibility has already been investigated? No, on the contrary, despite the major role which the left hand is traditionally alleged to play in magical and paranormal activity of all kinds, no attempt whatsoever at the investigation of left-handedness in this respect has been made at any time. The various organisations which exist for the study of the paranormal are, in fact, only marginally less obtuse than the academic establishment itself.

Since we are discussing 'biological imperatives' this is an appropriate point to look at the archetype, a concept built upon above all by C.G. Jung. The essential and central attribute of an archetype is that it arises, and can only arise, from the biological history of the species concerned.

Most heterosexual individuals, for example, have an idealised image of a hypothetical member of the opposite sex with whom they will fall in love for ever, as indeed that person will with them. This archetype of the 'magical' lover is heavily endowed with all the attributes that the opposite sex generally admires. So the female lover, for the male, will have matchless beauty and will also be a virgin. The male lover, for the female, 'Mr Right', will be appropriately 'tall, dark and handsome'. (Already the words 'tall' and 'right' suggest that we are dealing here with a Cro-Magnon archetype, see below, although the 'dark' is a little odd.) The ideal-lover archetype is strongest in us when we are young, in the years just after puberty in fact, when in our distant biological past pair-bonding would have occurred.

We can usefully divert here for a moment on the subject of pair bonding. My own view is that pair bonding – the permanent sexual union between two members of a species for life ('forsaking all others') – was a situation that arose in the biological evolution of Cro-Magnon, but not of Neanderthal. In apes, for example, we find pair bonding in the orang-utan and the gibbon, but not in the chimpanzee or the gorilla. In the last two we find what is crudely called the 'gang-bang', that is, promiscuous group sex. All members of the group have sex with all others, the males literally one after the other in group rank order with any female who happens to come into heat. Here I think we see, quite clearly and beyond question, the biological origins of Neanderthal orgiastic behaviour. The biological make-up of Neanderthal contained an orgiastic archetype, in contrast to a pair bonding one.

Yet given that archetypal impulses are genetically inherited and determined, what then occurs in a species which is a hybrid cross between two parent species carrying essentially incompatible archetypes? This is a question we consider in a little more detail below – but we can say here that there are two possibilities: (1) one particular archetype may be weakened or watered down, (2) the two essentially incompatible archetypal impulses can both persist, intact, active and at full strength in the one individual.

Returning to the general concept of the archetype, the individual can have, and often necessarily does have, an in-built archetypal response to any biological situation. (There is a complication which need not detain us here, namely, that the higher primates appear to be in the process of evolving beyond the archetype, or rather its biological base, as a controlling mechanism, just as they have in fact already abandoned many other instinctive behaviours found in lower animals.) So, a further example, both male and female human adults have an idealised view both of the baby they intend to produce and the actual baby itself. This will be/is the golden child, the wonderful boy (yes, the archetype here *is* slanted towards the male child), the saviour (of the people, of the future) and so on. This wonderful-child archetype tends to 'wear out' as the youngster gets older (and in the face of its *actual* behaviour!).

Such are one or two clearly definable archetypes. There are other variations however. A related biological phenomenon, which Jung also calls an archetype, but which I prefer to call by a term of my own, the archestructure,[64] is when we respond archetypally to some aspect of our own nervous system and/or anatomy. Thus our two major brains, cerebrum and cerebellum, have, in all, four hemispheres. I consider that our involvement in four-fold arrangements or mandalas (including possibly the four points of the compass), to which Jung drew attention, arises from that structural circumstance (though Jung himself does not propose this). Jung did find however that the four-fold mandala did tend to appear in the dreams of his patients when they were nearing the end of a successful analysis. For myself, this would be when all four centres of the higher nervous system were working together harmoniously and not antagonistically. A more obvious and less debatable example of the physical archetype, or archestructure, is further found in our perceptions of right-handedness and left-handedness.

Another form of archetype concerns events or objects in our environment to which we, again, establish an archetypal relationship. But there *must*, for the situation to qualify, again be a definable *biological* connection between the external object/event and the individual. We see the mechanism concerned operating very clearly in lower organisms. For example, the young of game-birds will instinctively run for cover if the shadow of a hawk passes over their heads. Experimentally, however, we can produced a stylised hawk which does a better job of frightening the youngsters than the real thing! So these are not responding so much to an actual hawk as to 'hawkness'. As said, the external event need not be another organism – it can be a physical object, a place, a situation. All apes, for example, even those that spend much of their time on the ground, prefer to climb into trees to sleep for the night. We ourselves also have this same bias for going 'upstairs' to bed (and not, for choice, into the cellar for example). So the place 'up trees' or 'upstairs' has an archetypal appeal for all apes including ourselves. It reassures us.

The concept of the external archetype is important for the present book, for it does look as if Neanderthal had evolved an archetypal response to the moon – possibly because of the, again, possibly greater influence of the moon on the Neanderthal female menstrual cycle – while Cro-Magnon, for his part, had evolved an archetypal response to the sun. This last in Cro-Magnon would have been an outcome of evolving in conditions of low sunlight (perhaps on the plains of northern India or central Asia, which during ice ages would have had only a temperate climate and possibly much overcast skies). The action of sunlight on skin is one of our very few ways of obtaining vitamin D. Cro-Magnon resolved his problem, biologically, by developing a pale skin and equally a compulsive attraction towards lying in the sun – which is, why for example, most of us today seek sun-drenched beaches and sunny climes for our holidays and recreation. Neanderthal – being in any case, as I believe, nocturnal or semi-nocturnal in habit – never solved this biological problem, so that rickets, caused by lack of vitamin D, the sunshine vitamin, was always endemic in Neanderthal populations in Europe. This presence of rickets in Neanderthal is of course itself one further tangential argument in favour of his nocturnalism.

We can say then with confidence that human responses to the

numbers 3 and 7 and 13, to the 7-fold maze, to the snake and the spider are *not* archetypal, since we cannot identify in ourselves any *biological* situation of which they form part. Even the male response to menstruation, which we have extensively documented, is not archetypal, or only very marginally so (see below). These are all entirely sociological and historical matters, and our reaction to them purely the result of cultural conditioning. There are not seven etheric chakras in the body, as the Indian esotericists claim (no one else has found them), and still less do they correspond to the endocrine glands, as is often alleged, of which there happen to be nine. Nor are there seven openings in the body, unless you are prepared to count the two ears, the two eyes and the two nostrils as one each. The male reaction to menstruation also proves not to be archetypal for, if it were, millions of men today would not be able to share a bed with a menstruating wife without considerable psychological stress. For you cannot cause an archetype or its psychological effects to disappear by ignoring it, by pretending it does not exist. We probably all do have a marginally aversive achetypal response to the exuded body fluids of all *strangers*, both male and female, but that is about it. (Such aversion probably arises from the use of body scent as threat, or the risk of transmission of disease.) In the case of Neanderthal, he probably had evolved not a negative but a positive archetypal response towards, specifically, blood of all kinds, including menstrual blood.

In the circumstances, a good deal of nonsense has been written in recent years by psychoanalysts and feminist writers (of both sexes) on the alleged psychological (i.e., archetypal) significance of the items mentioned in the previous paragraph. But the clear position is that our response in these cases is to be understood as sociological and historical, as purely the outcome of cultural practice and conditioning. It is very important that we grasp this truth. For otherwise we shall have people continuing to claim that precisely designed seven-fold mazes, and the elaborate menstrual taboos of many peoples, are independently generated psychological 'archetypes' – and not therefore, and on the contrary, vital clues to the origins of our civilisation.

The total aggregate of innate, archetypal and still other kinds of instinctive tendencies, some of which are harder to define than the clear examples we have discussed, makes up what we might call the composite or average 'personality' of a species. (Thus cats in general have a different personality, or psychological style, from dogs in general.) There is an overall way of life which suits the members of a given species, and other ways of life leave them less than happy. For example, a baby squirrel can be successfully reared with a litter of kittens; but the eventual adult squirrel in these circumstances is not a cat, let alone a happy one.

Let us assume here, just for the sake of argument, that we ourselves are indeed a hybrid species, and that some of our members incline instinctively towards a 'Neanderthal' style of life that is not accommodated in our predominantly 'Cro-Magnon' society. (Some perhaps hanker after group sex, instead of one to one pair-bonded sex. Or perhaps rather again, *all* of us *sometimes* hanker after group sex, even though we remain loyal most of the time to the idea at least of 'true' and exclusive love – a situation we consider later.) Is it perhaps possible that these 'Neanderthal' type individuals, not necessarily on any fully conscious basis, would tend to be drawn to others like themselves and so form sub-societies and sub-groups? We have seen such a process apparently operating in the case of witches and Cathars, for example. But here, now, is what is not only a very striking instance of the process suggested, but one which contains equally striking anatomical support for the views of this book. The following information is drawn from a report in the *Sunday Times* in 1972.[34]

Excavations at Norton Priory discovered the skeletons of eighty-five individuals, most of them identifiable as monks. Dating from the twelfth century, these skeletal remains and associated artefacts had been preserved by reason of their interment in stone coffins. Forty of the eighty-five skulls had a sizeable bulge at the back of the head – that is, the extended occiput or 'occipital rose' of Neanderthal. In our present-day population such skull formation (the article claims) is found in only one in every 5000 individuals. It seems quite clear, then, that these physical 'Neanderthals' had withdrawn their 'Neanderthal' personalities into a closed social situation, where they felt able to be happy.

The next item is from the *Transactions* of the Lancashire and Cheshire Antiquarian Society, Volume II, 1884, kindly sent to me by R.C. Turner, County Archaeologist of Chester. The writer of this article, William Norbury, is discussing Lindow Bog, whence came Lindow Man, the leading subject of Chapter 13.

> *I will add a few remarks on the peculiar race of people who, until recently, dwelt on the verges of these old commons* [*i.e.* bogs]. *From actual observation of their physical characteristics and habits during the last fifty years, I am of the opinion that they are of a very ancient race, totally different from the surrounding people. The physical peculiarities are very marked. They have the long head, projecting eyebrows, high cheekbones, strong and coarse limbs, leaden aspect, slow motions, and, in a very marked degree, the Moorish skin – the colour of the skin very like the gypsy's, but very unlike in every other feature. Their habits and modes of life in the early part of the present century were peculiar.... This would lead them to the commons* [*bogs*] *and most neglected parts of the country.... They are expert in using twigs or osiers, in making besoms from birch and broom... in fact, in using all kinds of natural and ready products of the country.... They were very sly and suspicious.... Some of the fiercer kind, if close pressed, would fight with their mouths and bite like bulldogs. I may add that they in a general way shunned society, and appeared to be almost destitute of religious instincts.*[141]

Norbury then adduces other testimony to show that these 'bog peoples' were probably representatives of the neolithic, pre-Celtic inhabitants of the British Isles.

Exciting from our own point of view here is the long head (an extended occiput produces that effect), the projecting eyebrows, the strong and coarse limbs, the association with brooms (as with witches), the use of the mouth for fighting, and the alleged lack of religious instincts. The large and powerful prognathous mouth (of Neanderthal) would be a far more useful and natural weapon that the flat mouth (of Cro-Magnon). As for the lack of religious instincts, the situation everywhere in the world is that the more primitive a people, the stronger is their religion. What Norbury is noting, I think – unfortunately he is not here to be asked – is that these people did not join in the religious observance of their neighbours. I suggest that they were, in secret, following the ways of a much older religion.

These people from Lindow and other bogs were not pure Neanderthalers of course – but it seems obviously clear that they had a considerably greater genetic, and psychological, debt to Neanderthal than the Europeans in general of our own historical times.

So far we have been speaking of a kind of all or nothing situation – where individuals with marked Neanderthal psychological leanings withdrew in some sense from the mainstream of events around them. But what of the notion that each of us individually has both some Neanderthal and some Cro-Magnon allegiance?

Necessarily, of course, in all this reflection we are if not guessing then certainly speculating. For we simply do not know what happens to, or within, the personalities of highly complex creatures like ourselves, in the event of two widely differing varieties crossing to produce a hybrid offspring – this last being, of course, a central claim of the present book – though we do, however, have some idea of what occurs in simpler organisms (see below).

Nevertheless, it is certainly possible that the situation we are postulating might lead at the experiential level to the Faustian sense of 'two souls in one breast', to R.D. Laing's 'divided self', and the frequent imagery of 'a divided house', 'a nation divided', all of which ideas do certainly appeal to us strongly. We might then, in attempting to resolve this dilemma at a personal level, seek to become a whole or undivided person by emphasising one side of our personality at the expense of the other – even though this step is actually a non-solution, for the other half of us does not simply go away.

I believe that this attempt is a very typical – in fact an absolutely typical – 'solution' in present-day society at large. I believe it results in the existence of the Socialist-Conservative, Communist-Fascist, Democrat-Republican axes of the political spectrum. Socialism, I consider, is the political party of Neanderthal, Conservatism the political party of Cro-Magnon.

The demonstration that Socialism is the party of Neanderthal has occupied considerable sections of my earlier books, and cannot even be summarised adequately here.[53–5, 69] But we note that the Socialist anthem is the *Red Flag*, containing, for instance, the line 'the people's flag is deepest red'. Further, one of the entirely accurate charges levelled against early Socialists was that they preached 'free love', i.e., permissive sex. We note also that Socialism is referred to as the left wing – and while one appreciates that this is 'because' the Socialists sat on the left side of the *Assemblée Nationale*, that circumstance is itself no accident. We are, again, not speaking of wholly conscious decision or perception here, but we are certainly talking of deeply motivated 'Freudian slips'. Equally certainly also, the Socialist party has always fielded more female candidates in British general elections than the Conservative party. In an earlier chapter it was suggested that 'Neanderthal' tends to end up at the bottom of our social heap – as in the case of the Untouchables in the Indian caste system. The Socialist party is certainly the self-proclaimed party of the bottom of the heap. My prediction, based on my theoretical views and my own informal observation, is that if examined a sample of Untouchables would be of shorter stature, have stronger brow ridges and eyebrows, have curlier hair and more left-handedness than a sample of Brahmins at the top end of the caste scale. Equally certainly, I am sure that a sample of members of the Labour Party would show a higher incidence of left-handedness than a sample of members of the Conservative party. (Note, we are saying here 'party members', so that the floating voter is specifically excluded.) I have also no doubt that red hair would be more prevalent among Socialists. (As chance will have it, the current leader of the Labour Party, Neil Kinnock, has red hair.)*

The following account is instructive.

The Peach-Faced lovebird, when in the process of building its nest, tears off strips of bark or leaves for this purpose. These it tucks into its rump feathers before flying to the next site. When Fischer's lovebird is nest building, however, it transports the same strips of bark and leaves in its beak. The hybrid cross between these two varieties of lovebird is found to have the instinctive behaviour of both parents. The unfortunate offspring tears itself a

* The aim of the Conservative party is to 'Cro-Magnonise' our planet, and this same endeavour is what Adolf Hitler was engaged in. The aim of Socialism is to 'Neanderthalise' our planet. Thus many of the people Stalin and the present Russian leadership imprisons are intellectuals; and in the late 1930s a number of scientists who produced evidence that intelligence is genetically inherited were shot.[39] Neither of the two parties' aims are in any way desirable, let alone possible.

strip of bark. This its Peach-Faced ancestry instructs it to push into its rump feathers, which the bird does. However, the also inherited Fischer instinct refuses to allow the bird to release the material from its beak, for it is not yet at the nest site. So the bird assumes the ready-to-fly position with the bark still in its mouth. The Peach-Faced side of its nature, however, noting that nest material is in the beak, again instructs the bird to place this in its rump feathers. So the cycle repeats itself without conclusion.[175]

Animals breeders often cross distantly related varieties of animal - say, a Tibetan cow with a Scottish bull –in order to produce new qualities and so-termed hybrid vigour. Unsuccessful crosses of any kind, including psychologically 'difficult' animals, are discarded. The pure geneticist also sometimes deliberately crosses lions with tigers, or Japanese monkeys with African monkeys. But nobody - neither the farmer with his unsuccessful crosses, nor the geneticist with his weird laboratory products - ever allows these, as it were, mutants to develop into breeding populations. Therefore we do not know what happens to, and with, such strange mixtures of genetically-determined physical and psychological characteristics. Would that we did. We might then have more insight into our own condition.

Concluding Word

Once it seemed ridiculous to suggest that all the various physical continents of the world had at one time, hundreds of millions of years ago, been joined together in one great land mass. Now the idea is commonplace.

All that the present book essentially asks is that we extend the scope of modern human history back from its present boundary of 5000 years to a slightly older 100,000 years. Is this really such a terrible request?

(There is so very much to gain, as we have clearly seen, by thus extending our view of the reach of human history. Is it perhaps the case, by way of one more example, that world-wide legends of a mighty flood are not this time necessarily drawn from a common point of origin of great antiquity, but from a mere 10,000 years ago, when the glaciers of the last ice age melted? The release of so much flowing water previously locked as ice must certainly have produced not only direct floods but, along with the rising temperature, a colossal increase in the water vapour in the atmosphere, leading to prolonged torrential rains everywhere. But more likely, given the well-known close parallels between flood legends in all cultures,[50] we are here essentially dealing with a genuine Neanderthal memory of a much earlier melting, perhaps reinforced by the later melting.)

Yet if my request above *is* so very terrible, why might that be? We end with the comment of another alternative writer.

'I realise that the acknowledgement of these facts is bound to evoke howls and cries of anguish from those archaeologists to whom a drastic revision of their ideas is more painful than would be an amputation of all their limbs without an anaesthetic. Such are the hazards which go with the addiction and opiate pleasures of submersion in a body of orthodox theory.'[183]

Appendix

Skeletons in our Cupboard

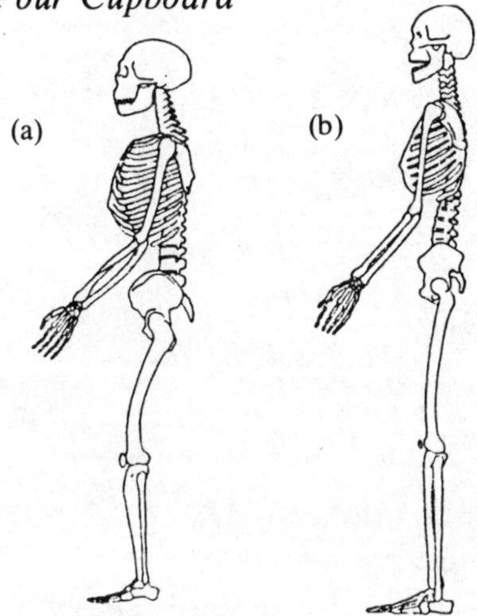

Figure 12
Full skeletons of (a) Neanderthal man. (b) Cro-Magnon man.

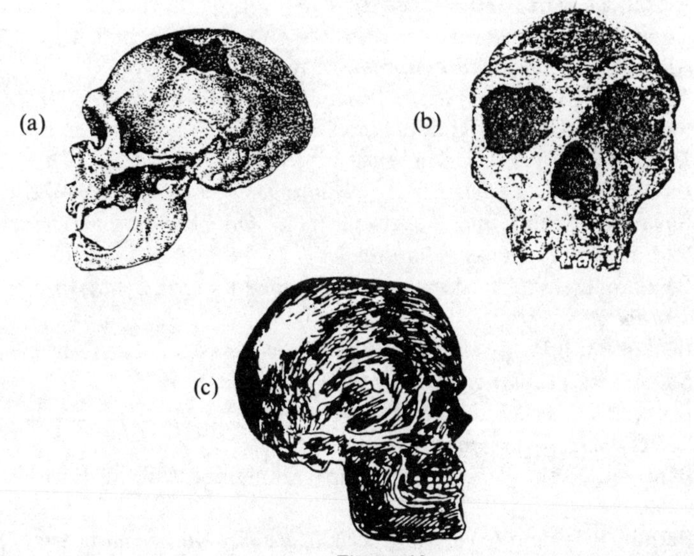

Figure 13
Skulls of (a) Neanderthal man, from France (b) Neanderthal variant from Rhodesia (40,000 B.P.) (c) Cro-Magnon man. Note backward projecting occiput (rear) of Neanderthal skull, and frontal 'horns'. Also the large eye-sockets, typical of a nocturnal creature.

Bibliography

1 Abbie, A.A., *The Original Australians*, Muller, London, 1969.
2 Alexander, H.B. (ed.), *The Mythology of All Races* (12 vols.), Cooper Square, New York, 1964; *see also* Macculloch, J.A.
3 Allen, L.A., *Time before Morning*, Crowell, New York, 1975.
4 Ashe, Geoffrey, *The Ancient Wisdom*, Macmillan, London, 1977.
5 Baigent, M., Leigh, R. and Lincoln, H., *The Holy Blood and the Holy Grail*, Cape, London, 1982.
6 Baskin, Wade, *A Dictionary of Satanism*, Owen, London, 1972.
7 Bayanov, Dmitri and Bourtsev, Igor, 'On Neanderthal *versus* Paranthropus', *Current Anthropology*, 17 June 1976.
8 Beaumont, B.P., 'Border Cave – a Progress Report', *South African Journal of Science*, 69, pp. 41–6, 1973.
9 Beaumont, B.P., 'The Ancient Pigment Mines of Southern Africa', *South African Journal of Science*, 69, pp. 140–6, 1973.
10 Beck, Brenda E.F., 'The Right-Left Division of South Indian Society'; *see* Needham, Rodney.
11 Benedict, Ruth, *Patterns of Culture*, Houghton Mifflin, Boston, 1959.
12 Berndt, R.M. and C.H., *The World of the First Australians*, Angus & Robertson, London, 1964.
13 Bettelheim, Bruno, *Symbolic Wounds*, Thames & Hudson, 1955.
14 Boshier, A.K., 'Mining Genesis', *Mining Survey*, Johannesburg, 1970.
15 Boshier, A.K. and Beaumont, P.S., 'Mining in Southern Africa and

the Emergence of Modern Man', *Optima*, Johannesburg, 1972.
16 Boule, M. and Vallois, H.V., *Fossil Men*, Thames & Hudson, 1957.
17 Breuil, Henri and Lantier, Raymond, *The Men of the Old Stone Age*, Harrap, London, 1965.
18 Briffault, Robert, *The Mothers* (3 vols.), Allen & Unwin, London, 1927.
19 Burkert, Walter, *Greek Religion*, trans. Raffan, John, Blackwell, Oxford, 1985.
20 Burl, Aubrey, *The Stone Circles of the British Isles*, Yale University Press, London, 1976.
21 Burland, C.A., *The Magical Arts*, Barker, London, 1966.
22 ——, *The Gods of Mexico*, Eyre & Spottiswoode, London, 1967.
23 ——, *Echoes of Magic*, Davies, London, 1972.
24 ——, *The Aztecs*, Orbis, London, 1980.
25 Burland, C.A. and Forman, Werner, *Feathered Serpent and Smoking Mirror*, Orbis, London, 1975.
26 Burt, Cyril, *The Backward Child*, University of London, 1937.
27 Campbell, Joseph, (ed.), *The Mysteries*, Pantheon, New York, 1955.
28 ——, *The Masks of God* (4 vols.), Secker & Warburg, 1960–68.
29 Cavendish, Richard, *The Black Arts*, Routledge, London, 1967.
30 Chadwick, John, 'Life in Mycenean Greece', *Scientific American*, October, 1972.
31 Chelhod, J., 'A Contribution to the Problem of the Pre-Eminence of the Right'; *see* Needham, Rodney.
32 Churchward, James, *The Sacred Symbols of Mu*, Spearman, London, 1960.
33 Clark, Graham, *The Stone Age Hunters*, Thames & Hudson, London, 1967.
34 Connolly, Robert, 'The Monks Who are on Loan from the Grave', *Sunday Times*, 30 January, 1972.
35 Considine, P.E. and G.D., *Van Nostrand's Scientific Encyclopedia*, London, 1983.
36 Cook, S.A., 'Serpent Worship', *Encyclopaedia Britannica*, 11th edition, 1910.
37 Cooke, H.B.S. *et al.*, 'Fossil Man in the Lebombo Mountains, South Africa', *Man*, vol. XLV, pp. 6–13, 1945.
38 Daly, C.D., 'The Role of Menstruation in Human Phylogenesis and Ontogenesis', *Int. J. of Psychoanalysis*, vol. 24, pp. 151–70, 1943.
39 Darlington, C.D., letter, *The Times*, 23 November 1976.
40 Day, Michael H., *Guide to Fossil Man*, Cassell, London, 1967.
41 ——, *Fossil Man*, Hamlyn, London, 1969.

42 Delaney, J., Lupton, M.J. and Toth, E., *The Curse: a Cultural History of Menstruation*, Dutton, New York, 1976.
43 Devereux, George, 'The Psychology of Feminine Genital Bleeding', *Int. J. of Psychoanalysis*, vol. 31, pp. 237–57, 1950.
44 Dewan, E.M., 'Rhythms', *Science and Technology*, vol. 20, 1969.
45 Drabble, Margaret, 'Words', BBC Radio, 14 September 1975.
46 Drake-Brockman, H., *Australian Legendary Tales*, Angus & Robertson, London, 1953.
47 Eliade, Mircea, *Birth and Rebirth*, Harvill Press, London, 1961.
48 ——, *The Forge and the Crucible*, Rider, London, 1962.
49 ——, *Myths, Dreams and Mysteries*, Collins, London, 1968.
50 ——, *Patterns in Comparative Religion*, Sheed & Ward, London, 1971.
51 ——, *Australian Religions*, Cornell University Press, London, 1973.
52 ——, *Occultism, Witchcraft and Cultural Fashions*, University of Chicago Press, London, 1976.
53 Elkin, A.P., *The Australian Aborigines*, Angus & Robertson, Sydney, 1956.
54 Ernst, B. and de Vries, T.E., *Atlas of the Universe*, trans. Welsh, D.R., Nelson, London, 1961.
55 Evans-Pritchard, E.E., *Nuer Religion*, Oxford University Press, 1956.
56 Ewen, C.H. L'Estrange, *Witchcraft and Demonaism*, Cranton, London, 1933.
57 Faron, Louis C., 'Symbolic Values and the Integration of Society among the Mapuche of Chile'; *see* Needham, Rodney.
58 Fox, James J., 'On Bad Death and the Left Hand'; *see* Needham, Rodney.
59 Frazer, J.G., *The Golden Bough* (13 vols.), Macmillan, London, 1922.
60 Gleadow, R., *The Origin of the Zodiac*, Cape, London, 1968.
61 Glob, P.V., *The Bog People*, trans. Bruce-Mitford, R., Faber, London, 1969.
62 Golding, William, *The Inheritors*, Faber, London, 1964.
63 Gooch, Stan, *Total Man*, Allen Lane, London, 1972.
64 ——, *Personality and Evolution*, Wildwood House, London, 1973.
65 ——, The Neanderthal Question, Wildwood House, London, 1977.
66 ——, *The Paranormal*, Wildwood House, London, 1978.
67 ——, *Guardians of the Ancient Wisdom*, Wildwood House, London, 1979.

68 ——, 'Right Brain, Left Brain', *New Scientist*, 11 September, 1980.
69 ——, *The Double Helix of the Mind*, Wildwood House, London, 1980.
70 ——, *The Secret Life of Humans*, Dent, London, 1981.
71 ——, 'Left-handedness', *New Scientist*, 22 July, 1982.
72 ——, *Creatures from Inner Space*, Rider, London, 1984.
73 Gooch, Stan and Pringle, M.L.K., *Four Years On*, Longmans, London, 1966.
74 Goodall, Jane van Lawick, *In the Shadow of Man*, Collins, London, 1971.
75 Grand, P.M., *Prehistoric Art*, Studio Vista, London, 1967.
76 Granet, Marcel, 'Right and Left in China'; *see* Needham, Rodney.
77 Graves, Robert, *The Greek Myths*, Penguin, Harmondsworth, 1960.
78 ——, *The White Goddess*, Faber, London, 1961.
79 ——, *Mammon and the Black Goddess*, Cassell, London, 1965.
80 Greenway, John, *Down among the Wild Men*, Little, Brown & Co., Boston, 1972.
81 Grimal, Pierre, *Larousse World Mythology*, Hamlyn, London, 1965.
82 Guirand, Felix, *New Larousse Encyclopedia of Mythology*, Hamlyn, London, 1968.
83 Hall, Manley Palmer, *Masonic, Hermetic, Qabbalistic and Rosicrucian Symbolical Philosophy*, P.R.S., Los Angeles, 1947.
84 Harding, Esther, *Women's Mysteries*, Pantheon, New York, 1955.
85 Hastings, J., *Encyclopedia of Religion and Ethics*, T. & T. Clark, Edinburgh, 1917.
86 Hawkes, Jacquetta, 'In Pursuit of Strange Gods', *Sunday Times*, 15 September 1974.
87 Hertz, Robert, 'The Pre-eminence of the Right Hand: a Study in Religious Polarity'; *see* Needham, Rodney.
88 Heyerdahl, Thor, *American Indians in the Pacific*, Allen & Unwin, London, 1952.
89 ——, *Aku, Aku: the Secret of Easter Island*, Allen & Unwin, London, 1958.
90 Hitching, Francis, *World Atlas of Mysteries*, Collins, London, 1978.
91 Holloway, R.L., 'The Casts of Fossil Hominid Brains', *Scientific American*, October 1974.
92 Hughes, T.P., *Dictionary of Islam*, Cosmo Publications, New Delhi, 1978.

93 Izumi, Tomoko, Japanese artist, personal communication.
94 Jackson, S.M., *The New Schaff-Herzog Encyclopedia of Religious Knowledge*, Funk & Wagnall, New York, 1909.
95 Jay, Thomas, *The Encyclopedia of Facts and Fallacies*, Elliot Right Way Books, New York, 1958.
96 Jennings, Hargrave, *The Rosicrucians*, Routledge, London, 1887.
97 Jobes, Gertrude, *Dictionary of Mythology, Folklore and Symbols*, Scarecrow Press, New York, 1961.
98 Jung, C.G., *Alchemical Studies, Collected Works*, vol. 13, Routledge, London, 1967.
99 ——, *Psychology and Alchemy, Collected Works*, vol. 12, Routledge, London, 1968.
100 ——, *The Archetypes and the Collective Unconscious*, vol. 9, Part 1, Routledge, London, 1969.
101 Jung, Emma and Von Franz, Marie-Louise, *The Grail Legend*, Hodder, London, 1971.
102 Kerényi, C., *Eleusis: Archetypal Image of Mother and Daughter*, Routledge, London, 1967.
103 Kerényi, C., *Zeus and Hera*, Routledge, London, 1975.
104 Kirk, R.L., *Aboriginal Man Adapting*, Clarendon, Oxford, 1981.
105 Klein, E., *A Comprehensive Etymological Dictionary of the English Language*, Elsevier, New York, 1946.
106 Kluger, Rivkah Schärf, *Psyche and Bible*, Spring Publications, Zurich, 1974.
107 Kroeber, A.L., 'Handbook of the Indians of California', *Bureau of American Ethnology Bulletin*, 78, 1925.
108 Kruyt, A.C., 'Right and Left in Central Celebes'; *see* Needham, Rodney.
109 Kusche, L.D., *The Bermuda Triangle Mystery Solved*, New English Library, London, 1975.
110 Lacey, Louise, *Lunaception*, Warner Books, New York, 1976.
111 Lancaster Brown, Peter, *Megaliths, Myths and Men*, Blandford Press, Poole, 1976.
112 Le Gros Clark, W.E., *History of the Primates*, British Museum, London, 1965.
113 Leakey, R.E. and Lewin, R., *Origins*, Macdonald & Jane's, London, 1977.
114 Lechler, Alfred, *Das Rätsel von Konnersreuth im Lichte eines Neuen Falles vonStigmatisation*, Elberfeld, 1933.
115 Lehane, Brendan, *The Companion Guide to Ireland*, Collins, London, 1985.
116 Lethbridge, T.C., *Witches: Investigating an Ancient Religion*, Routledge, 1962.

117 Lewis, I.M., *Ecstatic Religion*, Penguin, Harmondsworth, 1971.
118 Llewellyn-Jones, Derek, *Everywoman: a Gynaecological Guide for Life*, Faber, London, 1971.
119 Lloyd, Geoffrey, 'Right and Left in Greek Philosophy'; *see* Needham, Rodney.
120 Macculloch, J.A., (ed.), *The Mythology of All Races* (13 vols.), Marshall James, Boston, 1930; *see also* Alexander, H.B.
121 Maddock, Kenneth, *The Australian Aborigines*, Allen Lane, London, 1973.
122 Mallery, Garrick, *Picture-Writing of the American Indians*, Dover, New York, 1972.
123 Marshack, Alexander, *The Roots of Civilisation*, Weidenfeld & Nicolson, London, 1972.
124 Massey, Gerald, *A Book of Beginnings* (4 vols.), Williams & Norgate, London, 1881–3.
125 Mathers, S.L. MacGregor, *The Kabbalah Unveiled*, Kegan Paul, London, 1926.
126 Mathews, R.H., 'The Bora or Initiation Ceremonies of the Kamilaroi Tribe', *Journal of the Royal Anthropological Institute*, XXIV, 1895.
127 ——, 'The Burbung of the Wiradjuri Tribes', *Journal of the Royal Anthropological Institute*, XXV, 1896; and XXVI, 1897.
128 Matthews, W.H., *Mazes and Labyrinths*, Longmans, London, 1922.
129 Menaker, W. and A., 'Lunar Periodicity in Human Reproduction', *Obstetrics and Gynaecology*, vol. 17, pp. 905–14, April 1959.
130 Moody, R.L., 'Bodily Changes during Abreacation', *Lancet*, no. 251, part 2, 1946; and no. 254, part 2, 1948.
131 Morris, D. (ed.), *Primate Ethology*, Doubleday, New York, 1969.
132 Morrison, Tony, *Pathways to the Gods*, Granada, London, 1980.
133 Murray, Margaret, *The Witch Cult in Western Europe*, Clarendon, Oxford, 1921.
134 ——, *The God of the Witches*, Faber, London, 1952.
135 Mylonas, G.E., *Eleusis and the Eleusinian Mysteries*, Routledge, London, 1961.
136 Myres, J.L., 'The Holy Grail', *Encyclopaedia Britannica*, 11th Edition, 1910.
137 Napier, John, *Bigfoot*, Cape, London, 1972.
138 Needham, Rodney, *Left and Right*, University of Chicago Press, 1973.
139 Neugebauer, O., 'Tamil Astronomy', *Osiris*, vol. 10, no. 252, 1974.
140 Nicholson, Irene, *Mexican and Central American Mythology*, Newnes, Feltham, Middlesex, 1983.
141 Norbury, William, 'Lindow Common as a Peat Bog', *Transactions*

of the Lancashire and Cheshire Antiquarian Society, vol. II, Manchester, 1884.
142 Ovid, *Metamorphoses*, trans. Innes, M.M., Penguin, Harmondsworth, 1955.
143 Owen, A.L., *The Famous Druids*, Clarendon, Oxford, 1962.
144 *Oxford English Dictionary*, Clarendon, Oxford, 1933.
145 Palmer, G. and Lloyd, N., *A Year of the Festivals*, London, 1972.
146 Palmer, M., Man-Ho, K. and Brown, K., *Three Lives*, Century Hutchinson, London, 1987.
147 Patai, Raphael, *The Hebrew Goddess*, Ktav Publishing, New York, 1967.
148 Pauwels, L. and Bergier, J., *The Dawn of Magic*, Gibbs, London, 1963.
149 Perry, W.J., *The Children of the Sun*, Methuen, London, 1927.
150 Peterson, John M., 'Left-Handedness: Differences between Student Artists and Scientists', *Perceptual and Motor Skills*, vol. 48, 1979.
151 Phillips, W.A., 'Dragon', *Encyclopaedia Britannica*, 11th Edition, 1910.
152 Piggot, Stuart, *The Druids*, Thames & Hudson, London, 1968.
153 Porshnev, B.F., 'The Troglodytidae and the Hominidae in the Taxonomy and Evolution of Higher Primates', *Current Anthropology*, *15*, 1974.
154 Pringle, M.L.K., *11,000 Seven Year Olds*, Longmans, London, 1976.
155 Purce, Jill, *The Mystic Spiral*, Thames & Hudson, London, 1974.
156 Redgrove, H.S., *Alchemy – Ancient and Modern*, Rider, London, 1922.
157 Roheim, Geza, *Children of the Desert*, Basic Books, New York, 1974.
158 Romer, A.S., *Man and the Vertebrates*, Penguin, Harmondsworth, 1963.
159 Rose, Ronald, *Living Magic*, Rand McNally, New York, 1956.
160 Russell, Jeffrey Burton, *Witchcraft in the Middle Ages*, Cornell University Press, 1972.
161 Sandars, N.K., *Prehistoric Art in Europe*, Penguin, Harmondsworth, 1968.
162 Santillana, Giorgio de, *The Origins of Scientific Thought*, Weidenfeld & Nicolson, London, 1961.
163 Schliemann, H., *Troja*, Murray, London, 1884.
164 Selfe, Lorna, *Nadia – a Case of Extraordinary Drawing Ability in an Autistic Child*, Academic Press, London, 1977.

165 Seligman, Kurt, *Magic, Supernaturalism and Religion*, Allen Lane, London, 1971.
166 Shackley, Myra, *Neanderthal Man*, Duckworth, London, 1980.
167 ——, *Wild Men: Yeti, Sasquatch and the Neanderthal Enigma*, Thames & Hudson, London, 1983.
168 Shuttle, P. and Redgrove, P., *The Wise Wound*, Gollancz, London, 1978.
169 Skeat, W.W., *An Etymological Dictionary of the English Language*, Oxford University Press, 1946.
170 Slater, Philip E., *The Glory of Hera*, Beacon Press, Boston, 1971.
171 Smith, Grafton Elliot, *The Ancient Egyptians and the Origins of Civilisation*, Harper & Row, 1923.
172 ——, *Essays on the Evolution of Man*, Milford, London, 1927.
173 Solecki, Ralph S., *Shanidar: the Humanity of Neanderthal Man*, Allen Lane, 1972.
174 ——, 'Shanidar IV: a Neanderthal Flower Burial in Northern Iraq', *Science*, vol. 190, November 1975.
175 Sparks, John, *Bird Behaviour*, Hamlyn, London, 1969.
176 Spence, E.L., *Myths and Legends of the North American Indians*, Harrap, London, 1914.
177 Stead, I.M., Bourke, J.B. and Brothwell, D., *Lindow Man: the Body in the Bog*, British Museum, London, 1986.
178 Stephens, W.N., 'A Cross-Cultural Study of Menstrual Taboos', *Genetic Psychology Monographs*, *64*, pp. 385–416, 1961.
179 Stobart, J.C., *The Glory that was Greece*, Sidgwick and Jackson, London, 1984.
180 Summers, Montague, *The History of Witchcraft and Demonology*, Routledge, London, 1973.
181 Summers, R., 'Ancient Mining in Rhodesia', *Memoir No. 3*, National Museum, Salisbury, Zimbabwe 1969.
182 Taylor, F.S., *The Alchemists*, Henry Schuman, New York, 1949.
183 Temple, Robert, *The Sirius Mystery*, Sidgwick & Jackson, London, 1976.
184 ——, 'Coincidence or Contact: Magnetism in the New World', *Second Look* September, 1979.
185 ——, 'Olmec Magnetism and the Human Brain', *Second Look*, November 1979.
186 Teng, E.L. *et al.*, 'Handedness in a Chinese Population', *Science*, p. 193, 1976.
187 Tinbergen, N., *The Study of Instinct*, Oxford University Press, 1951.
188 Tindale, N.B. and Lindsay, H.A., *Aboriginal Australians*, Angus & Robertson, London, 1963.

189 Tomas, Andrew, *We are not the First*, Sphere Books, London, 1972.

190 Ulanov, Ann Belford, *The Feminine in Jungian Psychology and in Christian Theology*, Northwest University Press, Evanston, 1971.

191 Vaillant, G.C., *Aztecs of Mexico*, Penguin, Harmondsworth, 1965.

192 Van Waters, Miriam, 'The Adolescent Girl among Primitive Peoples', *Journal of Religious Psychology*, *6*, p. 4, 1913; and *7*, p. 1, 1914.

193 Vlcek, Emmanuel, 'Old Literary Evidence for the Existence of the "Snow Man" in Tibet and Mongolia', *Man*, 59, 1959.

194 Vogh, James, *The Thirteenth Zodiac* (originally published as *The Sign of Arachne*), Mayflower, London, 1979.

195 Vries, Ad de, *Dictionary of Symbols and Imagery*, North-Holland Publishing, London, 1981.

196 Waite, A.E., *The Secret Doctrine in Israel*, Rider, London, 1913.

197 Walcott, C., Gould, J. and Kirschvink, J.L., 'Pigeons have Magnets', *Science*, vol. 205, no. 7, 1979.

198 Walker, Charles, *The Atlas of Occult Britain*, Hamlyn, London, 1987.

199 Warner, W.L., *A Black Civilisation*, Harper & Row, New York, 1958.

200 Watson, Lyall, *Lifetide*, Hodder & Stoughton, London, 1979.

201 Werner, E.T.C., *Myths and Legends of China*, Harrap, London, 1922.

202 Whymant, Roger, 'Short Guts for Good Looks', *Sunday Times*, London 16 March 1975.

203 Wieschoff, H.A., 'Concepts of Right and Left in African Cultures'; *see* Needham, Rodney.

204 Willard, R.D., 'Breast Enlargement through Visual Imagery and Hypnosis', *American Journal of Clinical Hypnosis*, vol. 19, no. 4, 1977.

205 Williams, Mary (ed.), *Glastonbury: a Study in Patterns*, Research into Lost Knowledge Organisation, London, 1976.

206 Willoughby-Meade, G., *Chinese Ghouls and Goblins*, Constable, London, 1928.

207 Wright, Pearce, 'Neanderthals Take a Place in the Family Tree', *The Times*, London 4 August 1986.

208 Young, H.B. and Knapp, R., 'Personality Characteristics of Converted Left-Handers', *Perceptual and Motor Skills*, vol. 23, 1965.

209 Zerchaninov, Yuri, 'Is Neanderthal Man Extinct?', *Moscow News*, 22 February 1964.

210 Zimmer, H., *Myths and Symbols in Indian Art and Civilisation*, Princeton University Press, New Jersey, 1972.

Index